After Multiculturalism

After Multiculturalism

The Politics of Race and
the Dialectics of Liberty

John F. Welsh

LEXINGTON BOOKS

A division of
ROWMAN & LITTLEFIELD PUBLISHERS, INC.
Lanham • Boulder • New York • Toronto • Plymouth, UK

LEXINGTON BOOKS

A division of Rowman & Littlefield Publishers, Inc.
A wholly owned subsidiary of The Rowman & Littlefield Publishing Group, Inc.
4501 Forbes Boulevard, Suite 200
Lanham, MD 20706

Estover Road
Plymouth PL6 7PY
United Kingdom

British Library Cataloguing in Publication Information Available

Library of Congress Cataloging-in-Publication Data

Welsh, John F., 1951–
  After multiculturalism : the politics of race and the dialectics of liberty / John F. Welsh.
    p. cm.
  Includes bibliographical references and index.
  ISBN-13: 978-0-7391-1882-5 (cloth : alk. paper)
  ISBN-10: 0-7391-1882-X (cloth : alk. paper)
  ISBN-13: 978-0-7391-1883-2 (pbk. : alk. paper)
  ISBN-10: 0-7391-1883-8 (pbk. : alk. paper)
  1. Multiculturalism—United States. 2. Pluralism (Social sciences)—United States. 3.
Racism—United States. 4. United States—Race relations. I. Title.
  HM1271.W455 2008
  305.800973—dc22   2007032111

Printed in the United States of America

∞™ The paper used in this publication meets the minimum requirements of American
National Standard for Information Sciences—Permanence of Paper for Printed Library
Materials, ANSI/NISO Z39.48-1992.

To Wendy Welsh . . .

Her name, everything she is, and everything she does
has a cheerful lilt to it.
My love and gratitude to you.

Contents

Acknowledgments

I value the opportunity to thank the many scholars and friends who inspire me on a daily basis. Ed Arquitt, Neil Luebke, and the late Ivan Chapman were enormously helpful and encouraging to me during and subsequent to my doctoral studies at Oklahoma State University. Among my faculty colleagues, I particularly need to thank Don Viney, Bob Antonio, Wayne Ross, Sandra Mathison, Carolyn Rude-Parkins, and Tom Reio for their support and many insights about how to improve my work. I also want to thank my former supervisors who helped me become a professional: the late Dale Frihart, Martine Hammond-Paludan, the late Stanley Koplik, and Carol Garrison. Bill Docking and John Hiebert were also very helpful and inspiring to me during the time I spent working for the Kansas Board of Regents. Special appreciation is due to Sylvia Robinson, Fashaad Crawford, Terri Carr, and Wanda Adams-Taylor who patiently helped me struggle through some difficult conversations. There are no chasms if we climb the right mountain. I owe my beautiful and brilliant wife, Wendy Welsh, everything.

Chapter One

Multicultural Thought

Reactionary Tribalism versus the Dialectics of Liberty

THE ELEMENTS OF MULTICULTURAL THOUGHT

Contemporary theory and policy discourse on race and racism in the United States are dominated by collectivist principles that entail a fundamental contradiction: Racism historically required and continues to require state power for its implementation, but the prevailing interpretations and challenges to racism are those that also foster collective social identities and seek to influence and direct the use of state power in the interests of particular racial and ethnic groups. Despite their many and profound differences, liberals, socialists, ethnic nationalists, and even compassionate conservatives are all agreed that the most appropriate strategy for responding to racism is the collective acquisition and exercise of state power on behalf of racial and ethnic collectivities.

While collectivist and statist thought dominates contemporary dialogue on race and ethnicity, what is left undemonstrated is an explanation of why collective identities, experiences, and needs of racial and ethnic groups must be elevated above individual identities, experiences and needs. It is also undemonstrated why the acquisition and exercise of state power is thought to be a helpful component of the challenge to racism. To what extent can the collectivist and statist ideas of prevailing antiracist thought actually help liberate persons from racist domination? What are the alternatives to the collectivist and statist formulations of antiracist thought?

Contemporary conceptions of race, ethnicity, and racism are largely framed through the interpretive lens of multiculturalism. Multiculturalism is the dominant label or idée fixe that is used to characterize the current state, development, and goal of racial and ethnic group relationships in American society. As

1

the prevailing incarnation of antiracist ideology, multiculturalism reflects and structures political process and organizational life in the United States. Although it is difficult to identify the central texts that outline its components, the basic tenets of multiculturalism are (1) race and ethnicity are inherent and significant features of all social interactions, (2) racial and ethnic stratification are persistent characteristics of all social life, from informal everyday interactions to the formal, secondary interactions that occur within complex organizations, and (3) racial and ethnic constructs should be the primary consideration in understanding the distribution of all forms of social desiderata, including power, prestige, and access to income and wealth. Most significantly, the telos of the social and theoretical critiques of racism by multiculturalists is not the transcendence or elimination of racial and ethnic identities, but their advocacy and promotion.[1]

Multiculturalist thought best expresses the idea that concepts of identity, community, and political legitimacy are rooted in and ultimately constrained by race and culture. In heterogeneous social environments, such as the United States, there is not just one America, and not just one American democracy, but many Americas that are differentiated and separated by race and culture.

> If democracy is rule of the people, then we confront, in practice, not democracy but democracies: the rule of different peoples, each people ruling in its own way, each rule bearing the marks of particular pasts, particular conflicts, particular aspirations.[2]

Americans now speak of the "African American community," the "Asian American community," the "Latino community," and the "Native American community" as though these constitute fully integrated, fully homogenous wholes that are fully distinctive from each other. "Community" may be an overly optimistic euphemism that, in fact, signifies an ethno-racial bloc defined and enforced by the power of the federal government. These private ethno-racial enclaves may prove to be extremely abstract concepts that reflect little about the everyday experiences or aspirations of people. The sharp differentiation of ethno-racial blocs in culture and politics may function to reproduce elements of racist social patterns.

As a political ideology and social process, multiculturalism superseded other perspectives on race and ethnic group relations that prevailed in earlier historical periods in the United States. "Americanization" and "assimilation" were once concepts that suggested that there was something distinctive about America and about being American. Assimilation, especially, entailed the idea that being American implied not an identity based on race or ethnicity, but a commitment to a set of values and principles. Americanization and assimilation are held in wide disrepute in the United States today, as is any perspective that suggests that race and ethnicity should have little meaning in personal identity and social relationships. As Nathan Glazer remarks, "(n)either liberals nor neoliberals, conservatives nor neoconservatives, have much good to say about assimilation, and only a branch of paleoconservativism can now be mustered in its defense." Glazer believes that we are all multiculturalists today. But he also believes that it is somewhat tragic that elements of assimilation are no longer part of the national dialogue on race and ethnicity. The ascendance of multicultural thought as the ruling paradigm of race relations in the United States adumbrated the death knell of any concept of identity and community based on "adherence to ideals, to universal principles."[3]

Dialectical social theory suggests that, since multiculturalism arose at a particular historical juncture in American society, it will likely be superseded and replaced by another paradigm or perspective that reflects and structures conceptions of race, ethnicity, and racism. If so, it is important to ask questions about the elements of multiculturalist thought and what might be some of the theoretical alternatives to it. One set of important questions pertains to the nature of concepts about race, ethnicity, and racism. Are race and ethnicity inherent, essential qualities of individuals? Is racism an invariant social fact? Or, are race and ethnicity social, historical constructions that ultimately emerge from the interactions of individuals? How do concepts about race and ethnicity emerge from, and how are they shaped by, social and historical processes?

A second set of questions pertains to some of the specific problems or consequences of multicultural thought. Is multiculturalism a completely integrated logical whole, or are there problematic and contradictory ideas within it? What are the inner tensions within multicultural thought? To what extent can the basic elements and assumptions of multiculturalism contribute to the liberation of people? Or, in what ways does multiculturalism frustrate the interests of individuals and society in overcoming all forms of domination, including those based on race and ethnicity?

A third set of questions pertain to alternatives to multiculturalism and a vision of individuality and society after multiculturalism. Who are the theorists, and what are the schools of thought, that provide an antiracist vision, but do not reproduce the collectivism and statism of multiculturalism? Are there antiracist theories that promote individualist ideas about the relationship between the individual and society and libertarian ideas about the role of the state in society?

After Multiculturalism has three purposes. The primary aim of this book is to critique the notion that collectivist and statist ideologies "own" racism as a social and public policy issue. The book demonstrates that individualist and libertarian theorists developed critiques of racism and multiculturalism that emanate directly from the foundations of individualist and libertarian thought. Second, the book develops an argument that multiculturalism is unlikely to promote the types of actions and changes that are necessary to overcoming racism in American society. Third, it argues that individualist and libertarian ideas offer important contributions toward the realization of a social world free of racial domination. *After Multiculturalism* develops a perspective on racism and the struggle against it that is different from multiculturalism. It also develops a perspective that differs from that of the critics of multiculturalism who oppose the multiculturalist reduction of persons to their racial identities, but who still argue in favor of the reduction of persons to other collectivist abstractions, such as class, state, and nation. A critique of multiculturalism that is differentiated from other forms of collectivism must begin with a discussion of the meanings and origins of race, ethnicity, and racism.

A DIALECTICAL PERSPECTIVE ON RACE AND ETHNICITY

Despite the nearly universal and uncritical elevation of multiculturalism as the only theoretical alternative to racist ideology, there are ambiguities and conflicts in the multiculturalist view of the world and its agenda for managing crises in society. The concept of "racism," like "elitism" and "sexism," is today used in policy discourse as a pejorative catchall that supposedly describes and explains an infinite array of attitudes, behaviors, and facts that are thought to be unfortunate from the viewpoint of those using the term. The term "racist" is frequently used to stigmatize and discredit individuals and groups who run afoul of diversity elites who possess the ability to define and control behavior within the government, media, and major social institutions. If other persons are stigmatized by the attribution of racist attitudes or racist implications of their ideas, then one's credentials and ideas are elevated in policy discourse. Political actors mobilize support if they successfully stigmatize their opposition as "racist." The term "racist" connotes much in political discourse, but frequently denotes very little that is descriptive or helpful in the critique of domination.

Nevertheless, race is a social fact that has profound consequences for the life-chances and the life-experiences of individuals because racism is also a social fact. If racism is to be overcome and if the role of race in society is to be adequately understood, it is important to examine the social processes by which both race and racism become social facts. An assessment of multiculturalism as an alternative to racism is also dependent upon an understanding of how conceptions of race and ethnicity are produced in the interactions of persons. Berger and Luckmann's classic dialectical perspective on the nature of social reality provides a theoretical framework for understanding the construction of race and ethnicity. It also helps explain how racism is a departure from ordinary processes of social interaction and how persons make sense of their everyday world.[4]

Berger and Luckmann conceive reality construction to be a dual process in which the subjective meanings of individuals become experienced as objective facts and the objective facts shape the subjective meanings of individuals. Their dialectic of reality construction is comprised of three moments or sub-processes: externalization, objectivation, and internalization.

In the process of externalization, active human agents create society and culture as external to individuals in the forms of significant symbols, material artifacts, social institutions, values, and belief systems about the external world. Berger and Luckmann understand externalization as an active process in which gestures are tied to meanings and intentions, a sense of social order is created, and social interactions are structured. Their notion of externalization is based upon George Herbert Mead's concept of the creation of significant symbols and it captures the classic sociological notion of culture as a phenomenon that emerges from human interaction. In this formulation, racial and ethnic categories, as well as any notion about the superiority or inferiority of different groups, are ultimately rooted in the interactions of persons in everyday life.

Objectivation is the moment in the process of reality construction in which the externalized outcomes of social interactions become an objective reality, or they become experienced as an objective reality. The result of objectivation is the creation of institutional patterns that tend to structure human behavior and thought. The objectivated products of social interaction are encountered as an "out there" reality and eventually become part of the reality that individuals take for granted. Thus, while racial and ethnic categories are initially created by individuals in interaction with significant symbols, they acquire an "objective" reality and have an external and, at times, constraining effect on individuals.

In turn, the externalized and objectivated reality is internalized by individuals and constitutes guidelines for their future conduct. The externalized and objectivated social products of interaction are learned by individuals as objective facts and subsumed within their consciousness. People within the same sociocultural environment tend to typify situations similarly and rarely negate or question the origins or ultimate sources of these typifications because they have internalized the objectivated constructions in their society. Thus, constructions about race and ethnicity, including both group categories and beliefs about qualities associated with them, are internalized by individuals in socialization processes occurring through the family, the school, the media, the church, and the polity.

6 *Chapter One*

Social reality, then, is the result of this dialectical process in which people actively create the social world and are created by it. As Berger and Luckmann sum up the process, "Society is a human product. Society is an objective reality. Man is a social product."⁵ Berger and Luckmann view the dialectic of social life as an "anthropological necessity." Reality construction is essential to human survival and it defines what human being are, at least in a behavioral sense. Human beings are essentially culture-producing beings. A big part of what it means to be human is to participate in the social construction of reality. The implications of their viewpoint for theory about race and ethnicity are that (1) the knowledge used to place people into racial and ethnic categories is socially and humanly produced, and (2) this knowledge is reproduced in socialization processes.

Each of the three moments in the process of reality construction is comprised of elements that structure the variable nature of societies and cultures. The moment of objectivation is the central moment in which human beings embody their thoughts, attitudes, and values in objective or intersubjective products that are available to self and others as elements of a common life-world. These products can include material artifacts and cultural meanings tied to gestures and symbols. One element in the moment of objectivation is a process in which persons establish distance between themselves and the products of their interactions. That is, people begin to lose sight of the fact that they are the creators of the social world they experience. This occurs so that human beings can make the products of their interaction objects of their consciousness. The objectification of social constructions still allows for a connection between the producers, the acts of production, and the products themselves. It still allows for the connection between objective and subjective reality. Objectification is a necessary of part of reality construction and what it means to actively participate in the creation of a material and symbolic universe, but it implies that persons begin to take the external world for granted and, at times, deny that they are responsible for its production and reproduction.

Berger and Luckmann do not view human knowledge as a mere reflection of the external world. Human beings do not cognitively discover a ready-made world. Instead, they create it in their practical, everyday activity. The material resources they create knowledge with, however, are usually not evenly distributed throughout society and may even be denied to individuals or to entire categories of individuals. Under these conditions, the dialectic of social life does not function in a fully participatory manner. Obstacles to the fully human and fully participatory construction of reality can appear at any point in the process of reality construction. In fact, throughout human history the dialectic of social life has broken down quite frequently. The dialectic of social life may be anthropologically necessary, as Berger and Luckmann indicate, but it is not always achieved. Berger and Pullberg argue that significant departures from the fully human and fully participatory dialectic of social life are the de facto condition of human existence.[6]

Where there exists an interference in the process of reality construction so that categories of individuals are excluded from full participation, the link between the producers, the acts of their production, and the products themselves is severed. Stratification systems, whether they are based on social class, political power, or race and ethnicity, tend to orient the resources available to people for reality construction to the exclusive use of elites and their functionaries. In the parlance of the social construction of reality, this process is called alienation. It is a distorted form of objectivation since all persons have not had similar opportunities to participate in the creation of the objective world. Alienation exists in hostile contrast to the more fully human and participatory processes of objectivation and objectification. Reification is a moment in the process of alienation in which the characteristic of "thinghood" becomes the standard of objective reality. Reification is the personification of things and the "thing-ification" of persons. It is the inversion of the dialectic of social life in that what was once the subject becomes the object, and what was once the object becomes the subject. Reification is objectification in an alienated mode, or it is how objectification operates in an alienated lifeworld. Under alienated conditions, human beings do not create, but are subordinate to a fixed, ready-made, and hostile external world.

RACE, ETHNICITY, AND REIFICATION

Berger and Luckmann's concept of reification can be fruitfully applied to the analysis of race, ethnicity, and racism. The term "race" itself is far from conceptually clear in cultural and policy discourse in North America, but it has acquired a reified status in large part because the federal government classified the physical qualities of individuals into fixed, codified racial categories as a means of identifying protected classes of people.[7] Multicultural discourse tends toward the conceptualization of race as a trans-human fact that has an ultimate reality that is fixed and not an outcome of human activity, thus uncritically reflecting the state's imposition of a reified concept of race. This theoretical tendency is found in discourse on race and ethnicity that maintains or implies that racial and ethnic categories are persistent, universal features of social interaction and social organization. These reified concepts of race are frequently conceived as either physical or biological substrata to human existence that exist and operate independently of human thought and social practice in organizations and social institutions.

Reified concepts of race and racism come in two forms: those that focus on the sociocultural realities of race and those that focus on the biological and genetic realities of race. An interesting discussion of the perspective that race always constitutes a biological and social substratum in organizational life is Stella Nkomo's essay on race in organizations. Nkomo argues that the main problem with educational, corporate, and governmental organizations today is that they retain a legacy of the logic of assimilation which assumes that everyone within the organization or who is served by the organization can adapt to a set of common or universal goals. She argues that the realities of racial and cultural differences render this belief a tool that is used to favor some groups and disadvantage others.[8] For broader discussions of the same "race is real" cultural viewpoint, the academic celebrities Cornell West and Michael Eric Dyson are important resources.[9] West and Dyson critique "color-blind racism" or attempts to transform society and improve the lives of people without including race as the primary factor that structures human experience. It is important to acknowledge that West has argued for a genealogy of racist ideology, implying that racist thought and the concept of race itself have historical origins, but the fundamental precept of his writing is that race is the invariable determinant of human experience. Politically, Nkomo, West, and Dyson argue for a multiculturalist form of socialism that places race, not social class, at the center of its analysis and advocate the exercise of state and institutional power as a lever to create a greater equalization of cultural and social desiderata across racial and ethnic groups.

The themes of the persistence and primacy of race in social life is developed at length by Eduardo Bonilla-Silva in his book *Racism without Racists*.[10] Bonilla-Silva also advances the idea of "color-blind racism," which he defines as the notion of the "color-blind treatment" of people, or treatment of people without regard to their race or ethnicity. He argues that "color-blind racism" is the new form of racism in American society because "color blindness" does not help address historical or structural inequalities in society. The crux of Bonilla-Silva's conceptualization of racism is that race and ethnicity must continue to be central categories of social thought and political practice *in perpetuity*, otherwise racism will continue to flourish. Persons who attempt to think in nonracial categories and treat others in nonracial forms are merely "unwitting racists" whose "sincere fictions" only reinforce subtle and institutional forms of racial domination. In his view, the eradication of race-based thinking and treatment of people is a new form of racism. "Color-blind racism" in Bonilla-Silva's formulation is a reification that institutionalizes the multiculturalist belief that race and ethnicity must forever be central to the way humans think and behave. The notion of "color-blind racism" transcends neither race nor racism, but fixes both in social thought and practice.

The argument that race always constitutes a critical foundation for human interaction and knowledge is a sword that appears to cut both ways, culturally and politically. Nkomo, West, Dyson, and Bonilla-Silva view their philosophies as important contributions to the creation of an antiracist culture. However, some of the literature that assumes or argues that race constitutes a persistent biological or physical base for human behavior is not sympathetic at all to the multicultural impulse for greater tolerance and equality, and reaches conclusions that Nkomo, West, Dyson, and Bonvilla-Silva find repugnant. Instead, this research literature argues that the behavioral differences and inequalities among racial and ethnic groups is due to fundamental differences in human genetics. For instance, there are numerous academic treatments of race that search for the biological or physical roots of racial differences. These studies share a reified notion of race but have radically different political conclusions from Nkomo, West, and Dyson.

In *Race: The Reality of Human Differences*, Vincent Savich and Frank Miele argue that, rather than an obsession with race, America has an obsession with "color blindness" that contradicts the facts about race.[11] Their book outlines arguments and evidence against the idea that race and ethnicity are social constructs. They focus several chapters on DNA studies and IQ studies to build the argument that there are significant empirically demonstrable differences among the races. Further, they argue that these differences cannot be ignored in social and educational policy. While these differences have clear implications for racial and cultural superiority and inferiority they are not a legitimate basis for discrimination. Similarly, J. Philippe Rushton argues in *Race, Evolution and Behavior: A Life History Perspective* that discoveries in population genetics refute notions that race is a social construct and that racial differences are entirely determined by environmental influences.[12] Jared Taylor and George McDaniel develop arguments in *A Race against Time: Racial Heresies for the 21st Century* that there are not only scientific but philosophical and cultural reasons why it is important to retain the concept of race and knowledge of racial differences and accomplishments. Among other things, Taylor and McDaniel are concerned that the abandonment of prevailing racial categories will also result in the abandonment of the European and Judeo-Christian heritage of the United States, much to the detriment of the society's scientific, cultural, economic, and political life.[13]

The cultural and biological arguments for the "reality of race" can be critiqued from the perspective of the sociology of knowledge to examine the sources and consequences of these ideas. The multiculturalist argument in favor of a reified concept of race and ethnicity has a political agenda, whether open or hidden, that seeks greater cultural and political advocacy for some racial and ethnic groups, usually at the expense of others. The scientific or genetic argument in favor of a reified concept of race also has a political agenda, explicit or implicit, which propagates acquiescence to inequities and patterns of discrimination and prejudice, which are believed to be outcomes of biological or genetic dynamics. Despite their different political agendas, both offer a reified concept of race. One perspective harnesses individuals and society to a cultural and political perspective that seeks to overcome perceived racial inequalities through state power, cultural advocacy, and the preferential treatment of individuals based on a racial or ethnic identity assigned by the government. The other perspective subordinates individuals and society to a natural science methodology that masquerades as absolute truth about the nature of individuals and their relationships with others, and seeks to affect public policy and structure social relationships accordingly.

An alternative to both the cultural and biological arguments that race and ethnicity eternally structure human thought and action is the position that there are social facts that arise and dissipate according to specific sociohistorical circumstances. Historically, the federal government played an enormously important role in the contemporary formation of ethno-racial groups in the United States from the 1950s to the early twenty-first century. In the specific case of black Americans, F. James Davis explored the legal, social, and cultural mechanisms that are used to differentiate white and black Americans. The answer to the question "Who is black?" in the United States has long been that a black is any person with any known African black ancestry. In the south, the measure became known as the "one-drop rule," stipulating that a single drop of "black blood" is sufficient to signify that a person is black. The rule was initially created in the slave South, where miscegenation was widespread, to force all racially mixed individuals with any known black ancestry into the status of slaves. Later the rule buttressed the Jim Crow system and other patterns of segregation and discrimination. This became the nation's norm and was backed by law. Determined white enforcement of the one-drop rule brought persons with a wide range of racial traits together in the black community, and centuries of shared experience resulted in a common ethnic identity.

Initially, the black community was forced to accept the one-drop rule and socialize succeeding generations in how to cope with it. David Hollinger writes that the structure of race and ethnicity in the United States is best characterized as an ethno-racial pentagon, comprised of five "blocs": African Americans, Asian Americans, Latinos, Native Americans, and white Americans. The formation of the ethno-racial blocs was grounded in the Civil Rights Act of 1964. The political categorization of persons into ethno-racial blocs was deemed necessary to ensure that the antidiscrimination and affirmative action policies of the federal government were enforced and assessed. As Hollinger points out, "Affirmative action runs on numbers."

The most significant event that prompted the contemporary differentiation of one bloc from another was a policy directive that the Office of Management and Budget issued in 1977 that enabled government bureaucrats to force persons into ethno-racial categories as part of their data collection activities. Statistical Directive 15 instructed all federal agencies to classify people into one of the five blocs of the ethno-racial pentagon. The consequence of this seemingly innocuous accountability mandate was that the federal government fixed and reified contemporary understandings of ethno-racial categories. The social facticity of race, to borrow Berger and Luckmann's terminology, is not due to an artifact of either biology or civil society, it is the result of the racial activism of the federal government.[14]

The theoretical approaches that reify race and racial stratification are diametrically opposed to a more humanist idea that race is a socially constructed, humanly experienced reality that varies spatially and historically. Following Berger and Luckmann, race and racism are social constructions and mechanisms through which human activities and experiences may, or may not, be organized. For humans, and because of humans, the ultimate reality of race and racism are what humans create and live. Race and racism exist as sociocultural constructs that are created, communicated, and known through symbolic interaction supported by political power. Race and racism are both measured or known only through socially produced cultural artifacts, which includes the procedures and technologies of the physical and biological sciences. While race may be thought to constitute a biological substratum to human experience, it is important to understand that even the biological and physical realities of race enter the realms of human activity and experience only as they are identified and made meaningful through symbolic interaction. The biological and physical dimensions of race do not speak or act for themselves. They become real and meaningful in human experience only because they are defined as such by human beings interacting in a symbolic and political environment that is frequently characterized by conflict, violence, and contradiction. The multiculturalist and the scientific conception of the "reality" or permanence of race are opposed by the notion that both race and racism must be understood from a *dialectical* and *humanist* standpoint which entails the ideas that race and racism are not fixed ideas or processes, but emerge from and are either maintained or transformed through the behaviors of individuals within a social and cultural context.

A philosophically adequate concept and theory of the transformation of race relations cannot conceive of race or racism as external, trans-human facts that are somehow autonomous from social and cultural life, nor can it adequately study race with an interest in discovering any ultimate nature apart from human thought and practice. The philosophical externalization and objectivation of race as a feature of social life serves the cultural and material interests of political and cultural elites, but it frustrates the visioning and achievement of a global totality free of domination and stratification based on race, ethnicity, and other social categories. To the extent that multiculturalism reifies race and racial stratification as universal features of social life, it proffers a flawed concept of social relations and social transformation. An alternative interpretation of the persistence of racism is not that the forces of discrimination are so strong, but that the philosophy of change is so weak. If the goal is to construct and promote a society free of domination, a multiculturalist critique is insufficient.

RACISM AND MULTICULTURALISM: MIRROR IMAGES?

The concept of racism in critical thought historically entailed the notion that universal cultural, economic, social, political, and psychological dynamics undergird the identification and subjugation of people based on biological, cultural, and/or linguistic categories. Racism in a variety of contexts could be understood using the same or similar theoretical constructs and measures. Thus, despite the particular manifestations of racism, which vary by time and space, critical inquiry initially explored the basic or generalized principles that contributed to our social self-knowledge of forms of prejudice, discrimination, and violence based on biology, culture, and language. Indeed, an important argument of those who offered empirical, theoretical or conceptual critiques of racism was that an understanding of the broad, generalized, or universal dynamics of racism is central to social progress, justice, and the transformation of society into a form that better serves human purposes. Hence, the cultural and historical understanding of any one particular manifestation of racist social relations may not be sufficient to overcome even that one expression of racism. Whatever the contributions of particular studies of race and ethnicity, the telos of critical inquiry should also include a contribution to a generalized understanding of race and ethnicity and a universal philosophy of human freedom. It is very doubtful that multiculturalist thought fulfills or promotes this vision. The primary issue is whether multiculturalism actually promotes an epistemological break with racism, or reproduces significant features of racist theory and practice.[15]

Multiculturalism offers a flawed theoretical stance on race and culture, and promotes ideas and actions that negate individual liberty. This section elaborates on this assertion by discussing five dimensions of multiculturalist thought: collectivism, cultural relativism, statism, tribalism, and determinism. Taken together, these five dimensions of multiculturalism help define it as an ideology and a social process. They illustrate where multiculturalism departs from racism as an ideology, but also where racism and multiculturalism converge. Multiculturalism is not the philosophic transcendence of racism, but only its negative recognition. When analyzed from these five perspectives, multiculturalism is revealed as the mirror image of racism.

Collectivism

One of the fundamental elements of racist thought is that it is a *collectivist*, not individualist, ideology since it promotes the idea that the collective qualities and attributions of racial, ethnic, and linguistic groups matter more than the character and behaviors of individuals in cultural symbols and public policy. Racism defines and proscribes human identity and behavior in collective constructs purportedly rooted in biological, cultural, and/or linguistic phenomena. Through its advocates, racist thought attempts to affect or determine public policy through the seizure of political power to impose a regime of social relations that actualizes the collectivist constructs that categorizes persons into racial and ethnic groups. The self-fulfilling component of racist thought is not left to chance; instead, racist political activists seek to ensure that their definition of the situation is made real through the levers of the state, the culture, and the hierarchical organizations within society.

As the mirror image of racism, multiculturalism is also a collectivist, not individualist, ideology in that it promotes collective notions of victimization and the idea that collective action is the only viable or conceivable response to racism. Similar to racism, multiculturalism also promotes the idea that human identity and action must be reduced to collective constructs rooted in biological, cultural, or linguistic phenomena. Of course, multiculturalist ideology interprets historical process and social facts from a partisan perspective; it purports to be on the side of those it defines as victims and views the knowledge process as an element in the liberation of the victims.[16] However, the experience of the victim and the liberation of the victim are always understood in terms of *collective characteristics*, *collective experiences*, and *collective needs*, not *individual characteristics*, *individual experiences*, and *individual needs*.

It is questionable whether the collectivism of racism can be meaningfully challenged by the collectivism of multiculturalism. Like racism, multiculturalism is also an ideology that promotes the subjugation of individuals to the collectivity and, thus, entails all of the social, personal, and political problems associated with collectivism. What sort of liberation is it when individuals are emancipated from one collectivist ideology only to be subjugated to another? How is multiculturalism an optimal response to collectivist notions and movements that promote or reinforce racial superiority?

Cultural Relativism

Originally based in the philosophic precept that racial groups should not be viewed as superior or inferior, multiculturalism sought to promote inclusiveness and tolerance in through the idea that there is a type of cultural equality, or, at least, the idea that no one society, culture or linguistic group can be demonstrated to be superior to others. In its nascent form, the multiculturalist critique of racism simply built on top of the "cultural relativist" notion of the early western ethnographers and anthropologists, who were concerned that the cultural filter of the western nations would be used to interpret discoveries about preliterate societies.[17] However, the cultural relativism of the multiculturalist critique of cultural differences has been transformed into an attack on western culture and concepts, placing inequities among the ethnoracial blocs at the center of its analysis. In culture, science, and politics, those theories, ideas, and scholarly studies that attempt to re-center discourse on social relations on other concepts have been nearly universally condemned as "racist" or "chauvinist." Many organizations in the United States, in fact, have adopted policies that identify philosophic or ideological challenges to the relativism of multiculturalism as "hate speech" and elevate multiculturalism as the final statement on race, ethnicity, and social relations. Any belief in common values or goals that attempt to transcend race and culture are derided as "paleoconservatism."[18]

Multiculturalism is a *relativist* ideology in that it promotes the notion that one culture or one cultural element cannot be shown or understood to be superior to another, and that each culture should be understood in its own context. While the multiculturalist philosophy of change includes a number of analytic dimensions and appears to be applicable to a wide array of social and cultural issues, at base, it entails a relativist notion that one society, culture, or group cannot and should not judge or evaluate another society, culture or group by its own standards or frame of reference.[19]

The intent underlying the relativism of multiculturalist ideology is to establish an epistemological equality among races, cultures, and linguistic groups so that all groups or cultures will be tolerated, at least in the abstract. The tolerance of multiculturalism, however, is very selective; there is infinite tolerance of cultural difference, but very little tolerance for ideological difference. In a relativist world, no standard, no social formation or cultural value can be demonstrated to be better than any another. For the consistent relativist, democracy cannot be demonstrated to be any better than dictatorship, the rule of law cannot be demonstrated to be any better than tyranny, liberty cannot be demonstrated to be any better than domination. Following the logic of cultural relativism, racist and multiculturalist thought must both be understood in their cultural context; multiculturalism cannot be demonstrated to be superior to racism in any ultimate way. For a cultural relativist, multiculturalism cannot be demonstrated to be superior to racism in any ultimate way since both must be understood and appreciated in their cultural and historical context. Cultural relativism does not offer a helpful roadmap toward the elimination of racism because, to be consistent, relativism must validate racist culture just as it validates antiracist culture.

Statism

Racism is a *statist* ideology in that it requires political authority, power, law, and public policy to enforce the domination and subjugation of racial, ethnic, and linguistic groups. Racist regimes revere the state and assign it a primary role in social life because it functions to protect the domination of one racial group by another. Multiculturalism is also a statist ideology in that it looks to the state, public, and institutional policy and enforcement mechanisms to ameliorate, rectify, or eliminate forms of prejudice, discrimination, and violence. Multiculturalism's vision for responding to coercion against disadvantaged social groups is the acquisition of state power and the application of its coercive resources to assist them and defeat their enemies, all of whom are presumed to be racists.

Multiculturalism assumes that the same authority and power structures that were used to dominate and subjugate people can and should be used to emancipate them. Certainly, the effectiveness of the use of state power to emancipate subjugated social groups can be questioned, but it is also important to note that multiculturalist ideology does nothing to challenge the relationship between the state and other social institutions; nor does it challenge the role of the state in society or the power of the state over the individual. It assumes that the state is a neutral social structure that can and should be used to implement any social or political policy on behalf of favored or protected social groups. The political goal for multiculturalists is to either seize the state apparatus, or to influence it, so that the state sufficiently responds to their social and cultural agenda. Multiculturalism is a statist ideology because it looks to the state for the solution of all critical social problems; like racism, it reveres the acquisition and exercise of state power.[20]

Tribalism

Racism and multiculturalism are also *tribalist*, or *exclusionist*, ideologies that particularize human characteristics, experiences, worth, values, and needs. Both undermine common bonds among people and both negate the notion that political, ethical and educational systems should operate on the basis of the application of universal principles. Racism and multiculturalism are forms of tribalism that promote the separation of individuals based on racial, ethnic, and/or linguistic characteristics. Tribalism is a type of social organization that creates and enforces social, cultural, and geographic boundaries that separate individuals, deny their inclusion, interaction, and common humanity.

Racism defends and promotes the philosophy and practice of differentiating and separating people for the purposes of domination and subjugation based on race, ethnicity, and/or linguistic group. It elevates some groups above others. It argues that the allocation of social desiderata should be based on racial or cultural identity. Multiculturalism particularizes by defending and promoting the philosophy and practice of differentiating and separating people for the purpose of subjugating them to the authority of political, cultural elites and educational elites, who are presumed to promote ideas and public policies oriented toward the emancipation of disadvantaged racial, cultural and linguistic groups.

Identity-based hiring practices, scholarship programs, and organizations that aim at the social, cultural, and political promotion of specific groups, are tribalist practices legitimated by multiculturalist ideology. Higher education financial aid programs targeted at African American students, while intended to help improve access to higher education, are preferential practices that exclude Hispanic, Native American, and Asian American students. Corporate and governmental hiring practices targeted at Hispanic workers are preferential practices that exclude African American and Asian American workers. When a mayor declares a major American southern city "a chocolate city," it implies the exclusion or diminution of individuals from other racial and ethnic groups. Preferential and exclusionist statements and programs of all types function to separate groups, engender intergroup conflict, and reinforce collective identities. They are based on the belief that the structures of prejudice, discrimination, and violence directed against racial, ethnic and linguistic groups are fundamentally different and, thus, require particular programs and policies for their amelioration. Preferential practices have been effectively and appropriately criticized by a variety of political interests as new forms of discrimination. To the extent that multiculturalism promotes the differentiation and elevation of some groups at the expense of others, it is a form of tribalism and an enemy of human liberation. At the very minimum, this dimension of multiculturalism eschews discourse on the universal meaning of human liberation as far as individuals are concerned in favor of discourse that focuses on reinforcing boundaries that separate ethnoracial blocs.[21]

Determinism

Racism is a *determinist* ideology that promotes the idea that race, culture, and linguistic identity structure the thought, proclivities, ability, opportunities, and achievements of individuals. Racism is a destructive ideology for many reasons. Perhaps its determinist element is the most important among these because it negates the ability of individual human beings to freely pursue their interests and to cultivate their talents. Racist social regimes implement limitations on human freedom and choice through laws, policies, and cultural symbols that derogate individuals, deny them opportunities, and exact official violence against them to punish challenges and to promote fear and helplessness against the regime. Racist science and cultural discourse implements limitations on human freedom though generalizations and predictions that circumscribe the patterns of human thought and behavior.

A very curious expression of this point appeared in the recent controversy over the comments that comedian Bill Cosby made about the black underclass in the United States. Cosby essentially said that there needs to be some accountability of individuals and families for the social disorganization experienced by far too many African Americans. Cosby's comments were savaged by Michael Eric Dyson, *Is Bill Cosby Right, Or Has the Black Middle Class Lost its Mind?* However, Cosby found support for his perspective from intellectuals such as Shelby Steele and Juan Williams, who, while not paragons of individualism, reject the idea that persons in the black underclass are infinitely and eternally the victims of white racism. The basic issue is, to what extent are individuals in the black underclass responsible for changing their life experiences? Dyson argues a determinist perspective, that the black underclass are victims of a racist society. Racial discourse that focuses on or encourages changes in the behavior of individuals only promotes the prevailing cultural racism, according to Dyson. Cosby, Steele, and Williams argue that there is some opportunity for individuals in the black underclass to affect their own future. They all argue that the determinist perspective expressed by writers such as Dyson functions to reinforce helplessness.[22]

Multiculturalism elevates culture to a determinant, not just mediating, role in the structuring of human thought, behavior, and experience. The more important the role that culture has in shaping thought and behavior, the more significant multiculturalism is as an ideology that interprets racial and ethnic phenomena. The less significant role that culture has in shaping thought and behavior, the less significant multiculturalism is in challenging forms of prejudice, discrimination, and violence. To the multiculturalist, culture is everything, the individual is nothing. The multiculturalist agenda must assign culture a determinant role in individual behavior. Multiculturalism, like racism, carries with it all of the problems of determinist ideology. Most significantly, it either excises notions of individual freedom, spontaneity, and autonomy from social and political discourse, or subordinates them to other beliefs and values. What sort of emancipation does multiculturalism really offer if it elevates culture to a determinant status and reduces human individuals to passive receptacles of the political, social, and cultural dictates of the regime?

THE DIALECTICS OF LIBERTY: A THEORETICAL FRAMEWORK

Critique and opposition to racism cannot be reduced to the multiculturalist understanding of race and ethnicity without inflicting serious damage to the interest in human freedom. The understanding of race and ethnicity does not need to be reduced to a single choice of "racism" or "multiculturalism." It is important to uncouple the critique of racism from the multiculturalist agenda. Multiculturalism falls short of being an efficacious philosophy of liberation. Instead, it is an ideology that negates individuality and reinforces existing authority structures. It promotes coercion and militates against individualist values of voluntary agreement, personal responsibility, and self-reliance. Although multiculturalism seeks to promote equality and tolerance, it offers very little in the way of a vision for a future that optimizes opportunities for the cultivation of individual human talent. It requires the rigid, institutional categorization of people along racial and ethnic lines. Multiculturalism is a type of collectivism that reduces individuals to racial and ethnic categories defined by the government. Taken together, its elements constitute a form of reactionary tribalism.

If multiculturalism is an inadequate framework, what type of approach can be adopted that will help critique racism but also negate the collectivist, relativist, tribalist, statist, and determinist elements of multicultural thought? One approach to articulating the elements of an alternative perspective is to identify and analyze what individualist and libertarian theorists and writers have said about race, ethnicity, and culture. It is time to explore what individualism and libertarianism have to offer to those who are interested in reconstructing social life without racial and ethnic domination. The remaining chapters in this book identify some ideas that may lead toward an approach that neither capitulates to racism nor adopts the reactionary tribalism of multiculturalism.

The theorists discussed in chapters 2 through 6 have many differences in their views of knowledge, society, and humanity, but there are two commonalities that unite their thought. First, each articulates a critique of racism. In one case, the critique is more implied than explicit, but the others are explicit, direct critiques of racism that have not received due attention in the contemporary discourse on race and ethnicity. Second, each theorist based a critique of racism on a philosophy of individual freedom and an antistatist view of the role of government in society. Because they are individualist, libertarian, and antiracist, their ideas do not fit neatly into the received political categories or theoretical paradigms of the social sciences. They are neither left nor right in their political ideas. They are neither racist nor multiculturalist in their views of race, ethnicity, and culture. An encounter with their theoretical ideas can open new vistas into how racism can be attacked through the promotion of individualist and libertarian philosophy.

In his book, *Total Freedom: Toward a Dialectical Libertarianism*, Chris Matthew Sciabarra outlines a philosophic perspective that seeks to integrate or fuse the basic elements of libertarianism with dialectical social theory.[23] *Total Freedom* develops many of the ideas that Sciabarra initially presented in his studies, *Ayn Rand: The Russian Radical* and *Marx, Hayek, and Utopia*.[24] Sciabarra's basic argument is that there are some important points at which dialectical and libertarian theory converge. *Total Freedom* is particularly eloquent on the points that dialectical thinking does not, by necessity, result in the collectivist and statist utopias attributed to Hegel and Marx. In fact, if the understanding of dialectics is expanded and traced back to Aristotle, the compatibility between dialectics and libertarianism becomes more apparent. In Sciabarra's formulation, dialectical analysis transcends antagonisms between nations, races, and social classes, and is applied more broadly to include the conflicts between the market and the state, cultural ideals and social practices, and the self and other. This is especially true in the thought of Ayn Rand, as Sciabarra demonstrates through an extended discussion of the philosophies of both Rand and Murray Rothbard.

With the exception of Max Stirner, the theorists associated with the Hegelian dialectic ultimately pursued collectivist agendas that Sciabarra and other libertarians cannot accept.[25] Yet, freedom is a central category in Hegel's philosophy. The young Hegel was vehemently antistatist and once commented that "the state must be abolished" because it inevitably treats persons as though they are machines. Hegel's dialectic purports to discover the process in which freedom is made actual in the world. In *The Science of Logic*, Hegel refers to the dialectic as the "self–bringing forth of liberty." He also states that "(o)nly that which is an object of freedom may be called an Idea," which, for Hegel, meant that the standard by which the validity of knowledge is assessed is not its correspondence to an inert "out there," but by its contribution to human freedom. It is pertinent that the young Marx, having discovered the Hegelian dialectic, stated that "the individual is the social entity," which hardly prefigures his so-called mature position that social classes are the primary social actors. Although they are not libertarians, Dinesh D'Sousa in *The End of Racism* and Peter Wood in *Diversity: The Invention of a Concept* provide arguments that race, ethnicity, and diversity are constructed phenomena, and advocate much more from an individualist point of view than the early Hegelians.[26]

Sciabarra provides a compelling argument that dialectical social theory should be freed from its Marxian fetters. He is not just interested in a dialectical interpretation of Rand's philosophy, but in examining how dialectical thought could help develop and promote individualist and libertarian ideas. He fully believes that there is a dialectical foundation to Rand's thought, in spite of her dramatic differences with Hegel and Marx. Sciabarra articulates a dialectical libertarianism as an integrated political philosophy that is distinct from other political perspectives, but every bit as comprehensive in its depiction of political sovereignty and legitimacy.

The vision of a dialectical libertarianism in this study is considerably more restricted than the comprehensive philosophy Sciabarra proposes. The "dialectics of liberty" is a very helpful framework for developing a critique of multiculturalism, particularly if it promotes an individualist and libertarian critique of the social reality of racism. Dialectical theory is strong in its interpretation of conflict, alienation, and change. Libertarian theory is strong in its defense of individuality and challenge to authority and political domination. Both purport to be philosophies of freedom. Both assign liberty a central role in philosophy and politics.[27] An optimal outcome of a dialectical libertarian critique of multiculturalism is a vision of individuality and society freed of racial domination and the collectivist reduction of persons to racial and ethnic categories. The dialectical libertarian vision of the individual bears a significant resemblance to Hegel's concept of the "free subject," which is conceived as a self-conscious, self-determining individual. A dialectical libertarianism offers the best hope for the articulation of a social theory that envisions individuality and society freed of the domination by racist ideology and the state.

Sciabarra's dialectical libertarianism is based on the notion that radical social theory

> recognizes the organic relationship between goals and context and seeks a resolution that is immanent to the conditions that exist. As such, it is opposed in principle to the construction of new institutional designs as if these were outside the historical process. It views social institutions as constituted by both human intentionality and unintended social consequences.[28]

Sciabarra envisions a tri-level model of power relations that emphasizes the reciprocal impact of each level on the others and opposes the isolation and abstraction of one level from the others, except for the purpose of analysis. Ultimately, each level cannot be extracted from the whole.

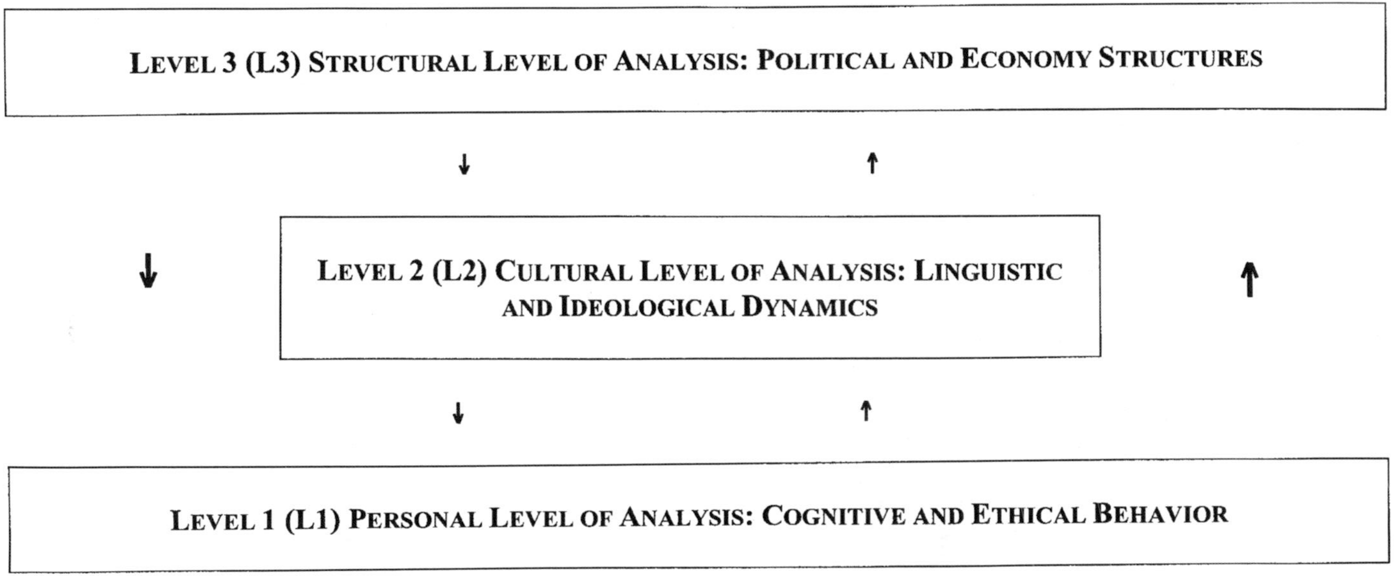

Figure 1. The Dialectical Libertarian Framework of Power Relations in Society

Note: Adapted from Chris Mathew Sciabarra, *Total Freedom: Toward a Dialectical Libertarianism* (University Park, PA: Penn State University Press, 2000), Page 380.

Level 1 (L1) refers to power relations as they are viewed from the perspective of the ethical and cognitive behaviors of the individual. When L1 is brought to the foreground of analysis, the focus is on the importance of individual and interpersonal ethical and cognitive behaviors that promote or challenge racism and alternatives to it. Level 2 (L2) refers to the analysis of power relations from the perspective of culture including language, values, norms, and ideology. When L2 is brought to the foreground of the analysis of racism and alternatives to it, the focus is on cultural traditions and ideologies that either promote, perpetuate, or challenge relations within and among ethnoracial groups. Level 3 (L3) refers to the structural level of the analysis of power relations from the perspective of political and economic structures, processes, and institutions. When L3 is brought to the foreground of the analysis of racism and alternatives to it, the focus is on laws, taxes, programs, and policies that either promote, perpetuate, or challenge racism. From Sciabarra's point of view, the dialectical libertarian framework requires an analysis and attack on the realities of racism at all three levels. He emphasizes the organic unity of the dialectical libertarian framework by quoting Rand's dictum that intellectual freedom, political freedom, and economic freedom are mutually dependent and mutually reinforcing. One cannot exist without the support of the others.[29]

Drawing from the framework Sciabarra developed, the basic elements of a dialectical libertarian approach to the critique of racism and multicultural thought might be founded on the following methodological precepts:

1. A focus on the conflicts and antagonisms in theory and society, and a suspicion that prevailing political ideologies are replete with internal tensions and conflict with social practice. From a dialectical libertarian point of view, a fundamental conflict in theory and society is between the authority of the state and the freedom of the individual.
2. A focus on the critique of force and fraud as central social processes, and a suspicion that social organization tends to be the outcome of coercion and manipulation rather than consensus, all of which tend to be rooted in the exercise of political power in society. Individuals and groups tend to resist constraints on their behavior. Force and fraud are important mechanisms for the imposition of state power.
3. A commitment to the description of social reality in historical or processual rather than static terms. Individualist and libertarian theorists tend to oppose reified conceptions of social institutions, particularly the state, which declare that the domination of individuals by the state is a permanent, necessary, invariant feature of human existence. Society and culture are not fixed; they are in flux, constantly challenged and potentially changing.

4. A commitment to a philosophy of knowledge that disputes the idea that human sciences must be identical in their assumptions and procedures to the natural sciences. Dialectical libertarianism must allow for indeterminacy and freedom in human behavior.
5. A belief that the goal of inquiry is not the discovery of eternal laws and universal order in social life, but the search for the sources of, and obstacles to, individual freedom.

These methodological precepts do not constitute an argument that the theorists examined in subsequent chapters consistently propound a dialectical libertarianism. Instead, the precepts are helpful in understanding individualist critiques of racism and in developing a dialectical libertarian critique of both racism and multiculturalism. A progressive critique of both racism and multiculturalism must include elements of dialectical methods in order to ensure that the understanding of these processes is grounded in human behavior. It must also include the philosophy and goal of liberating individuals from ideologies, practices, and movements that reduce their identities to racial and ethnic categories. An important first step in the development of a dialectical libertarian critique of multiculturalism is discovering (1) what individualist and libertarian theorists have said about race, ethnicity, and racism, and (2) how their views on race emerged from the broader context of their social thought.

The survey of the individualist and libertarian critiques of racism included in this book begins with Ayn Rand because of the clarity and force with which she outlined basic theoretical choices. The discussion then moves to a consideration of the market anarchism of Murray Rothbard, the theorists associated with the Libertarian movement in the United States, and the individualist anarchists Benjamin Tucker, Lysander Spooner, and Albert Jay Nock. The exploration concludes with a consideration of the ideas of Max Stirner because his trenchant, unrelenting critique of ideology provides a seamless entrée into the transracial and post-ethnic concepts discussed in the final chapter that foreshadow politics and identity after multiculturalism.

NOTES

1. Charles Taylor, ed., *Multiculturalism: Examining the Politics of Recognition* (Princeton, NJ: Princeton University Press, 1994); Peter Kivisto, ed., *Multiculturalism in the United States: Current Issues, Contemporary Voices* (Thousand Oaks, CA: Pine Forge Press, 2000); Lawrence Foster and Patricia Herzog, *Defending Diversity: Contemporary Philosophical Perspectives on Pluralism and Multiculturalism*

(Amherst: University of Massachusetts Press, 1994); Cynthia Willett, *Theorizing Multiculturalism: A Guide to the Current Debate* (Malden, MA: Blackwell Publishers, 1998).

2. Anne Norton, "The Virtues of Multiculturalism," in *Multiculturalism and American Democracy*, ed. Arthur Melzer, Jerry Weinberger, and M. Richard Zinman (Lawrence: University of Kansas Press, 1998), 130.

3. Nathan Glazer, "Is Assimilation Dead?" in *Multiculturalism and American Democracy*, ed. Arthur Melzer, Jerry Weinberger, and M. Richard Zinman (Lawrence: University of Kansas Press, 1998), 16–17. For a similar, wistful statement about assimilation in a multicultural age see Glazer's, *We Are All Multiculturalists Now* (Cambridge, MA: Harvard University Press, 1998). For collectivist perspectives that critique multiculturalism see Antonia Darder and Rodolfo Torres, *After Race: Racism after Multiculturalism* (New York: New York University Press, 2004); Peter McLaren, *Revolutionary Multiculturalism: Pedagogies of Dissent for the New Millennium* (Boulder, CO: Westview Press, 1997); Walter Benn Michaels, *The Trouble with Diversity: How We Learned to Love Identity and Ignore Inequality* (New York: Metropolitan Books, 2006); Richard Bernstein, *Dictatorship of Virtue: Multiculturalism, Diversity and the Battle for America's Future* (New York: A. A. Knopf, 1994); Henry A. Giroux, *Living Dangerously: Multiculturalism and the Politics of Difference* (New York: Lang, 1993).

4. Peter Berger and Thomas Luckmann, *The Social Construction of Reality: A Treatise in the Sociology of Knowledge* (New York: Doubleday, 1966). Berger and Luckmann's perspective on reality construction is not flawless. See my review of literature on their work and an early attempt to develop a dialectical critique of Berger and Luckmann in John F. Welsh, "Reification and the Dialectic of Social Life: Against the Berger Group," *Quarterly Journal of Ideology* 10 (Spring 1986): 12–23.

5. Berger and Luckmann, *The Social Construction of Reality*, 161.

6. Peter Berger and Stanley Pullberg, "Reification and the Sociological Critique of Consciousness," *History and Theory* 4 (Spring 1965): 196–211.

7. One example of the federal government's formal definition of racial and ethnic categories appears in the Bureau of the Census's summary of population characteristics of the United States. See http://www.census.gov/population/cen2000/phc-2-a-B.pdf.

8. Stella Nkomo, "The Emperor Has No Clothes: Rewriting Race in Organizations," *Academy of Management Review* 17 (1992): 487–504.

9. Cornell West, *Race Matters* (Boston: Beacon Press, 1993); *Democracy Matters* (New York: Penguin, 2004). Also, see Cornell West's argument that racism can only be addressed through the political framework of democratic socialism in "Toward a Socialist Theory of Racism," retrieved on January 22, 2007 from http://race.eserver.org/toward-a-theory-of-racism.html. Michael Eric Dyson, *Debating Race* (New York: Perseus Books, 2007).

10. Eduardo Bonilla-Silva, *White Supremacy and Racism in the Post–Civil Rights Era* (Boulder, CO: Lynne Rienner, 2001); *Racism without Racists: Color Blind-Racism and the Persistence of Racial Inequality* (Boulder, CO: Rowman and Littlefield, 2003); "The (White) Color of Color Blindness," *Race, Ethnicity, and Education*:

Racism and Anti-Racism in Education, in E. Wayne Ross. (Westport, CT: Praeger, 2006).

11. Vincent Savich and Frank Micle, *Race: The Reality of Human Differences* (Boulder, CO: Westview Press, 2004).

12. J. Phillippe Rushton, *Race, Evolution, and Behavior: A Life History Perspective* (Port Huron, MI: Charles Darwin Research Institute, 2000).

13. Jared Taylor and George McDaniel, *A Race against Time: Racial Heresies for the 21st Century* (Oakton, VA: New City Foundation, 2003). Another book that developed a similar argument is Steven Gregory and Roger Sajek, *Race* (New Brunswick, NJ: Rutgers, The State University, 1994).

14. See F. James Davis, *Who is Black? One Nation's Definition* (University Park: Pennsylvania State University Press, 1991) and David Hollinger, *Postethnic America: Beyond Multiculturalism* (New York: Basic Books, 1995). Also see Michael Omni and Howard Winant, *Racial Formation in the United States from the 1960s to the 1990s*, 2d ed. (New York: Routledge, 1994) and Werner Sollors, ed., *The Invention of Ethnicity* (New York: Oxford University Press, 1989).

15. Examples and discussions of pre- and non-multiculturalist scholarly critiques of racism include Gunner Myrdal, *An American Dilemma: The Negro Problem and Modern Democracy* (1954; Somerset, NJ: Transaction Publishers, 1995); George Fredrickson, *Racism: A Short History* (Princeton, NJ: Princeton University Press, 2003); Gordon Allport, *The Nature of Prejudice* (1954; New York: Perseus Books, 1979).

16. For multiculturalist discussions of this point see Ruth Sidel, *Battling Bias: The Struggle for Identity and Community on College Campuses* (New York: Penguin Books, 1994); William Tierney, *Building Communities of Difference: Higher Education in the Twenty-First Century* (Westport, CT: Bergin and Garvey, 1993); and William Tierney, "Cultural Politics and the Curriculum in Postsecondary Education," in *College and University Curriculum*, ed. Lisa Lattuca, Jennifer Grant Haworth, and Clifton Conrad (Boston: Pearson Custom Publishing, 2002), 25–35. Alternative perspectives are offered by Stephan Thernstrom and Abigail Thernstrom, *America in Black and White: One Nation, Indivisible* (New York: Simon and Schuster, 1997); Stephan Thernstrom and Abigail Thernstrom, *No Excuses: Closing the Racial Gap in Learning* (New York: Simon and Schuster, 2003); and J. Harvie Wilkinson, *One Nation Indivisible: How Ethnic Separatism Threatens America* (New York: Addison Wesley Longman, 1997).

17. For a critique of cultural relativism from the perspective of critical social theory, see Christopher Norris, *Reclaiming Truth: Contribution to a Critique of Cultural Relativism* (Durham, NC: Duke University Press, 1996) and *Against Relativism: Philosophy of Science, Deconstruction, and Critical Theory* (Malden, MA: Blackwell, 1997).

18. For a discussion of this point that is focused on higher education see David Sacks, Peter Thiel, and Elizabeth Fox-Genovese, *The Diversity Myth: Multiculturalism and Political Intolerance at Stanford* (Oakland, CA: The Independent Institute, 1996). Also relevant is Timothy C. Shiell, *Campus Hate Speech on Trial* (Lawrence: University of Kansas Press, 1998).

19. For a left-oriented discussion of this point see Douglas Kellner, "A Marcuse Renaissance?" in *Marcuse: From the New Left to the Next Left*, ed. John Borkina and Timothy Lukes (Lawrence: University of Kansas Press, 1994). More conservative perspectives are presented in Roger Kimball, *Tenured Radicals: How Politics Has Corrupted Our Higher Education* (New York: Harper and Row, 1990) and Sandra Stotsky, *Losing our Language: How Multicultural Classroom Instruction Is Undermining Our Children's Ability to Read, Write and Reason* (New York: The Free Press, 1999). A classic but very controversial statement on this point is Allan Bloom, *The Closing of the American Mind: How Higher Education Has Failed Democracy and Impoverished the Souls of Today's Students* (New York: Simon and Schuster, 1987).

20. See Lynn Cheney, *Telling the Truth: Why Our Culture and Our Country Have Stopped Making Sense—and What We Can Do About It* (New York: Simon and Schuster, 1995) and Tammy Bruce, *The New Thought Police: Inside the Left's Assault on Free Speech and Free Minds* (Roseville, CA: Prima Publishing, 2001). For great discussions about this point placed in an historical context see Peter Collier and David Horowitz, *Second Thoughts about the Sixties* (New York: Summit Books, 1990) and Richard J. Ellis, *The Dark Side of the Left: Illiberal Egalitarianism in America* (Lawrence: University of Kansas Press, 1998). These books demonstrate that the multicultural left in the United States has been consistently authoritarian in its approach to inquiry, politics, and culture.

21. Ayn Rand is the indispensable source for the tribalist concept. See Ayn Rand, *Return of the Primitive: The Anti-Industrial Revolution* (New York: Penguin, 1999). For more contemporary example of an Objectivist use of the concept of tribalism, see Gary Hull, "The Pied Pipers of Tribalism," http://www.aynrand.org/site/News2?news _iv_ctrl=1&page=NewsArticle&id=5395&security=1 (accessed January 26, 2007) and Peter Schwartz, "The Racism of Diversity," http://www.aynrand.org/site/News2? JServSessionIdr001=hqrs2gp9q8.app7a&page=NewsArticle&id=7915&news_iv_ctr l=1076 (accessed January 26, 2007). Also see Harold Isaacs, *Idols of the Tribe: Group Identity and Political Change* (Cambridge, MA: Harvard University Press, 1989). For a left-oriented discussion of tribalism that emerged after the collapse of postmodernist thought in Europe see Robert J. Antonio, "After Postmodernism: Reactionary Tribalism," *American Journal of Sociology* 106 (2000): 40–87.

22. Michael Eric Dyson, *Is Bill Cosby Right, Or Has the Black Middle Class Lost its Mind?* (New York: Basic Civitas Books, 2005). For perspectives that directly critique determinist views of race and define this element of multicultural thought as a departure from the vision of the early civil rights movement, see Shelby Steele, *The Content of Our Character: A New Vision of Race in America* (New York: St. Martin's Press, 1990); *A Dream Deferred: The Second Betrayal of Black Freedom in America* (New York: HarperCollins, 1998); and *White Guilt: How Blacks and Whites Together Destroyed the Promise of the Civil Rights Era* (New York: HarperCollins, 2006); Thomas Sowell, *Race and Culture* (New York: Basic Books, 1994) and *Black Rednecks and White Liberals* (San Francisco: Encounter Books, 2005); and Juan Williams, *Enough: The Phony Leaders, Dead-End Movements, and the Culture of Failure That Are Undermining Black America—And What We Can Do About It* (New York: Random House, 2006).

23. Chris Matthew Sciabarra, *Total Freedom: Toward a Dialectical Libertarianism* (University Park: Pennsylvania State University Press, 2000).

24. Chris Matthew Sciabarra, *Marx, Hayek and Utopia* (Albany: State University of New York, 1995); *Ayn Rand: The Russian Radical* (University Park: Pennsylvania State University Press, 1995).

25. Mikhail Bakunin, *Statism and Anarchy* (1873; Cambridge: Cambridge University Press, 1990) and Max Stirner, *The Ego and Its Own* (1844; Cambridge: Cambridge University Press, 1995). Karl Marx developed a dialectical, humanist, and constructivist view of racism in his early essay "On the Jewish Question," which is included in *Writings of the Young Marx on Philosophy and Society* (New York: Doubleday, 1983). Jean-Paul Sartre did the same in *Anti-Semite and Jew* (New York: Shocken Books, 1965). Also see Frantz Fanon, *Black Skins, White Masks* (New York: Grove Press, 1967) for a similar view. It is debatable whether any of these writings transcends a collectivist framework. However, Marx, Sartre, and Fanon appeared to struggle with the ways in which racism denigrates individuals and the role of individuals in the struggle against it.

26. Dinesh D'Sousa, *The End of Racism* (New York: The Free Press, 1995); Peter Wood, *Diversity: The Invention of a Concept* (San Francisco: Encounter Books, 2003). For a discussion of the centrality of the concept of freedom in Hegel's thought, see John F. Welsh, "The Unchained Dialectic: Theory and Research in an Era of Educational Reform," in *Neoliberalism and Educational Reform*, ed. Wayne Ross and Rich Gibson (Cresskill, NJ: Hampton Press, 2007), 217–35.

27. The notion of a dialectical libertarianism may not be as foreign as it first appears. No less of an authority on the Marxist dialectic than Bertell Ollman speaks approvingly of Sciabarra's project in *Dance of the Dialectic: Steps in Marx's Method* (Champaign-Urbana: University of Illinois Press, 2003), 7. For an argument that the dialectic should be "unchained" from its collectivist and statist moorings in Hegelian and Marxist thought, see Welsh, "The Unchained Dialectic," 217–35.

28. Sciabarra, *Total Freedom*, 4.

29. Sciabarra, *Total Freedom*, 383.

Chapter Two

Against the Predatory State and the Mystique of Race

The Objectivist Vision of Ayn Rand

OBJECTIVISM, RACE, AND DIALECTICS

In his hilarious and insightful personal history of the Libertarian movement in the United States in the early 1970s, *It Usually Begins with Ayn Rand*, Jerome Tucille suggests, with tongue-somewhat-in-cheek, that Ayn Rand is one of the preeminent theorists of individualist and libertarian thought because of her influence on a generation of young intellectuals and activists who were searching for viable alternatives to the traditional left-right formulation of political phenomena. In his recent "freewheeling" history of libertarianism in the United States, Brian Doherty also documents the tremendous impact that Rand had on the formation of the early libertarian movement.[1] By the early 1970s, of course, Rand was already an enormously successful novelist and essayist whose work was as controversial as it was popular, in part, because of the clarity and force that characterized her writings and the philosophical system she developed.

Rand had much more than a mere cult following at the time libertarianism emerged as a political movement in the United States in the early 1970s. In fact, a comprehensive philosophic, literary, educational, and psychological self-help industry had already developed around her by an inner circle of acolytes and publishers who were determined to promote her publications and philosophy, and to critique American politics and popular culture from the rational egoist point of view she developed. The philosophic movement and the organization Rand and her followers founded persist and appear to flourish to this day. *After Multiculturalism* begins a survey of individualist critiques of racism and multiculturalism with Ayn Rand primarily because an American academic audience is likely to be more familiar with her writings than with those of the other individualist thinkers discussed herein. An encounter with her work on racism and individualism also helps lay an intellectual foundation for many of the issues discussed in subsequent chapters.

Ayn Rand was born Alissa Rosenbaum in St. Petersburg, Russia, in February 1905 into an educated family that had an individualist and liberal political orientation. Rand herself was initially very enthusiastic about the emergent Russian Revolution in 1917 because she believed that it destroyed the tyranny of religious mysticism that dominated Russian culture and politics. For the first time in Russian history, the Revolution also created an opportunity for a republican form of government to emerge that would protect the rights of individuals. She enrolled in the university at Petrograd in 1921 and pursued a liberal education in the college of social science. She was significantly influenced by the preeminent Russian philosopher N. O. Lossky and may have learned and adopted a dialectical method of analysis in her thinking and writing.[2] With the victory of the Bolsheviks and the rise of Communism, however, Rand became increasingly disenchanted with the Revolution, believing that Marxist-Leninist theory and practice shared common features with the mysticism and authoritarianism of the Tsarist government. In her view, the Communists simply replaced the Tsarist God with an omnipotent collectivist state in their rush to create a new, but equally irrational society.

Attempting to escape Soviet Communism, she emigrated to the United States in 1926 and by the mid-1940s became a successful novelist and public intellectual. Rand is perhaps best known for her novels, *The Fountainhead*, which was originally published in 1943, and *Atlas Shrugged*, which was originally published in 1957. The entire corpus of her work includes two other novels, *We the Living* and *Anthem*, at least ten nonfiction books, screenplays, a stage play, and many essays, letters, and journals that include elements of her philosophy and criticism of political, literary, and cultural trends. Following her death in 1982, her followers pursued the development of the philosophy she founded through a variety of venues. Today, the Ayn Rand Institute manages her literary-philosophic estate and continues her work through educational programs and the publication of essays and studies that apply aspects of her thought to a wide array of philosophical, cultural, and political issues.[3]

A major theme in Rand's later political writings concerns how conflicting social and cultural forces tend to reflect similar underlying philosophic principles or premises. Methodologically, Rand frequently approached political and cultural topics through a discussion of the foundations of antagonistic ideas to reveal that one idea was a mirror image of the other. A critical feature of her analysis of these false oppositions is how they emerge from, interact with, and are resolved in a larger sociocultural context. This point has considerable relevance for understanding her critique of racism and the struggle against it. Her method has been characterized as a type of dialectical analysis that sought to understand, critique, and overcome false or artificial oppositions in order to reveal new, authentic alternatives to established social thought and practice.[4] From this vantage point—and given the premium her thought places on the freedom of the individual—Rand can be fruitfully understood as an important "dialectician of liberty."[5]

Although many academic philosophers and behavioral scientists still view her and her work with considerable disdain, Rand has been taken much more seriously in academia in recent decades. There is at least one scholarly journal, *The Journal of Ayn Rand Studies*, that is devoted exclusively to critical studies about her novels and philosophy. At least four other academic journals are either founded on, or greatly influenced by, her writings. In addition, important critical academic analyses of her work have emerged in recent years that range from studies that are virulently hostile to reflective critiques that situate her thought in the history of ideas.

For example, Chris Matthew Sciabarra has written extensively on the dialectical structure and radicalism of Rand's thought, describing her as one of the foremost modern examples of theorists working in that tradition. William O'Neill published an early scholarly study that was a fairly hostile account of Rand's ethics and politics. Roderick Long has written on the Aristotelian roots of Rand's thought and her relationship with classical philosophy. Other scholars, such as Tibor Machan, Douglas Den Uyl, and David Kelley have written on many aspects of Rand's work that demonstrate how she addressed the core problematics of modern philosophy. Despite the growing volume of serious scholarly study of Rand and her work, her ideas have not been widely infused or confronted in social and behavioral science literature. The relative lack of interaction with Rand's ideas in social and behavioral science may be due to the somewhat idiosyncratic use of her concepts and method. It may also be partially due to a tendency in these disciplines to exclude individualist thought that goes far beyond Ayn Rand.[6]

In her novels and many essays, Rand articulates an individualist, free will, pro-capitalist philosophy she called "Objectivism." At the outset, this moniker causes confusion for many scholars in the social and behavioral sciences since its suggests a philosophic stance that is diametrically opposed to "Subjectivism." While Rand's Objectivist philosophy is strongly opposed to subjectivism in all of its forms, it is not the diametric opposite of subjectivism. Rand's Objectivist philosophy does not state or imply that all reality is collapsed into the object, a position that she called "intrinsicism," in which meaning, value, and significance are thought to be "intrinsic" to objects external to human perception and conceptualization. Instead, Objectivism places an emphasis on the objective nature of the external world and the equally objective activity of human beings within it. Objectivism is a philosophy about the reality of concrete human beings living on earth. In Rand's view, subjectivism and intrinsicism are opposing, one-sided concepts about the nature of reality that share the same premise regarding the denial of the reality of human activity within an external world. Objectivism is her resolution of the false opposition between them. As far as human beings are concerned, Objectivism does not collapse reality into either the object or the subject, but instead understands reality as the dynamic interaction of both the objective and the subjective. Rand liked the term "existentialism" as descriptive of her thought, but certainly could not ally herself with that philosophical tendency.[7] In politics, Rand was a tireless critic of the left-right, liberal-conservative formulation of social problems in American politics and culture for pretty much the same reason that she adopted a stance that transcends the intrinsicist-subjectivist opposition: It obfuscates similarities in the two perspectives and fails to illuminate alternative conceptualizations and theories about social reality.

Rand developed what she believed was a comprehensive philosophy of human beings living on earth, which included broad commentary on political, social, and cultural phenomena. She initially resisted commentary on racism for many years because she believed that the left dominated discourse on this profound social problem. In the early 1960s she articulated a critique of racism that was grounded in her metaphysics, ethics, and politics. Her Objectivist philosophy includes a critique of both racism and multiculturalism, which her followers subsequently extended to the contemporary philosophic, educational, and political environment.[8] To understand Rand's critique of racism and multiculturalism, it is important to have a sense of the overall organization and basic principles of Objectivist thought. This chapter will discuss Rand's critique of racism and multiculturalism in the broader context of her rational egoist philosophy.

This chapter addresses four questions: First, what did Rand say specifically about racial, ethnic, and multicultural dynamics in her writings? Second, how do these ideas fit within the totality of her thought regarding the domination of society and culture by altruist and collectivist philosophies? Third, what are the implications of Rand's thought for race as a concept, and multiculturalism as an analytical tool and political agenda in the struggle against racism? Fourth, how should we assess Rand as a "dialectician of liberty"? Does her Objectivist critique offer a meaningful prospect of liberation from racism? The chapter proceeds by first analyzing the content and structure of Rand's philosophic thought, including her views on metaphysics, epistemology, ethics, and politics. The chapter then reviews her specific study of racism and the multiculturalist turn of the leadership of the civil rights movement. The chapter concludes with a discussion of the basic elements of the rational egoist critique of multiculturalism and its vision of society after multiculturalism.

PHILOSOPHY AND PURPOSE

The foundational theme of Rand's Objectivism is that the purpose of philosophy is to articulate the abstract and universal principles on which human beings must act if they are to live the life proper to humans. In order to live such a life, humans need philosophy. "As a human being you have no choice about the fact that you need a philosophy."[9] The only choice people have about the need for a philosophy is whether they define it through a rational and disciplined process, or whether they let their subconscious accumulate feelings and judgments that have been uncritically accepted. Her concept of philosophy is radically different from the formalized, organizationally compartmentalized, and systematized endeavor that today characterizes the academic discipline that exists today in colleges and universities in the United States. She views philosophy as a fundamental force that shapes *every* person and culture.[10]

It is no shame that Objectivism lacks a good fit within the pantheon of philosophic orientations that have achieved organizational legitimacy in academia. In fact, the "outsider" status of Objectivism is a badge of honor, since it helps distinguish the uniqueness of Objectivism and promote one of its primary features: its relevance to the everyday lives of people. For Rand, almost all of western and, certainly, modern academic philosophy has largely abdicated its responsibility to help human beings survive and adapt to the challenges and vagaries offered by the natural world. In her concept of Objectivism, the purpose of philosophy is to provide individuals, societies, and cultures with ideas that enhance the ability of persons to live a human life on earth. Philosophy is practice-oriented; it guides the natural conceptual faculty of human individuals, assisting in every activity that involves the human mind.[11]

Philosophy is not just an academic endeavor, consigned to the technical activities of detached professionals working in compartmentalized organizational units in academia. Instead, it is a practical activity directed toward solving the material, social and psychological problems that all individuals confront in everyday life. Objectivism purports to be an organized system of ideas that responds to interrelated questions about nature, human beings, and the interaction between human beings and nature. From an Objectivist viewpoint, philosophy is directed toward answering the basic questions of ontology, epistemology, and ethics: Where am I? How do I know it? What should I do?[12] In response to these fundamental questions, Objectivism purports to provide a hierarchical system of tightly defined, interrelated concepts and axioms that individuals can apply as they navigate their everyday lives.

Rand's philosophic position is difficult at times to comprehend from a systematic perspective because it is dispersed throughout her very large corpus of fiction and nonfiction. However, she systematized her epistemology in *An Introduction to Objectivist Epistemology*. Leonard Peikoff, heir to her estate, attempted a systematization of her entire work in *Objectivism: The Philosophy of Ayn Rand*. Perhaps the most succinct and best-organized statement of Objectivist philosophy is found in the lengthy "This is John Galt" speech from *Atlas Shrugged*.[13] Regardless of its level of philosophic systemization, Objectivism has a fairly clear organization that includes concepts and principles that serve as the foundation for more concrete inquiries into human experience and behavior in the context of everyday life. Rand's views of aesthetics, ethics, and politics, the three branches of philosophy important in her system, all follow from foundations she established in ontology and epistemology. Thus, her critique of racism is ultimately rooted in her egoist ethics and individualist politics, which are themselves based in ontological and epistemological principles.

Rand defines "metaphysics" as "the study of existence" and considers it to be the basic branch of philosophy that addresses the question of whether the external world is, or is not, organized by a system of natural law. Her Objectivist ontology is primarily directed against religious, mystical, and existential concepts that view the universe as chaotic, unpredictable, and replete with supernatural events. In her view, these philosophies are inherently antagonistic to human beings who are attempting to live their lives on earth.

Objectivism begins with the elaboration of three axioms pertaining to existence, consciousness, and identity. "Axiomatic concepts" cannot be reduced to smaller component ideas or concepts. As "irreducible primaries" they are beyond any demonstration of proof, although they can be validated by sense perception. Axiomatic concepts are simply the starting points of cognition or knowledge on which all other knowledge or proof depends, but they have an important function in that they are the "guardians of man's mind and the foundation of reason."[14] In *Atlas Shrugged*, the hero initiates his philosophic manifesto by saying, "Existence exists—and the act of grasping that statement implies two corollary axioms: that something exists when one perceives and that one exists possessing consciousness, consciousness being the faculty of perceiving that which exists."[15] The three axioms of Objectivism are:

1. Existence exists.
2. Consciousness is inherent in my grasp of existence.
3. To be is to be something, to have an identity.

O'Neill argues that the axiomatic concepts in Rand's philosophy mean that (a) the external or objective world is what is immediately perceived to be by human beings, (b) all people potentially or implicitly know the nature of the external world, and (c) the problem humans have in understanding the nature of reality and themselves is that they deny or mystify the objects of their perception.[16] The three axioms can be summarized by saying that there is an absolute, external, independent, objective world that can be known by human beings, and the ability to know the objective world is part of what it means to be human.

As far as Rand is concerned, the physical universe is orderly and operates on the basis of cause and effect. The natural order in the objective world is not imposed by a supreme being or a supernatural agency of any sort. Instead, causality and the natural law and order in the objective world are not metaphysical afterthoughts, but are "part of the fabric of reality as such."[17] The universe was not created and natural law was not caused. For Rand, the nature and reality of the objective, external world appears settled. Nature was not created and was not caused; it is metaphysically given as an absolute.

Rand's view of nature and existence has an important emendation: The absoluteness of the "metaphysically given" does not negate human creativity or exclude the reality of the human-made world. In fact, it is essential in Objectivist philosophy to differentiate between the "metaphysically given" and "human action." The formula inherent in the axiomatic concepts does not apply to the world or the part of existence created by or affected by human beings. In fact, Rand draws a very sharp distinction between the necessity or determinism that operates in the natural world and the freedom of choice that characterizes the world that humans create. There is no necessity in the behaviors, symbols, and objects that humans create. Ultimately, they are acts of choice. The ability of human beings to create or affect part of their environment does not contradict the absolutism of reality because it is the nature of human beings to create or to use their faculty of reason to survive, adapt, and construct features of the world they inhabit. Rand says, "to rebel against the metaphysically-given is to engage in a futile attempt to negate existence. To accept the man-made as beyond challenge is to engage in a successful attempt to negate one's own consciousness."[18]

Humans are, by nature, creators and producers. The facts of the human-made world are similar to the facts of the natural world in that they also exist regardless of whether a particular individual chooses to recognize them. "A man-made product did not have to exist, but, once made, it does exist."[19] It is a significant feature of Objectivism that human beings have the ability to create part of the environment they inhabit. To ignore this is to make one of two philosophic errors: to sanction the status quo by assuming that the human-made world is immutable or to rewrite reality by arguing that the natural world is alterable.

The implications of these ideas for race and racism are critical. The dualism in Objectivist ontology between the natural and the human-made worlds helps to understand that the physical or genetic *characteristics* of individuals may be unalterable by human thought alone, but that *concepts* and values pertaining to race are themselves human constructions. Objectivist ontology, therefore, includes an intellectual foundation for the idea that neither race nor racism are necessary to human existence, despite the fact that the physical qualities of persons are given. To the extent that it negates the ability of humans to live as human beings, racism negates the notion of human identity and may be critiqued on the basis of Objectivist ontology as irrational and antilife.

The axiomatic concepts about the nature of being might seem laboriously obvious and, therefore, unnecessary to those not familiar with or sympathetic to Rand, but they serve an important purpose in Objectivist philosophy. The axiomatic concepts establish the Objectivist view of the nature of the external world and they lay the foundation for the principles of Objectivist epistemology. They serve as the basis for the critique of what Objectivists consider false and artificial philosophic antinomies, as well as unnecessary social conflicts. They help distinguish the unique contributions of Rand's thought.

Rand is critical of almost the entirety of Western philosophy, with exception of Aristotle, on the point of the absolutism of existence, or the primacy of existence over consciousness. She argues that, with few exceptions, philosophy from Plato to Hume is characterized by the opposite argument that existence had a subordinate role to a supernatural consciousness, or that a supernatural consciousness is the cause of existence. Kant secularizes this religious viewpoint and argues that the human mind creates existence through innate forms of perception and cognition. Human consciousness, not God's will, is the metaphysical factor in Kantianism that underlies and structures everyday existence. In Rand's view, a cultural and historical version of Kant's perspective became much more explicit with the philosophies of Hegel and Marx.[20]

Another position Rand rejects is best represented by postmodernism, which essentially states that, although no individual can negate or create *ab novo* existence, humankind or diverse groups within it can and do create reality through social definition alone. Thus, there are numerous realities and knowledge or truth about them rests on the consensus of among thinkers within the groups.[21] Contrary to Objectivism, postmodernists argue that there are no objective facts but only humanly created truths which are deconstructed into knowledge that is valid only within the variable contexts of specific national, cultural, racial, ethnic, gender, or sexual orientation groups. The presupposition of the postmodern perspective is that "a group can override facts" or that facts are relative to different groups.[22]

The axiomatic concepts of Objectivism entail a rejection of all three of these positions as they are applied to conceptions of race and multiculturalism, historically and today. A central characteristic of contemporary multiculturalist thought is the postmodernist idea that different racial and ethnic groups possess different cultures or subcultures. Multiculturalists believe that different cultures construct, interpret, and experience the world in different ways, and that one culture may not be legitimately applied as a standard to assess or understand others. From the perspective of Objectivism, the multiculturalist view of reality denies the absoluteness of existence, our ability to know it, and the idea that there is a universal meaning to living as a human being. The multiculturalist denial of the three axioms adumbrates serious implications for reason and human freedom.

REASON AND FREEDOM: THE NATURE OF KNOWLEDGE

The Objectivist understanding of ontology lays a foundation for Rand's individualism and her critique of racism, but these are also predicated upon an understanding of her epistemology, or the relationship of human consciousness to existence. Objectivism rejects any notion that faith, feelings or instinct are viable means of understanding ourselves and our world. It also rejects any form of determinism, or the belief that human consciousness is determined forces beyond the control of humans, whether these forces are biological, psychological, or social in origin. Further, Objectivism rejects both Hume's skeptical view that absolute knowledge is impossible and Kant's view that reality can be divided into the knowable and the unknowable. Rand's epistemology argues that sense perception and human reason are the only valid means of gaining knowledge about self, others, and the world. Humans are by nature rational beings who are potentially aware of their real nature and that of the natural world as well. The rational nature of human beings entails the belief that all truth is knowable and self-evident on the basis of perception and conception or the innate abilities of persons to form concepts and develop abstract thought. "Those who tell you that man is unable to perceive a reality undistorted by his senses, mean that they are unwilling to perceive reality undistorted by their feelings."[23] Thus, Rand rejects any theory of knowledge that relegates truth to realms beyond human understanding.

She also rejects any form of idealism that asserts the primacy of consciousness over existence, or any notion that asserts that truth is found in a spiritual dimension or supernatural force. Rand is thus a thoroughgoing, un-compromising, and militant atheist. She does not just deny that God exists, she opposes the idea of God as irrational and contradictory to both the self-evident nature of the external world and the nature of humans as rational crea-tures. She also rejects any form of materialism that denies the reality or effi-cacy of consciousness in human activity. Materialism implies a type of existence without human consciousness. Materialism is anti-reason because it negates the possibility of any form of knowledge that is not determined by the external environment.

Rand frequently discusses the nature or essence of humans in their species-being, or what fundamentally defines humans as humans. Objectivism places its image of human existence at the center of its philosophic system. The Ob-jectivist view of human nature is based on its conclusions about ontology and epistemology, particularly the emphasis on reason, which is comprised of the dual processes of perception and conception, as humanity's sole means of learning about the world. Since Objectivists view reason as humanity's basic means of survival, they consider the activities of the mind to be indispensa-ble to the definition of humans in their species-being. "Man is a being of vo-litional consciousness."[24] There is no such thing as a group mind or collec-tive consciousness, both of which suggest the existence of a supernatural, transcendent thinking entity. Groups and organizations are phenomena that are derived from the behaviors of individuals, they do not think or act in any way. Society, culture, and any form of collective action are ultimately re-ducible to a rational process in which percepts and concepts are formed by in-dividuals, and then acted upon by others. Individuals are rational beings who choose to accept the validity of percepts, concepts, and values that others place on objects or symbols.

For Rand, individuals are a totality in that they are sovereign over their thoughts, emotions, and behaviors. The ability of the individual to think struc-tures or determines his or her thought, values, character, and behavior. "Man has been called a rational being, but rationality is a matter of choice—and the alternative his nature offers him is—by choice; he has to hold his life as a value—by choice; he has to learn to sustain it—by choice; he has to discover the values it requires and practice his virtues—by choice."[25] Persons are re-sponsible for all that they do and all that they evade, as well as any existen-tial consequences that follow from their action or inaction. This does not mean that persons are omnipotent or unaffected by the actions of others. In fact, there are numerous enemies of reason and freedom, including faith and force, as well as philosophies and cultural concepts that cultivate determinis-tic visions of human existence and behavior.

The Objectivist emphasis on reason means that humans, in their species-being, are not pawns of forces beyond their control, regardless of race, ethnicity, and circumstance. Humans are not the mere products of biological dynamics, conditioned reflexes, or cultural dictates. "In any hour or issue of your life, you are free to think or to evade that effort. But you are not free to escape your nature." [26] Volition, or freedom of the will, is the defining feature of human existence and behavior because it is essential to life, to self-formation, to daily work, and the choices that individuals make in everyday life. In Rand's formulation, reason is not separate from will, and will is not irrational or antithetical to reason. Choice and intellect define the freedom of persons in their species-being. Choice and intellect define what it means to be human in a behavioral sense.

EGOISM AS A VIRTUE: THE ETHICS OF OBJECTIVISM

Since reason is humanity's only means of acquiring knowledge, the primary standard for assessing values and behavior is the extent to which they contribute to the ability of humans to live as humans, or to exist in their species-being. Objectivism fuses its concept of human nature with a philosophy of ethics. Rand understands the practical dimension of ethics as a "code of values to guide man's choices and actions—the choices and actions that determine the purpose and the course of his life." [27] Objectivism stands in strong opposition to prevailing notions of ethics because of the dominance of mystical, collectivist, and altruist concepts in ethical inquiry. Mystical views of ethics have subordinated human reason and judgment to the demands of supernatural or supreme beings, mediated, of course, by the interpretations of the religious specialists who serve them. Mystical and supernatural foundations for ethics entail the sacrifice of the lives, thoughts, and resources of individuals to the supernatural and its human hirelings. Some social theorists, such as Auguste Comte and his followers in modern social science, tried to transcend the mysticism of ethical philosophy by articulating more scientific, social, and nonreligious foundations for morality. Social science alternatives to mysticism typically justify ethics on social grounds, substituting "society" or "the public interest" for God as the source of value and virtue. The "will of God" is transformed into the "good of society." [28]

Rand argues that the prevailing wisdom is that human value and virtue must be guided by something other than reason, whether it is faith, instinct, feeling, taste, urge, or whim. The major ethical battles fought in philosophy and society are over whose subjective preferences will govern, and not over values and virtues based on rational inquiry. In sharp opposition to mysticism, altruism, and popular culture, Rand grounds her theory of ethics on the basis of reason and human volition. She argues that humans confront basic choices about what they value and how they act. Persons have the choice to think and to be conscious, or not, which implies the choice of life or death. Consciousness, then, is the basic means of survival for those who possess it. For humanity, the means to survival is reason and knowledge, not faith, instinct, or whim. Human beings are free to choose whether they will think and focus, but they are not free to choose the consequences of unconsciousness. Thus, for humans, who are dependent on their ability to reason for their survival, existence implies ethics. Rand says, "every *is* implies an *ought*." [29] For human beings, the central question of ethics is, what are the values and virtues that their survival requires? "Since reason is man's basic means of survival, that which is proper to the life of a rational being is the good; that which negates, opposes or destroys it is the evil." [30] Morality cannot be equated with social mores, subjective feelings, or religious commandments. Ethics is an objective necessity for human survival that is inherent in the nature of being human.

Egoism is the central category in Objectivist ethics. Egoism subsumes all values and virtues, implying that individuals adopt consistent goals, think, and plan for the long-term, act on principle, and accept responsibility for the consequences of their actions. The egoism of Objectivist thought maintains that the primary moral obligation of each person is to pursue and achieve his or her own self-interest, well-being, and happiness. Thus, the primary beneficiary of each individual's behavior should be that individual. Egoism does not specify the particular actions that individuals should pursue, except that these should benefit or augment their self-interest.[31] The mystical and altruistic alternatives to egoism state that the person's primary moral obligation is to serve some external entity, such as God, the state, or the common good. These ethical theories require that persons subordinate or deny their own welfare for the good of the external entity.

Self-preservation, or existence, must be the ultimate goal of the voluntary behavior of human beings. For rational beings, to exist is to be selfish as an act of choice. Human life is the standard of value and rationality is the only legitimate means of pursuing it.[32] Objectivism does not recognize any ethical behavior or egoism outside the absolute of reason. Objectivism promotes a "rational egoism." The egoist is rational because of the recognition that any departure from rationality is harmful to human survival and well-being. Objectivist ethics are primarily concerned with humans living in their species-being, or in a manner consistent with being human. Ethics cannot be alienated from the concept of humans living the life appropriate to their species. Since rational egoism is the central principle of human survival, it applies to all individuals regardless of culture, race, gender, nation, or historical period. Rational egoism is absolute and universal.

The rational egoism of Objectivism maintains that human life is the standard of value and the individual's life is the ethical purpose of each individual. For the rational egoist, the ultimate value is his or her own life. To live for one's own sake means that the achievement of his or her own happiness is the highest moral purpose an individual can have. In Rand's view, individuals can achieve happiness only by recognizing that life is one's primary ethical value and by pursuing the rational values that life requires. The pleasure or satisfaction that results from nebulous or irrational emotional drives is neither ethical nor compatible with rational egoism.[33] Rationality means that the individual recognizes and accepts reason as the only source of knowledge, as the only measure of one's values, and as the only guide to one's actions.

The rational egoism of Objectivism rejects mysticism, altruism, and subjectivist forms of egoism as a sources of moral codes. Mysticism is rejected as an antilife basis for ethics because it is established in a supernatural, not human, dimension. Both altruism and subjectivist forms of egoism are rejected because they are on based the sacrifice of individuals. Altruism requires that individuals sacrifice themselves to other individuals or to collectivist abstractions. Altruism is a particularly pernicious antihuman, antilife theory of ethics because it views human beings as objects of sacrifice, entities that have no right to exist for their own sake. Altruist theories of ethics promote the notion that service to others is the only justification of existence, thought, and behavior. Sacrifice of self is regarded as the highest moral duty, virtue, and value. Altruism, like mysticism, establishes an antilife basis for human behavior by holding "death as its ultimate goal and standard of value."[34] Moreover, altruism is inherently irrational since there is no rational justification for the sacrifice of the lives, happiness and resources of some people to others. No objective criterion can possibly guide such sacrifice in human practice. Given the premium it places on sacrifice, Rand concludes that altruism elevates self-abnegation, self-denial, and every other conceivable form of suffering, including self-destruction, as the cardinal virtues of ethics.

Subjectivist forms of egoism, such as that frequently attributed to Friedrich Nietzsche, entail the sacrifice of others to the individual. Objectivism rejects the idea that human existence and behavior requires sacrifice and martyrdom, or that these phenomena constitute any type of human value or benefit. Objectivism argues that human existence, the nature of human being, is incompatible with sacrifice, regardless of who is chosen as the victimizer and the victim. Objectivist or rational egoism is based on the principle that individuals are totalities; they are ends in themselves, and should not sacrifice their lives, well-being, or resources for other people, the common good, or any form of institutionalized power. Any type of sacrifice of individuals is incompatible with humans living in their species-being. The fundamental social principle inherent in Objectivist ethics is summed up by John Galt, the hero of *Atlas Shrugged*, "I swear by my life and my love of it—that I will never live for the sake of another man, nor ask another man to live for mine."[35]

Objectivism maintains that every person should live *by* his or her own convictions, and *for* his or her own interests. Each individual should pursue the values and practice the virtues that are required to live as a rational, independent, creative, and productive human being. Goods, services and other desiderata can be legitimately acquired from others only by means of voluntary exchange in which all parties agree that such exchange in beneficial. Objectivist ethics rejects domination and coercion as the bases of social order, in favor of voluntary exchange among individuals.

It is only through the principles of rational egoism that humans can live together in a free, peaceful, prosperous, and rational society. Each person is conceived in Rand's philosophy as a totality, or to use her terminology, each individual is an end in himself or herself. Thus, she rejects any form of collectivism, altruism, or ideology that bases morality on living or sacrificing for God, others, or society. The implications for race and racism include the conclusion that racial solidarity, racial preference, and racial superiority can never be ethical foundations for behavior. To the extent that any of these concepts or phenomena require or imply the sacrifice of individuals, or inhibit individuals from pursuing their own happiness and well-being, they are unethical and irrational. Just as Objectivist ethics entails a central social principle, Rand argues that every form of social and political system is founded on or derived from a theory of ethics. It is therefore important to examine the Objectivist perspective on social and political formations, as well as their implications for the critique of racism and the struggle against it.[36]

INDIVIDUAL RIGHTS AND POLITICAL LEGITIMACY

Rational egoism forms the basis of Objectivist social ontology and politics since (1) no individual or group has the right to initiate physical force against others, and (2) no individual or group has the right to seek economic value or any form of desiderata from others. Furthermore, Rand's concept of politics is founded on the notion that ethical principles constitute the sole criterion for assessing social and political systems and, thus, determine the legitimacy of the state or the political regime. For Rand, politics is essentially the practical application of ethics to social and political questions. Rational egoism maintains that there can be some benefit to living in society, but only if society promotes reason and is configured in a manner that supports individuality and individual rights. Rand's political philosophy and her theory of racism are focused on the basic questions regarding political legitimacy: What kind of society and what kind of political system best enhances the ability of humans to live their lives as rational beings?

The fundamental idea of Objectivist political philosophy is that individual rights are absolute. Conversely, social and political systems must be understood in terms of their implications for individual rights. Normatively, the legitimacy of these systems is founded on the extent to which they articulate and protect the rights of the individual. The concept of "right" points to the interstice where ethics and politics overlap. It refers to the juncture at which the governance of the behavior of the individual intersects with the governance of the behavior of others. Right has a dual nature in that it articulates the behavioral requirements that others expect of the person, but it also is a means of subordinating society to the ethical principles of rational egoism. For Objectivists, the role of right in sanctioning, protecting, and preserving individual behavior in a social environment is paramount. Morally and politically, individual rights cannot be infringed without the behavior of the other losing legitimacy. Thus, from an Objectivist point of view, the basic challenge of politics is not the acquisition, legitimation, and use of political power, but the subordination of the social and political system to the rights of the individual.[37]

All rights of the individual derive from the right to life, which is itself derivative of the struggle to survive. The concept of "right to life" carries with it some connotations in contemporary political discourse that Rand and Objectivists do not support. The Objectivist meaning of the "right to life," is that an individual has an ethical and political right to his or her own life as the basis of all other rights. All forms of liberty are dependent upon and contribute to the right of the individual to struggle to survive. Without the individual's right to life, other rights are meaningless. Following from the right to life, the major categories of individual rights are the rights to liberty, property and pursuit of happiness, each of which is founded on a basic human need, serves an important individual and social purpose, and entails an array of actions that constitute its practical expression.[38]

The right to personal liberty is rooted in the basic need of human beings to protect and sustain their lives by effectively navigating and using the external world they inhabit. The purpose of the right to personal liberty is to enable individuals to use their rational abilities to survive and flourish as they interact with each other and the external world. The practical expression of this right includes the right to think, to choose, and to act on the basis of one's judgment.

The right to property is founded on the need to create the material means to survive. Its purpose is to possess the things that are necessary to the individual's ability to live as a material being. The practical expression of this right is to create, gain, keep, exchange, and consume material value in accordance with the individual's own judgment. The right to pursue personal happiness is grounded in the need of human beings to be governed by specific motives or to have their behavior oriented by practical goals. The purpose of the right to pursue happiness is to enable individuals to define and pursue their own welfare. Practically, this right entails all of the behaviors and constrained explicitly stated or implied in the basic principle of Objectivist ethical theory that is to live for one's own sake and fulfillment and to resist all forms of sacrifice.[39]

Rand argues that individual rights constitute a logical whole; one cannot be extracted or subordinated to others without undermining all of them. She argues that in our contemporary political discourse and practice, the right to property is frequently under attack, particularly by those who seek to promote egalitarianism and expand the powers of the state. The argument historically propounded especially by the political left is that the right to property conflicts with or negates" the public interest," "human rights," or the presumed rights of some collectivity or political category. More recent incarnations of this argument include the assertion by developers and city planners that the absolute right to property inhibits "economic development."[40] From an Objectivist viewpoint, however, individual rights are not absolute if one can be alienated from the others, or if abstractions like "human rights," "social justice," and "economic development" are elevated above individual rights. The right to property means that individuals have the right to convert their activity into material values. The right to think, to work, and to choose how to dispose of the material outcomes of one's activity is the right to property. If the right to property is extracted from the totality of individual rights, other rights are necessarily diminished or exterminated.

> The right to life is the source of all rights — and the right to property is their only implementation. Without property rights, no other rights are possible. Since man has to sustain his life by his own effort, the man who has no right to the product of his effort has no means to sustain his life. The man who produces while others dispose of his product, is a slave.[41]

The absoluteness of individual rights is also negated by notions that collectivities, such as societies, nations, classes and races, have rights. From an Objectivist point of view, it is not the collectivity, but the individuals who may or may not be part of a collectivity, who have rights. In addition, the effort to collectivize the idea of rights means a diminution or negation of the rights of individuals. Thus, Rand offers a sharp critique of the notion of "collective rights" based on her theory of ethics and social ontology.

Rand viewed society and all groups or collectivities, including classes, races, and nations, as ultimately reducible to the individuals who comprise it. A society or group within it is only a number of individuals who interact with and identify with each other. All social entities are ultimately abstractions that have no reality except as concepts that individuals employ to understand themselves and their external environment. They do not act, think, feel, choose, bleed, sweat, or suffer except as the individuals within them act, think, feel, choose, bleed, sweat, and suffer. Rights do not transcend individuals nor do they have any existence apart from individuals. Since rights are based in ethics, it is impossible to attribute to collectivities the same sort of expectations and sanctions for action that are attributed to individuals. A group can have no rights other than those that are derived from the rights of their members.

> In a free society, the "rights" of any group are derived from the rights of its members through their voluntary, individual choice and *contractual* agreement, and are merely the application of these individual rights to a specific undertaking. Every legitimate group undertaking is based on the participants' right of free association and free trade.[42]

Since groups are nothing but the individuals who comprise them, the notion of "collective rights" can mean nothing more than the idea that rights belong to some individuals but not to others. Hence, some individuals acquire the power and authority to control and dispose of the life, liberty, and property of others. The source of this authority is simply that some individuals succeed in controlling the political process and technology of coercion. Rand argued that the conceptual switch from individual to collective rights occurs as a consequence of numerical superiority, force or fraud, rather than ethics or any political legitimacy. Collective rights entails the application of altruist ethics to social and political life, thereby placing a premium on sacrifice and coercion. In fact, the notion of collective rights boils down to the dictum that "anything society or the collectivity does is right because it chooses to do it," a negation of ethics and political legitimacy. "Collective rights" stands in hostile opposition to individual rights.[43]

Rand's insistence on the absoluteness and objectivity of individual rights provides the foundation for her philosophy of the state and its legitimacy. In all ethical, social and political issues, the individual is the unit of analysis and value. Individualism is the political corollary of the rational egoist ethical principle that each individual is an end in himself or herself. An individualist social and political system is founded on, protects, and preserves individual rights, and militates against the elevation of other values above individual rights. The state in Objectivist philosophy is a social agency that has the singular purpose of protecting individual rights. Rand defines the state as "an institution that holds the exclusive power to enforce certain roles of social conduct in a geographical area."[44] The state is the creature of a voluntary social contract and has no legitimate power or authority not assigned to it by the individuals who created it. The state is conceived as the sole entity within society that has the legitimate power to protect the rights of individuals. Rand was not an anarchist; she articulated an individualist political philosophy that bases the limited functions and legitimacy of the state on the need to protect individuals from those who use force or fraud to deprive them of their life, liberty, property, and/or ability to pursue their own happiness. This clearly involves the need to use force against those who would use it against innocent citizens.

Rationality requires that individuals agree to delegate their right of self-defense and self-protection to the state in order to eliminate caprice and subjectivity in the use of force in society. The purpose of the state is to prohibit the use of force by individuals against each other for any reason. There are only three legitimate functions of the state. First, the state has a policing function that is intended to protect citizens from criminals. Second, the state has a legitimate function in protecting individuals of a country from armed, foreign invaders. Third, the state has an adjudication function to settle disputes among people in courts operated according to a system of objective laws. Any additional features or functions necessarily entail the state's initiation of force against innocent citizens, which makes its behavior illegitimate and criminal. The insistence that the functions of the state be limited to the protection of individual rights is extended even to democratic states. Majority rule is legitimate only if it is limited in the scope of its powers. The "consent of the governed" does not include any right of the democratic majority to deprive any individual of life, liberty, property, or the pursuit of happiness, even if the people elect to do so with unanimity. The source of the state's legitimacy is not in the arbitrary decisions of the people. Instead, it is found in the objective and absolute principle that the rights of individuals must be protected. The only legitimate purpose of the state, which was best illustrated by the nascent American political system, is to protect the individual from criminals, the mob, and the inappropriate use of political power.[45]

Rand made a forceful case for the idea that social and political systems are not equal; some are better than others in that they provide a rational and ethical foundation for the exercise of political power. The legitimacy of a social and political system varies directly with the degree to which it functions to protect the rights of individuals. "Statist" political systems are those that concentrate power and authority in the state and diminish the rights and freedoms of individuals. Statism thus subsumes an array of social systems such as Nazism, fascism, communism, democratic socialism, and Islamist fascism, which may vary in their ideologies, form, and tactics. However, they are all similar in that they elevate collectivist and subjectivist values above reason, freedom, and individual rights.

For Objectivism, the primary political dialectic is not between the state and anarchy, but between statism and individualism. The emergent political form that dominates the American social landscape is the "mixed economy," which purports to be the most reasonable and propitious combination of freedom and constraint, self-interest and altruism, democratic civility and pressure group warfare. For Rand the "mixed economy" is an unprincipled and irrational political contradiction. It is a social system that places a premium on compromise and pragmatism as it manufactures demands and "false rights" that emerge from any subculture that is able to place its interests on the public agenda. The "mixed economy" is not a legitimate compromise nor a "third way" between capitalism and socialism. Rather, it is a transitional stage toward a full-blown statist transformation of the political culture in the United States.[46]

The only social system that consistently bars the use of physical force from human social relationships is laissez-faire capitalism, which is based on the importance of reason and the recognition of all individual rights, including property rights, as absolute. Rand's vision of laissez-faire capitalism was radically different from the type of capitalism or mixed economy that exists in our world. For Rand, capitalism was an "unknown ideal" that was frustrated by religious mysticism, altruistic ethics, and the intrusion of the state in the economy. Political philosophy identifies the principles that should govern the relationships among individuals and their relationship with the state. It includes the articulation of the principles of production, distribution, and consumption of economic value that are appropriate to the ability of people to live their lives as human beings. Thus, Rand bases her view of economics and defense of laissez-faire capitalism on her ethical and political philosophy, and not on the historical efficiency and productivity of capitalist social systems. Capitalism may, in fact, be a superior economic system in many aspects of its performance, but its legitimacy is established by its foundation in the ethics of rational egoism and the politics of individual rights. This includes the right of individuals to own property and the assurance that all property is owned privately. In the Objectivist concept of capitalism, the state is not a capitalist, it does not foster economic development, and it sets no economic standards or value.[47]

The moral basis of laissez-faire capitalism is found in the fact that it enables people to work, produce, trade, and consume voluntarily. It allows for people to think, to choose, and to act according to their convictions. It is a social system that promotes the notion that each individual is an end in himself or herself. Each person can be the beneficiary of his or her own actions, which is the antithesis of any system that places a premium on sacrifice and self-denial. In addition, laissez-faire capitalism has an element of objectivity in it that is not characteristic of economies based on command. The price or the value of labor or item for sale is determined by the laws of supply and demand; value is not established by subjective wishes but is at the same time the highest price that the seller can command and the lowest price the buyer can find. Economic value, under the "unknown ideal" of laissez-faire capitalism, is neither intrinsic to the commodity nor reflective of the subjective caprice of the individuals involved. It includes elements of objective value: people who value the object, a sense of purpose or benefit in owning the object, knowledge of the object, and alternatives to its purchase.[48] The values and social relations inherent in laissez-faire capitalism are diametrically opposed to those of statism. Laissez-faire capitalism is essentially a positive social system that offers individuals choice, rewards, incentives, and value, while statism is a negative social system that entails constraint, plunder, threats of injury, and motivations based on fear. The implications of the opposition between the moral foundation of laissez-faire economics and the social realities of political systems for race are developed in detail by Rand in an essay on racism she published in 1963.

RACISM, MULTICULTURALISM, AND THE POLITICS OF OBJECTIVISM

As the national civil rights legislation that was expected to put an end to 350 years of institutional racism was introduced in the United States Congress, Rand published an essay devoted directly to racism and the struggle against it.[49] Rand resisted writing anything about race or racism for many years primarily because the Left dominated discourse on both topics. She decided to articulate an Objectivist position on racism because some of its opponents in the leadership of the nascent civil rights movement in the United States had abandoned the individualist foundation of their critique of racism in favor of a collectivist and statist argument. Rand believed that it was important to restate a strong individualist position on racism in the hope of reversing the emerging collectivist orientation of the civil rights movement. In her 1963 essay on racism, Rand outlines the basic elements of the Objectivist critique of racism as well as a critique of the forms of political opposition to racism that were evolving in American political culture. She also offers a commentary on the historical development of racist thought and social policy in Europe and America from the nineteenth to the mid-twentieth century.

It is no surprise that Rand's critique of racism carefully follows from and reinforces positions she had previously articulated on ontology, epistemology, ethics, and political economy. She argues that racism is the crudest and most primitive form of collectivist thought and offers the most obvious and thoughtless form of identity and association—one based on racial characteristics. Racial tribalism is, unfortunately, a form of identity and association that appeals to some people under certain historical circumstances. In her theory the basic elements of racist thought include:

1. The ascription of moral and behavioral significance to an individual's genetics,
2. The idea that intellectual and personality traits are somehow produced and transmitted through an individual's chemistry,
3. The belief that an individual's commitments, values, and behaviors are determined by physical factors beyond his or her control, and
4. The denial that human beings posses a mind or a rational faculty that differentiates them from all other living beings.[50]

Racism is an ideology that negates the two fundamental elements that define human beings as human: their abilities to think and to choose their own behavior. Instead, racist thought reduces human "being" to the legacies of genetics and the behaviors and values of ancestors. Racism, thus, is a form of determinist thought that promotes the notion that human behavior is controlled by a biological, chemical, or physical substratum that is external to control by human volition or reason.

The collectivist foundation of racist thought is generally expressed in two ways. The first is through the claim or the celebration of the accomplishments of individuals as though they are outcomes of the superiority or the greatness of a nation, a culture, or a race, or through the collectivization of human activity. Rand viewed this expression of racism "as revolting a spectacle of collectivist expropriation, perpetuated by racists, as an expropriation of material wealth perpetuated by communists."[51] This point is primarily focused on exceptionally talented persons whose accomplishments receive national or international acclaim or visibility and are then demeaned as expressions of the presumed collective qualities of the nation, culture, or race. The implication is that racist ideology reduces all individual achievement to factors external to the individual's talents, convictions, values, thoughts, and behaviors. The second expression of the collectivist nature of racism is found in the opposite attribution in which a nation, culture, or race is defined as inferior in some way because of the failures, malice, or brutish behaviors on the part of some of its members. Since there is no such thing as a collective mind or racial mind, there can be no collective or racial achievements, failures, or crimes. The two expressions of racism are, in fact, two sides of the same collectivist and determinist coin. Both mean that individual thought, values, and behaviors are rooted in and must be understood by their association with a nation, culture, or race.[52]

Rand further developed the relationship between collectivism and racism in a discussion of the historical development of racism. While collectivism and racism characterize the preponderance of political behaviors in human history, Rand argued that racist ideology emerges and dissipates as collectivist thought and regimes rise and decline. She argues that statism is the political form that is necessary to implement and maintain racist thought. Racism is inconsistent with and contradictory to political formations that place a premium on individual rights. Statist regimes are difficult to legitimate because there is no rational justification for their absolute rule. Racism thus emerges as a "mystique" in the absolute state to promote tribal warfare and the fixed idea that persons of one group are the "natural prey" or natural enemies of other groups. Race is a mystique because it mystifies. It distorts the individualist base of collective constructs and elevates a collective attribution to the status of an absolute. It confers legitimacy on the illegitimate social and cultural expropriation of individual identity and behavior. It generates and reinforces divisions and antagonisms among people. It degrades human thought and action by grounding them in an irrational, biological substratum of human existence. The bureaucratic apparatus of the racist state implements all of the organizational and culture weapons of physical and ideological social control, including taxation, education, and law enforcement, to institutionalize the tribal warfare. The "mystique" of race is a tool of statist social control in that it promotes submission to the power and authority of state for the tribes that are presumably elevated in the regime's political culture and those that are forced to suffer it.

Individualism and the laissez-faire political culture it entails is the only way that racism can be effectively challenged because individualism elevates the inalienable rights of individuals and voluntary exchange as the primary political and cultural values. In Rand's view, laissez-faire capitalism, the unknown ideal, is the only conceivable social system that fully negates racism. Within an authentically laissez-faire capitalist system, ancestry and descent, biology and genetics do not matter. People are defined and rewarded only by their individual accomplishments. Capitalism also tends to militate against racism because it penalizes all forms of irrationality, including racism. Historically, she argued that capitalism and free trade broke down national and racial barriers, abolished slavery and serfdom, and encouraged immigration, integration, and all forms of intergroup tolerance and interaction.[53] In the United States, for example, people of many races and cultures immigrated freely and were able to form new lives and succeed on the basis of their talents and productivity. Social unity, to a great extent, was based not on race or ethnicity but on the commitment to protect and promote individuality.

But capitalism remained an unknown ideal and the performance of capitalist social systems on racial and ethnic issues was not perfect, or even very good, at times. In the United States, the enslavement of Africans, the genocide of Native Americans, and the subsequent institutional discrimination against both groups are particularly odious examples of the contradiction between the social ideals of the American political and economic system. In Rand's view, the extant racism in the United States was not due to capitalism, the individualist ethos, or to the relatively open political system, but was due to the persistence of contradictory elements of collectivism, altruism, and statism in American politics and culture. To their credit, the capitalist social systems entailed a degree of political pluralism and respect for individual rights so that critique and opposition to racism became part of the political discourse and permitted some progress toward the elimination of racism, unlike racist regimes that are founded on an authoritarian state and a command economy. The existence and persistence of racism within capitalist social systems is more of an expression of contradictory collectivist and altruist cultural legacies than capitalist social ideals or prerequisites of a capitalist social order.

In the United States, even as early as the 1960s, progress toward the elimination of racism was largely reversed because of the growth of a collectivist welfare state that is dedicated to responding to racism and all other policy problems through collective blame and increased governmental control. In Rand's view, the consequence of the increased collectivization and incipient statism in the United States was the birth of a "new, virulent growth of racism."[54] Racism increased as the programs and controls of the welfare state expanded. Rand argues that the "mixed economy" forced the fragmentation of the country into an "institutionalized civil war" in which different advocacy groups based on ethno-racial tribes fight for "legislative favors and special privileges at the expense of one another" and with a complete disregard for the implications for ethics and the values of an individualist culture.

Chris Matthew Sciabarra calls this new political formation "the predatory state" which imposes an altruistic and collectivist ideology that legitimates the sacrifice of individual rights to the so-called public good and expropriates the economic value created by individuals for distribution by the state. The mixed economy functions through an absolute state that preys upon individuals and groups in order to promote the agenda of the advocacy groups that prevail in the public policy process. The predatory state exacerbates racial and ethnic tension by setting individuals and groups against each other because of the arbitrary and unearned expropriation and redistribution of resources and other social desiderata. The state, not the market and not civil society, is the social institution that defines individual, social and cultural value and allocates desiderata accordingly. Thus, the state engenders conflict between the groups who are conferred privileges by the state and the groups whose rights and resources are expropriated in the state's policy process. The predatory state thus mirrors the functioning of the racist regime in that individuality is diminished or extinguished while race or ethnicity becomes a primary element of identity, advocacy, decision making, and policy.

The leadership of the American civil rights movement initially offered a critique of racist thought and practice that included all of the basic elements of individualism. However, Rand criticized the theoretical turn the civil rights leadership made in the early to mid-1960s away from the elimination of racism as official social policy and toward the transformation of the philosophy of the antiracist struggle into a collectivist advocate within the predatory state. The transformation of the civil rights movement reinforced the predatory state by defining all forms of social and personal disorganization as rooted in race and ethnicity. With support from the multiculturalist left, the predatory state elevated the "racial mystique" to an analytical and political absolute. It also sought to manage the resultant social and personal disorganization through increased intervention in society, economy, and culture. From an Objectivist viewpoint, the evolution of the predatory state was disastrous for race relations, individualism, and the moral foundation of society and economy. Far from mitigating social and personal disorganization, the predatory state expanded and intensified the conflict, disorganization, and suffering of individuals. The outcomes include increased racial antagonism, wider achievement gaps, higher crime, diminished economic opportunity, and the subversion of social solidarity.

The prevailing political discourse on race in the United States offers very little hope that these trends will be reversed anytime soon. Consequently, Rand carefully dissociated herself from both the right and the left. The right in the United States has always promoted contradictory ideas, and has been consistently on the wrong side of racial and ethnic issues. Until the mid-1960s, the conservatives promoted limited government, individual freedom, capitalism, and property rights, while simultaneously espousing governmentally-based race discrimination and race hatred. The political contradiction of the right in the United States is that it originally advocated a little more freedom in the sphere of economics, but demanded broad governmental controls on individual behavior, much of which was focused on race. Conservatives now identify themselves as "compassionate conservatives," claiming to promote limited government, individual freedom, capitalism, and property rights while they now advocate for affirmative action, eminent domain, surveillance, and promote the growth and expansion of federal controls, entitlements, and subsidiary programs for citizens, illegal residents, and foreign governments alike. Compassionate conservatism is little more than the right's current effort to legitimate the altruist ethic of sacrifice for the goals of the security state.

The multicultural left espouses similar contradictions in a different form. Liberals and leftists seek to subordinate all individual rights to unlimited governmental predation in the interest of "society" or "the people," all the while presenting themselves as advocates for the rights of ethno-racial minorities and other presumed victims of societal dynamics. When the liberal-left vision is extended into the realm of foreign policy, the altruism evolves into a form of racism that helps prop up dictatorships and terrorists who are devoted not only to the elimination of individual rights, but to the extermination of racial and ethnic groups that oppose their mysticism and totalitarian agendas. The sympathy of the multicultural left for the Islamic Fascist states and movements is a particularly repugnant expression of this political contradiction, especially given the efforts by Islamists to exterminate Israel and Judaism. In the formulation of the multicultural left, Israel and Jews are to be sacrificed so that Muslims can be emancipated, at least in the sense that the Islamic Fascists understand emancipation. In its war against individual rights, the multicultural left consistently ignores the facts that (a) the individual is the smallest minority, (b) minority and victims groups are comprised of individuals, and (c) the individual is the most significant victim today of the interventionist, predatory state the left sees as the lever for social progress.

The Objectivist perspective on race and racism is that neither the right nor the left advocates helpful positions to the extent that they seek to promote collectivism and utilize the coercive technologies of the state to solve or manage individual and group problems. Rand argues that two things are needed to overcome racist thought and practice. First, there must be a transformation in the philosophy of the society toward rational egoism and the promotion of individual rights. Second, the ability and the right of the state to intervene in society, economy, and culture must be eliminated. Some critics of Ayn Rand and Objectivism, however, inaccurately portray on occasion her arguments on race and racism in a fashion that suggests her individualist position is racist or is at least inconsistent with those who seek improvements in race relations.

For example, in his analysis of Objectivism, O'Neill argues that Rand's philosophy can never be reconciled with antiracist thought because of her strong support of property rights. Without providing any documentation or analysis, O'Neill argues that Rand's position is that (a) property rights take precedence over all others and (b) all rights can be reduced to two basic categories: property rights and free trade. Objectivism, according to O'Neill, cannot be reconciled with racial equality because Objectivists are unwilling to sacrifice the inviolate nature of property rights to promote racial equality.[55]

It is true that Rand views property rights as absolute, but it is not accurate to say that property rights take precedence over all other individual rights. Nor does she say that all individual rights can be reduced to property rights, or that all freedoms are reducible to free trade. She argues consistently that property rights cannot be extracted from the totality of individual rights without undermining all individual rights. This does not mean that property rights have precedence over all others, but that individual rights have integrity *only as a totality*. It also means that the statist argument that achievement of racial equality requires the sacrifice of the property rights of individuals is contradictory, since it requires that the rights of some individuals must be sacrificed for the advantage or benefit of others. While this argument provides ideological support for the enhancement of the power of the state, it is not clear how it emancipates anyone, how it benefits individuals of minority groups, or how it improves relations among people.

THE DIALECTICS OF RACE AND LIBERTY

Ayn Rand's critique of racism as a brutal form of collectivism, also opposes multiculturalism as irrational, unethical, and statist. Multiculturalism maintains that there are racial or ethnic groups whose members are victims of racist thought and practice. The political agenda of multiculturalism is the acquisition and employment of state power in the service of the presumed victims of racism. Functionally, this means the reallocation of rights and other desiderata by the state from some individuals to other individuals. Multiculturalism is a form of predatory statism that promotes the sacrifice of the autonomy, property, and resources of some individuals for the benefit of others. Objectivism opposes multiculturalist ideology for its negation of the values of individuality and rationality, and for its advocacy for the sacrifice of individuals and their rights to the collectivist state. Racism and multiculturalism share the same philosophic premise that it is appropriate for the state to sacrifice individual rights because of the race or ethnicity of the individuals involved. The implications of the political project of Objectivism for racism and multiculturalism cannot be understood through the traditional lens of a one-dimensional political spectrum. Objectivism is neither left nor right. It is both antiracist and anti-multiculturalist. It seeks to transcend both of these false oppositions. It is an antiracist philosophy which grounds a political concept of individual rights on an ethical theory which is itself grounded in a view of ontology and epistemology.

The Objectivist understanding of racism as a social system is found in Rand's ethics, politics and economics. Rand advocates for a social system that generalizes the principle of rational egoism and limits the state's role to the protection of individual rights. In the Objectivist vision, the state must not collectivize human activity or pursue altruist agendas that sacrifice the rights of some individuals for others. Objectivism opposes the use of state power to impose racist policies or multiculturalist abstractions, such as "social justice," onto the interactions of people in everyday life. Laissez-faire capitalism is the preferred social system because it relies totally upon the market and civil society, not the state, for the allocation of social desiderata and the solution of individual and social problems not related to the protection of individual rights. Each individual is morally responsible for the creation, acquisition, exchange, and use of material value. Objectivism is both antiracist and anti-multiculturalist because it critiques the sacrifice of any individual's rights and refuses to confer any special privileges on any individual or group. At the most fundamental level, Objectivism propounds the need to move to a social system in which race and ethnicity are irrelevant because individual rights are absolute.

Objectivism is a normative philosophy that primarily seeks to advocate for a specific social system and a specific concept of human existence within a social context. Not just any culture and not just any social system will do. A fully human existence requires a culture and social system that promote and defend individual rights. Objectivist analysis, thus, is largely the articulation of a critique of philosophy, culture, and society that is not bound or mitigated by space or time. It is a *transcendental* critique in which a predefined set of concepts and standards, or a philosophy of a fully human existence, are used to analyze and critique a social system.[56] Rand's ethical and political concepts can be targeted at any social system to understand the fundamental issues pertaining to racism and individual rights. Her preferred method is to understand nature, society, and humanity in terms of Objectivist concepts and principles.

The emphasis Rand places on a *transcendental* critique may limit the scope and power of Objectivist thought. Rand is much more of a polemicist than a societal analyst. Consequently, Objectivism is not as helpful as a sociological theory and dialectical method as it might be. For example, it is very clear that Rand makes room in Objectivism for a social ontology, or the study of the humanly constructed world. Rand expresses deep appreciation of the interaction between the individual and the social system. However, she rarely attempts to contrast what social systems say about themselves with how they actually function. Her focus is almost entirely on the interpretation and critique of the philosophic premises of societies and cultures from an Objectivist standpoint. Objectivism, as Rand articulated it, predominantly understands dialectics in terms of the contradiction and struggle of philosophic ideas, but not as facts of the social world that individuals inhabit. Her critique of racism is an important exception to this point.

Her analysis of racism and multiculturalism includes elements of both a *transcendental* and *immanent* critique. *Immanent* critique is a form of dialectical analysis that is more focused on contradictions as social facts. It is a dialectical methodology that requires the analyst to first understand how a social system defines or understands itself. It then compares and contrasts this presentation of self with the realities of the social system. Immanent critique is ultimately concerned with the extent to which there is a match or mismatch between what a social system says about itself and how it actually operates. The false correspondence of the ideal and the real is elaborated in the first instance as a method of social analysis, but it has an historical or a political meaning as well: to make the ideal a reality, or to eliminate the false correspondence between societal goals and societal realities.

By differentiating the human-made world from the natural world, Rand distinguishes the two realms by arguing that the natural world operates on the principle of cause-effect, while human beings are creatures of volitional consciousness. But she does not tell us much about how the human-made world operates. It is important for any theoretical perspective, including individualist theories such as Objectivism, to understand how the human-made world produces racism as a social fact and how it can be overcome through cultural and political processes.

What are the social dynamics that produce racist ideologies and racist regimes? If people have free choice throughout all time and space, why is it that they tend to choose racism, collectivism, and statism? Why is it that racist, collectivist, and statist ideologies tend to dominate human history? What are the conditions under which an antiracist, individualist political movement might emerge? Objectivists are not conservatives, they seek change in society, culture, and everyday life. What are the circumstances that might prompt the changes that Objectivists seek in the social system?

One place where Rand utilizes an immanent critique is in her analysis of racism and the multiculturalist turn of the civil rights leadership in the United States. In this analysis, she very effectively demonstrated that racism is not an expression of societal ideals, but a contradiction of them. She also demonstrated that when American capitalism functioned best, it was the negation of racism. In her immanent critique of racism, laissez-faire capitalism did not produce racism, but helped dismantle large segments of the social and cultural supports for racism.

Conversely, racism intensified as the state and multicultural ideology became more aggressive forces in society, culture, and economy—against the founding ideals of American society. Rand certainly envisions a direct and mutually reinforcing relationship between racism and the cultural supports for statism. One does not exist without the other. Her defense of the state and her critique of anarchism, however, can be turned against her argument on the role of the state in repairing racial inequities. She believes that the state can function to limit its role to protect, innocently and neutrally, the rights of individuals. This belief may be as much of a fantasy as the multiculturalist belief that the statist promotion of particularist ethnic agendas will lead to universal liberation. If the state has a legitimate role in the protection of the rights of individuals, why can't the multiculturalist promotion of "social justice" be legitimately included under this rubric? Practically speaking, at what point, and through what sort of process, can state power be limited to the protection of individual rights? Exactly how is state power to be restricted to the political project that Objectivists see as legitimate?

Despite this problem in her political project, Rand was able to supplement a transcendental critique with an immanent critique of racism in America perhaps because of the uniqueness of the individualist ideals in the United States. Rand's immanent critique of racism and multiculturalism in American society is an important expression of the critique of contemporary social formations and the renewal of individual liberty within them. Her work has been and should continue to be an important source of perspective and inspiration for individualists and libertarians who are concerned about the dynamics of racism and the multiculturalist agenda for responding to them. Among those who were both profoundly influenced by, and critical of, Rand's critique of statism are Murray Rothbard and the Anarcho-Capitalists, who are the focus of chapter 3.

NOTES

1. Jerome Tucille, *It Usually Begins with Ayn Rand* (San Francisco: Fox and Wilkes, 1972). Tucille's sequel, *It Still Begins with Ayn Rand: Part Two of a Libertarian Odyssey* (Mill Valley, CA: Pulpless.Com, 1999) continues his observations on the interactions of Rand's philosophy with the libertarian movement, and the political follies in the United States through the Reagan, Bush Sr., and Clinton administrations. Also see Brian Doherty, *Radicals for Capitalism: A Freewheeling History of the Modern American Libertarian Movement* (New York: Public Affairs, 2007).

2. Chris Matthew Sciabarra, *Ayn Rand: Her Life and Thought* (Poughkeepsie, NY: The Objectivist Center, 1996). For a more detailed discussion about Rand's early life and the influence of Lossky on her philosophic development, see Chris Matthew Sciabarra, *Ayn Rand: The Russian Radical* (University Park: Pennsylvania State University Press, 1995).

3. The web site for the Ayn Rand Institute can be found at www.aynrand.org. The sources for Rand's four novels are: Ayn Rand, *We the Living* (New York: Dutton, 1995); *The Fountainhead* (New York: Bobbs-Merrill, 1993); *Anthem* (New York: Dutton, 1995); *Atlas Shrugged* (New York: Signet, 1996).

4. In his discussion of the intellectual relationship between Lossky and Rand in *Ayn Rand: The Russian Radical*, Sciabarra first developed his controversial but groundbreaking thesis that Rand should be considered to be a dialectical philosopher. See especially pages 45–64 and 84–95. Also see Chris Matthew Sciabarra, "The Rand Transcript," *The Journal of Ayn Rand Studies* 1, no. 1 (Fall, 1999): 1–25.

5. For a critical perspective on the notion that Rand belongs in the dialectical tradition of analysis and a broader assessment of the notion of dialectical libertarianism, see Roderick Long, "The Benefits and Hazards of Dialectical Libertarianism," *The Journal of Ayn Rand Studies* 2, no. 2 (Spring 2001): 395–448. Also see Roderick Long *Reason and Value: Aristotle versus Rand* (Poughkeepsie, NY: The Objectivist Center, 2000).

6. Robert Antonio, "Nietzsche's Antisociology: Subjectified Culture and the End of History," *American Journal of Sociology* 101, no. 1 (July 1995): 1–43. While Antonio's essay is focused on Nietzsche, the argument that antisociological or individualist social theory contributes to the rethinking of the foundations and practices of social science also applies to individualists such as Ayn Rand, Murray Rothbard, and Max Stirner. Nietzsche counterposed a theory of the forms of domination against the abstract analysis of sociology that largely serves to reify society and culture and, thus, supports the domination of the individual by the state and society. For examples of important scholarly treatments of Rand and her work see Douglas Den Uyl, *The Fountainhead: An American Novel* (New York: Twayne Publishers, 1999); Tibor Machan, *Ayn Rand* (New York: Peter Lang, 1999); David Kelley, *The Evidence of the Senses* (Baton Rouge: Louisiana State University Press, 1986). Also see Chris Matthew Sciabarra, *Total Freedom: Toward a Dialectical Libertarianism* (University Park: Pennsylvania State University Press, 2000) that develops and expands some of themes that first appeared in *Ayn Rand: The Russian Radical*.

7. Ayn Rand, *Philosophy: Who Needs It?* (New York: Penguin, 1982), 70; Ayn Rand, *The Virtue of Selfishness: A New Concept of Egoism* (New York: Penguin, 1964), 123–24. Rand's efforts to overcome the left-right, materialist-idealist, objective-subjective dichotomies is also a major theme of Sciabarra's analysis. See Sciabarra, *Ayn Rand: Her Life and Thought*, 5.

8. Rand's primary statement on racism appears in Ayn Rand, "Racism," *The Virtue of Selfishness*, 147–57. The web site of the Ayn Rand Institute includes many essays by Rand's followers that apply her concepts to the analysis of contemporary racial and cultural issues including affirmative action, welfare, and education. Another important essay that addresses multicultural themes is "Global Balkanization," which appears in *Return of the Primitive: The Anti-Industrial Revolution* (New York: Penguin, 1999). This volume also contains a pertinent essay by Rand's colleague Peter Schwartz on "Multicultural Nihilism" which ridicules the moral relativism of multicultural thought.

9. Rand, *Philosophy: Who Needs It?* 5.

10. Rand, *Philosophy: Who Needs It?* 2–3.

11. Rand, *Philosophy: Who Needs It?* 8; Leonard Peikoff, *Objectivism: The Philosophy of Ayn Rand* (New York: Penguin, 1991), 1.

12. Ayn Rand, *Introduction to Objectivist Epistemology* (New York: Penguin, 1979), 1–3; Rand, *Philosophy: Who Needs It?* 2.

13. Rand, *Atlas Shrugged*, 923–79. Also see Peikoff, *Objectivism*. For a fascinating discussion about Peikoff's attempt to systematize Objectivism and his claim that it is the official systematic expression of Objectivism, see David Kelley, *The Contested Legacy of Ayn Rand: Truth and Toleration in Objectivism* (New Brunswick, NJ: Transaction Books, 2000). The use of Peikoff as a source in this chapter does not imply any agreement with either side in the argument about what constitutes the official statement about Objectivism. Peikoff is at the bare minimum a highly credible source of information about Objectivism. He summarizes important points about it in a very helpful manner.

14. Rand, *Introduction to Objectivist Epistemology*, 60.

15. Ayn Rand, *Atlas Shrugged* (1957; New York: Penguin, 1992).

16. William O'Neill, *With Charity Toward None: An Analysis of Ayn Rand's Philosophy* (Totowa, NJ: Littlefield, Adams, & Co, 1972), 27.

17. Peikoff, *Objectivism*, 17.

18. Rand, *Philosophy: Who Needs It?* 27.

19. Rand, *Philosophy: Who Needs It?* 31.

20. Rand's summary dismissal of most of western philosophy appears in several places, but see her 1964 interview in *Playboy* magazine that is reprinted in Alvin Toffler, "The *Playboy* Interview with Ayn Rand" in *The Libertarian Reader: Classic and Contemporary Writings from Lao-Tzu to Milton Friedman*, ed. David Boaz (New York: The Free Press, 1997). Kant's position appears in *Critique of Pure Reason* (Cambridge: Cambridge University Press, 1988) and *Critique of Practical Reason* (Cambridge: Cambridge University Press, 1988); See also G. W. F. Hegel, *Phenomenology of Spirit* (London: Oxford University Press, 1977); and Karl Marx, *Economic and Philosophic Manuscripts 1844* (Amherst, NY: Prometheus Books, 1988). For an excellent discussion about Rand's philosophic relationship with Kant, see Machan, *Ayn Rand*, 117–18.

21. Pauline Marie Rosenau, *Postmodernism and the Social Sciences: Insights, Inroads and Intrusions* (Princeton, NJ: Princeton University Press, 1992); Steven Best and Douglas Kellner, *Postmodern Theory: Critical Interrogations* (New York: The Guilford Press, 1991).

22. Peikoff, *Objectivism*, 22.

23. Rand, *Atlas Shrugged*, 948.

24. Rand, *Atlas Shrugged*, 926.

25. Rand, *Atlas Shrugged*, 927.

26. Rand, *Atlas Shrugged*, 926.

27. Rand, *The Virtue of Selfishness*, 13.

28. Rand, *The Virtue of Selfishness*, 15.

29. Rand, *The Virtue of Selfishness*, 24.

30. Rand, *The Virtue of Selfishness*, 25.

31. Peikoff, *Objectivism*, 229–30.

32. Rand, *The Virtue of Selfishness*, 24; Peikoff, *Objectivism*, 229–30.

33. Rand, *The Virtue of Selfishness*, 24–25.

34. Rand, *The Virtue of Selfishness*, 38.

35. Rand, *Atlas Shrugged*, 979.

36. Rand, *The Virtue of Selfishness*, 38.

37. Rand, *The Virtue of Selfishness*, 108.

38. Rand, *The Virtue of Selfishness*, 110.

39. Rand, *The Virtue of Selfishness*, 111.

40. See the background materials on this issue prepared by the National Council of State Legislatures at http://www.ncsl.org/programs/natres/emindomain.htm. The basic policy issue addressed but not solved by the Supreme Court's decision in the Kelo vs New London case is whether the state has the right to appropriate and transfer private property from an individual to other individuals for the sake of economic development in the "public interest." Objectivism clearly opposes the use of political power to appropriate the property of individuals.

41. Rand, *The Virtue of Selfishness*, 111.

42. Rand, *The Virtue of Selfishness*, 119.

43. Rand, *The Virtue of Selfishness*, 118–24.

44. Rand, *The Virtue of Selfishness*, 125.

45. Rand, *The Virtue of Selfishness*, 127–30.

46. Rand, *The Virtue of Selfishness*, 91–92.

47. Rand, *The Virtue of Selfishness*, 117; Ayn Rand, *Capitalism: The Unknown Ideal* (New York: Penguin, 1967),11–34.

48. Rand, *The Virtue of Selfishness*, 147–57.

49. Rand, *The Virtue of Selfishness*, 147.

50. Rand, *The Virtue of Selfishness*, 148.

51. Rand, *The Virtue of Selfishness*, 148–49.

52. Rand, *The Virtue of Selfishness*, 148–49.

53. Rand, *The Virtue of Selfishness*, 151.

54. Rand, *The Virtue of Selfishness*, 149.

55. O'Neill, *With Charity Toward None*, 230–31.

56. Robert J. Antonio, "Immanent Critique as the Core of Critical Theory: Its Origins and Development in Hegel, Marx and Contemporary Thought," *British Journal of Sociology*, 32 (Fall 1981): 330–45. Also see my discussion of immanent critique in John F. Welsh, "The Unchained Dialectic: Theory and Research in an era of Educational Reform," *Neoliberalism and Educational Reform*, ed. Wayne Ross and Rich Gibson (Cresskill, NJ: Hampton Press, 2007), 217–39.

Chapter Three

Fusion and Transcendence

Murray Rothbard and the Anarcho-Capitalist Critique of Racism

THE SOURCES OF ANARCHO-CAPITALIST THOUGHT

Of all of the social theorists included in this volume, Murray N. Rothbard is by far the most prolific writer as measured by his scholarly output as an academic economist and his polemical publications that reflected his work as a political activist.[1] Among individualist and libertarian theorists, Rothbard's productivity as a scholar and public intellectual certainly superseded that of even Ayn Rand, although he cannot match her renown or infamy as a philosopher and novelist. In a life that spanned the sixty-nine years from 1926 to 1995, Rothbard published over two dozen scholarly books and hundreds of academic journal articles. He edited four journals—*Left and Right*, *The Libertarian Forum*, *The Review of the Austrian School of Economics*, and *The Journal of Libertarian Studies*. The last two of these journals persist to this day.

Rothbard was also a principal in the founding of three academic and policy research institutes—the Cato Institute, the Ludwig von Mises Institute, and the Center for Libertarian Studies. Rothbard is also arguably the most influential libertarian writer upon faculty in higher education in the United States, again superseding Rand. In the first decade of the twenty-first century, there are dozens of libertarian scholars in a variety of disciplines, but especially in economics, who were directly influenced by the writings of Murray Rothbard. While the Chicago School of Economics is probably much better known, the Austrian School of Economics is arguably much more rigorous in its espousal and defense of free-market capitalism, in large part, because of Rothbard's voluminous and compelling writings on the economy and the state.[2]

It is misleading, however, to think of Murray Rothbard "merely" as the academic economist, who is known for several standard works, including *The Panic of 1819: Reactions and Policies, America's Great Depression, The Mystery of Banking, The Case Against the Fed*, and *Man, Economy, and State*. In fact, Rothbard was an exemplary interdisciplinary scholar. As a historian, he published a four-volume work on the American Revolution entitled, *Conceived in Liberty*. As a sociologist, he contributed to the study of cults in *The Sociology of the Ayn Rand Cult* and to the philosophy of social science in *Individualism and the Philosophy of the Social Sciences*. As a political philosopher, he wrote *The Ethics of Liberty* and *For a New Liberty: The Libertarian Manifesto*. In *Power and Market: Government and the Economy*, he outlined how a society based on libertarian principles might operate.[3]

Murray Rothbard was also a political activist who participated tirelessly in the anti–Vietnam War campaigns of the 1960s and 1970s, collaborated with New Leftists in the Peace and Freedom and Party in a variety of grassroots protests in New York City, and was one of the founders of the Libertarian Party, which became the largest third party in the United States. In his political writings, Rothbard developed an "internal colonialist" theory and critique of racism that was woven into the libertarian philosophy he created. As an individual, by all accounts, Rothbard himself appears to have been an engaging and ebullient person who was adored by his colleagues, political coconspirators, and students alike. If Ayn Rand had a "sense of life," Murray Rothbard had a "zest for life."[4]

Rothbard's biographer, Justin Raimondo, identified three important influences on the development of Rothbard's thought: the isolationist or noninterventionist Old Right, Ludwig von Mises and the Austrian School of Economics, and Ayn Rand and her Objectivist colleagues. While Rothbard was an economist by profession, he attempted to fuse the ideas he developed in economics with an analysis of politics and ethics in order to help popularize libertarian and individualist ideas in American society. In Rothbard's view, foremost among these was an opposition to an aggressive foreign policy and the war-making powers of the state propounded by the Old Right in the 1930s through the 1950s. Rothbard's opposition to an interventionist foreign policy by the United States government prompted him to seek an alliance with the critics and social theorists of the Old Right, who believed that a government with strong powers inevitably adopts an aggressive policy in external relations, and that an interventionist foreign policy leads to the increased domination of state over the lives of individual citizens. As a young man, Rothbard found great affinity with the pre–World War II writers H. L. Mencken, Frank Chodorow, Garet Garrett, Isabel Patterson, Rose Wilder Lane, and Albert J. Nock, each of whom argued that the rise of the welfare-warfare state in the

United States was disastrous for individual liberty and prompted the political right to abandon its own traditions and principles in favor of a very strong, interventionist government.[5] Chodorow and Nock, both of whom were students of the writing of German sociologist Franz Oppenheimer, were especially important to Rothbard's intellectual development because of the delineation they drew in their writings between the "political," or coercive, means and the "economic," or voluntarist, means of meeting human needs.[6]

After World War II, with the United States confronting the menace of the Soviet military abroad and attempting to manage communist infiltration and subversion at home, the noninterventionist ideology of the Old Right was effectively supplanted by the New Right, which was best represented by William F. Buckley and the intellectuals associated with the *National Review*. Buckley and the New Rightists supported the free market and traditional American values, but believed that the growth of governmental intrusion into the economy and society was warranted by the Soviet threat abroad and the communist threat at home. The New Right argued implacably for an aggressive military posture toward the Soviet Union. Rothbard had written articles for the *National Review* that championed the free market and limited government, but he was treated as an eccentric by the Buckleyites and was never a good fit with the New Rightist agenda that included a hastening of a military confrontation with the Soviet Union to defeat the communists internationally.[7]

Rothbard and the small group of radical libertarians associated with him during the 1950s were all for protecting America and defeating communism, but they believed, with remarkable prescience, that the structural contradictions in economy and society in the Soviet Union would lead to its own internal collapse. Further, Rothbard and his associates were not willing to compromise civil liberties at home in order to militarize the conflict with the Soviet Union. Most of all, Rothbard and his associates believed that there was a huge contradiction in the New Rightist advocacy for noninterventionism in the economy, but total comfort with the use of state power to separate the races and to subjugate black Americans and other minority groups. In the late 1950s and early 1960s, Rothbard considered himself to be a rightist but rejected the party of the right and the philosophic core of its new, statist incarnation. He knew that something more than the ideas of the Old Right and the New Right was needed to help understand the social and political context of the postwar era.

In 1949, while still a student in the doctoral program in economics at Columbia University, Rothbard met the central figure in the Austrian School of Economics, Ludwig von Mises, and was immediately attracted to Mises's brand of laissez-faire economics. Mises had immigrated to the United States in 1940 to escape Nazi-occupied Europe. Mises had already established himself as a world-class economic theorist whose "praxeology" grounded a vigorous defense of free market economics in a theory of human behavior. Mises published his comprehensive statement on economics, *Human Action*, in 1949 while working part-time at the Foundation for Economic Education in New York City. Rothbard joyously reviewed *Human Action* for the Chodorow's libertarian journal *Analysis*, applauding its "thoroughgoing portrayal of the vicious effects of every type of governmental intervention in economic life."[8] Rothbard believed that *Human Action* corrected important theoretical errors made by Mises predecessors in the history of economic thought. Furthermore, it laid a solid foundation for libertarianism because of its uncompromising *laissez-faire* orientation.

> In all matters, from theoretical to political, Mises was the soul of rigor and consistency. Never would Mises compromise his principles, never would he bow the knee to a quest for respectability or social or political favor.[9]

Mises also taught a seminar on economics at New York University which Rothbard soon began attending. Mises's theory was based on the notion that economics must be studied as a category of individual, not collective, human action. Mises did not view economics as the study of the interaction or conflict of social classes or other collectivist abstractions. The goal of the Austrian approach to economics was to discover the laws of "praxeology," or the fundamental principles that define human social and economic behavior. Mises rejected the statistically-based methodology of institutional economics, and the mathematical modeling methods of the Keynesians, as well as their content supporting collectivization in economic analysis and policy. The praxeological approach that emphasized qualitative and theoretical analysis set Mises and the Austrian School apart from all of the major economic paradigms typically taught in graduate programs at universities in the United States at that time. Rothbard believed that, for the first time, a firm methodological base for economic theory had been finally articulated by Mises in *Human Action*.

> [*Human Action*] is economics made whole, based on the methodology of praxeology that Mises himself had developed, and grounded in the ineluctable and fundamental axiom that human beings exist, and that they *act* in the world, using means to try to achieve their most valued goals. Mises constructs the entire edifice of correct economic theory as the logical implications of the primordial fact of individual human action.[10]

In response to this realization, Rothbard wrote *Man, Economy, and State*, which he conceived to be a comprehensive statement of the history of economic thought from an Austrian or Misesian perspective. Rothbard differed with Mises on a number of points, particularly on the need for the state. Mises believed that the state was an unfortunate necessity to protect individuals and private property, although, at bottom, the state is nothing more than coercion, compulsion, and police power.[11] Rothbard was an anarchist who worked for the dissolution of the state. However, because of the groundbreaking approach of *Human Action* to economics in both method and content, Rothbard identified with the Austrian School of Economics and considered Mises to be a scholar, creator, hero, and "preeminent theorist of our time."[12]

In the mid-1950s, prior to the publication of *Atlas Shrugged* and Ayn Rand's abandonment of her career as a novelist to pursue philosophy, Rothbard was briefly affiliated with Rand and the group of New York intellectuals associated with her. Both Rothbard and Rand embraced a very radical form of individualism and were ardent supporters of a philosophy of free-market capitalism that was grounded in a natural law justification of property rights. However, there were significant philosophical differences between Rand and Rothbard, and the two individualists never really got along very well. Rothbard also believed that the Objectivist environment was an emergent cult that isolated Rand from broader philosophic debate and the cultural, political, and economic dynamics that preoccupied her. Eventually, Rothbard concluded that the valuable elements in Objectivism did not really originate with Rand and that his philosophic position, despite areas of agreement, was not the same as Rand's, although he expressed deep admiration for *Atlas Shrugged*.

Rothbard could never accept what he considered to be the dull and mechanical emphasis of Objectivism on reason and the exclusion of emotion in philosophy and life. Rothbard was interested in human action in all of its facets and believed that a libertarian political movement should strive for a balance and integration of reason and emotion in its analysis of events and its advocacy for change. Without a passion for individualist ideals based on a rational understanding of the basic elements of libertarian thought, Rothbard believed that any philosophy would fail as it attempted to enter the realm of political movements and social practice.[13] The difference between Rothbard and Rand on the role of reason and emotion in human action is an important source of another difference between them: Rand was not a political activist. She attacked both the left and the right and articulated a radical individualist political position, but she remained aloof from political organizations and movements. She preferred to isolate herself from the political process to propagate her philosophy among her readers. She limited her political-philosophic engagement to interactions within a relatively small group of true believers, which, organizationally, only reinforced a strict demarcation between Objectivism and the morally tainted external world. Rothbard, on the other hand, was an activist as well as a scholar. From the 1950s to the 1980s and into the early 1990s he worked tirelessly to promote his own form of libertarianism in political organizations just as he pursued his scholarship with theoretically diverse environments. On many occasions, this meant developing political coalitions with groups that did not share his ideals, which Rothbard believed he could pursue without compromising his important philosophic principles.[14]

Further, Rand philosophically defended the need for political authority, ridiculed anarchism, argued that the state's primary purpose is to protect the rights of individuals. Rothbard was an anarchist who argued that the state should be abolished in favor of an arrangement in which private firms provided internal and external security. Rand was a committed atheist and believed that atheism is an important component of a rational philosophy of life. To her detractors, she was intolerant of religion. Rothbard was tolerant of religious ideas. Rand articulated many genuinely libertarian ideas and was concerned with how the collectivist state homogenizes persons and oppresses successful business people and others who create, invent, and produce. Rothbard was more concerned with how big business colludes with the state to oppress the poor and marginalized groups. Rand based her laissez-faire economic and political philosophy on a rigidly structured articulation of individualist ethics that was derived from her ontological and epistemological positions. As an individual, Rothbard was certainly concerned with ethics throughout his career, but he did not publish a statement of his ethical system until 1982, long after he had outlined the elements of an anarcho-capitalism philosophy, including his analysis of race and racism. In Rand's Objectivist system, an individualist ethics structured the critique of racism; in Rothbard's anarcho-capitalist system, the critique of racism followed, in part, from his view of political change.

Rand viewed racism as an irrational cultural legacy that contradicted basic American ideals of individualism and autonomy. Racism also frustrated the rationality and ethics of her Objectivist utopia. Rothbard articulated an "internal colonialist" critique that defined racism as a form of exploitation that inevitably emerges from the formation of a social system dominated by an authoritarian government. In the realm of political practice, Rothbard sought out alliances with the Old Right and factions of the New Left to attack racism and to implement all aspects of a revolutionary anarcho-capitalist agenda that promoted individual liberty and autonomy above all other societal values.[15]

The purpose of this chapter is to examine Murray Rothbard's critique of racism. This chapter discusses Rothbard's internal colonialist thesis in the context of his broader vision of anarcho-capitalism. The chapter addresses three questions: First, what are the basic elements of Rothbard's anarcho-capitalist theory? Second, what did he say about race, racism, and multiculturalist thought and how do these ideas fit into the broader context of anarcho-capitalism? Third, what are the implications of Rothbard's thought for race as a concept, and multiculturalism as an analytical tool and political agenda, in the struggle against racism? The chapter proceeds by first analyzing the content and method of Rothbard's economic and political thought. It then discusses Rothbard's analysis of racism and multiculturalism. The chapter concludes with a discussion of the basic elements of the anarcho-capitalist critique of multiculturalism and an assessment of anarcho-capitalism as a vision for a transracial and post-ethnic society.

THE FOUNDATIONS OF ANARCHO-CAPITALIST THOUGHT

The central idea in Rothbard's anarcho-capitalist thought is the principle of nonagression, which means that individuals should be free to do as they wish as long as they do not initiate any aggressive action toward another person.[16] Not only does the state have no right to intrude on individual freedom, it should ultimately be abolished in favor of a system that protects individual rights through private security firms. While Rand based her political and economic philosophy on an atheistic, rational egoist ethical position, Rothbard based his principle of nonagression on the social science concept of methodological individualism and Austrian economics. The necessary point of departure for understanding Rothbard's economic and social theory is the methodology of Austrian economics, especially that of Mises, which essentially holds that knowledge about economic life is derived from theoretical analysis, not from the study of history or the quantification of economic phenomena. The Austrian discovery of the subjective theory of value, its emphasis on deductive reasoning and axiomatic concepts, its methodological individualism, and its articulation of the opposition between the market and the state constitute the foundation of Rothbard's theory of the relationship between the individual and society.[17]

There are four critical elements of Rothbard's individualist approach to epistemology, which he outlined in *Individualism and the Philosophy of the Social Sciences*: a critique of scientism, an inclusion of the notion of freedom of the will, a rejection of mechanical and organic analogies of social life, and the praxeological method of Austrian economics. In his discussion of methodology, Rothbard is very disturbed by the trends in sociology and economics promoted by positivists and pragmatists to equate scientism with science. He argues that the prevailing tendency in all of the social sciences, including economics, was to "credit scientism too highly and accept at face value its claim to be the one and only scientific method."[18] He regards scientism as the attempt to uncritically apply the philosophy and method of the physical sciences to the study of human action. The primordial fact about the nature of human action is that human beings have freedom of the will and a rational consciousness that distinguishes them and their behavior from the rest of the natural world. To ignore the basic fact of human existence and to impose an inappropriate set of methodological precepts derived from the study of the natural world Rothbard considers "profoundly unscientific." To the extent that it generates valid knowledge, social and economic science must proceed by first understanding that humans choose their behavior in order to bring about an end or goal in the near or distant future. That is, humans must act with purpose.

In Rothbard's view, this basic reality of the subject matter of the social sciences entails a rejection of positivist, empiricist, and mathematical methodologies, just as it implies a refutation of any causal or determinist philosophy of history, society, or personality. The existing arguments demonstrating the reality of free will are sound, but as Rothbard examines the philosophic foundations of social and economic science he concludes that the arguments in favor of determinism can be refuted by both experience and logic. He argues that the case for determinism in human action is merely a scientistic agenda for the future in which individual behavior is described, predicted, and controlled. "After several centuries of arrogant proclamations, no determinist has come up with anything like a theory determining all of men's actions."[19] Thus, the determinist ideas of the behaviorists, positivists, Freudians, Marxists, and multiculturalists are basically efforts to impose an ideological agenda upon individuals and society. Moreover, determinism is a self-contradictory idea when it is applied to the human sciences since the person who articulates it implicitly relies on free will. From a determinist point of view, the ideas held by the determinist are determined by external factors just as the ideas of the person who believes in freedom of the will are determined. How, then, can determinists claim any special insight? Rothbard argues that they invariably claim a special exemption for themselves and place themselves and their theories outside the realm of determined behavior. Even determinists must employ freedom of the will to argue their case, promote their ideas, and convince others of their veracity. It is important, therefore, to ensure that the notion of freedom of the will grounds the image of the subject matter and the methodological precepts of social and economic science.

The conclusion that the purposive action of human beings structures social institutions and social processes, and not the obverse, helps understand many facets of social life. Social and economic phenomena always have a human base and that humans are ultimately responsible for the organization and functioning of social institutions. Social institutions are not "just there," they are not inherent in the natural world, and they are not provided by God or some other supernatural entity. They do not precede human interaction in any way. However, the fact that social reality is humanly constructed does not mean that human individuals are completely equal in their ability to affect or influence societal outcomes. Rothbard warns that we should not confuse freedom of the will with either political power or power over nature. Persons may have the ability to choose their own beliefs, values and actions, but this does not mean that they can abolish natural law or that they always have an equal ability to fulfill their aspirations. It does mean, however, that it is a mistake to conclude that human behavior is determined by either nature, society, or culture. The philosophy of the social sciences is inherently opposed to *any* form of determinism, including biological, cultural or social determinism. Thus, differences among the behaviors of individuals and groups cannot be attributed to culture or society without, first, forgetting that it is individuals who create, reproduce, and change their culture and social institutions and, second, arguing that humans are the slaves to, or victims of, their culture and society. Thus, the interest of scientism in the social and economic sciences in the prediction and control of behavior is illusory and ideological.[20]

An important consequence of the inclusion of the notion of freedom of the will and its corollary principle that social reality is humanly constructed, is that mechanical and organic analogies cannot be meaningfully applied to the study of human action. Mechanical analogies, inherent in behaviorism, social engineering, mathematical and causal modeling, and all forms of psychometrics, sociometrics and econometrics, cultivate the assumption that human beings are machine-like in their unreflective response to external stimuli. In their search to understand the external causes of human behavior, the scientistic theorists who adopt mechanical analogies forget that humans are the cause of their own behavior. Methodological approaches in the social sciences based on survey and experimental designs are particularly prevalent research strategies that base their claims to validity and reliability on the notion that persons and groups respond in an unmediated fashion to the stimuli of the questionnaire or controlled variables in the psychology lab. The belief is that the research design will provide valid and reliable information about human behavior if the researcher follows established methodological protocols, due to the assumption that human beings have a mechanical nature. But this is an approach that propounds the assumption that human behavior is subsumed and determined by external entities.

Another example of the scientistic reduction of human behavior is the tendency to ascribe consciousness or agency to social collectivities or collective abstractions. In organic analogies, humans are "reduced to mindless cells in some sort of social organism."[21] Concepts such as "the public good," or "the common good," or "the national interest" are all based on the idea that a supra-individual organic entity known as "society" or the "public" exists, has purposes and acts to achieve them. Rothbard also points out that some friends of free market economics make the same mistake when they describe the market as though it has a corporeal existence and acts on its own behalf. In reality, "the market," "the community," and "the public" are merely labels for the interactions and interrelations of individuals. When social and economic theorists depart from this idea, they scientifically reify the objects of their analysis by personifying things and "thing-ifying" persons. Rothbard's methodological individualism was a humanist critique of the scientific reification of all collectivist abstractions.

The methodological stance Rothbard applies to his economic and political studies is not blindly negative in its opposition to scientism. It is positive in its adoption of the basic elements of the methodology of the Austrian economics. Historically, perhaps the most significant discovery of Austrian economics is its articulation of the subjective theory of value. Prior to the work of the Austrians, the classical economists, the Marxists, and the historical school of economics all propounded an objective theory of value or the idea that the value of a good or a thing had an objective existence that was inherent in the object itself. However, Rothbard, Mises, and their predecessors in the Austrian School, such as Carl Menger, elaborate a theory of value that refuted classical notions, and argued for the idea that value is attributed to objects or goods by human beings.[22] Value is not inherent in objects and cannot be separated from the thoughts and actions of human beings. Thus, human choice or preference, not structural nor institutional factors, is the primary determinant of the meaning that objects have for people. Even the individual valuing objects, goods or social relations cannot reduce the valuation to objective or measurable terms, but can only articulate preferences of some things over others, or increments of some things over increments of other things. Preferences are shaped by the individual's expectation of the satisfaction that the object will bring and not by any sort of external, objective measure. The extent to which an object brings satisfaction is personal and varies by time and space, but it is always grounded in the subjective valuation of the individual who is making choices.

While other economic schools of thought today have adopted the subjective theory of value, in part because of its promulgation by Menger, Mises, and Rothbard, the Austrian School grounds its theories of exchange, money, and the market on the notion that meaning is attributed to objects by human beings; meaning is not inherent in objects. The Austrian school rejects the positivistic, scientistic, and natural science approaches to the study of social phenomena in general and economic behavior in particular. Austrian-oriented economists also reject the empiricist argument that it is impossible to discover knowledge that is universally valid and based on reason, not observation. The Austrians favored a more philosophic and interpretive approach to

economic theory that is guided by a set of methodological and epistemological principles. This places the school in strong opposition to the use of math-
ematics or statistical testing in economic research. The methodological stance
views economics as an a priori or deductive system in which analyses of specific economic dynamics are derived from more general, basic principles or
axioms. "Praxeology" is the process through which the theorist attempts to
discover the fundamental axioms of human action and to derive valid deduc-
tions regarding economic behavior from them.[23]

Austrian economic analysis proceeds from theoretical-deductive reasoning
and not through empirical observation based on the measurement of narrowly
defined variables. Economic behavior occurs in a complex sociocultural environment that is too complex and fluid to permit the use of experimental
methods favored in the natural sciences or its approximation in the survey research or quasi-experimental methods favored in the social and behavioral
sciences. Thus, Austrian theory is opposed on philosophic grounds to statistical analysis or the reduction of scientific thought to statements that are supposedly validated by the probability curve. The Austrian School views qualitative, conceptual understanding, not quantitatively validated empirical
regularities, as the telos of economic inquiry. At the center of the type of
analysis adopted by Mises, Rothbard, and their colleagues is the complex interaction among human nature, human values and actions, and the limitations
and challenges that the external world provides them. The last of these includes human error, fallibility, uncertainty, and the vagaries of time and space
In this image of economics, the complexities or mysteries of even advanced
economic systems are analyzed using basic axioms to reveal the essential elements and causes of the market, production, exchange, and governmental intervention.[24]

The most fundamental axiom that both Mises and Rothbard articulate is
that individual human beings exist and act. Individuals exist as objective actors and make conscious, purposive choices about their values and behavior
among an array of alternatives. From Rothbard's point of view, economic
analysis and all of social science is the elaboration of the nature and consequences of the choices and exchanges made by free individuals. Rothbard's
anarchism is ultimately rooted in his analysis of the opposition between individuals acting freely and governmental intrusion.[25] The praxeological concept
of purposive human action enables modern economics to demonstrate the
positive and objective consequences of the free market for efficiency in production and resource allocation, material prosperity, and personal and societal development against the poverty, chaos and primitivism engendered by
governmental intervention. Thus, economic dynamics are the outcomes of individual behavior pertaining to production, exchange, and consumption.

While individual behaviors may occur within a broader environment, they are not the product of abstract or reified social, cultural, or historical forces, such as social classes or market forces. The economic totality must be understood through the analysis of the behaviors of individuals. A methodological posture that emphasizes individuality and freedom of the will places Rothbard in complete opposition to the scientism, collectivism, and statism of modern social science. Rothbard himself delighted in the conflict between the methodological individualism of the Austrian School as the "science of the free society" and scientism of modern sociology as the "science of social control."

In addition to the axiom that humans act purposefully, Rothbard identifies three additional axioms that constitute the foundation of his political philosophy. First, Rothbard deduces the axiom of the absolute right of self-ownership, that each individual owns his or her mind, self and body. The other options include slavery, in which some persons own others, and communism, in which each person is owned by all others. The concepts that estrange or externalize the ownership of the self cannot work in society and economy.

> Absolute self-ownership for all rests on the primordial fact of natural self-ownership by every man, and on the fact that each man may only live and prosper as he exercises his natural freedom of choice, adopts values, learns how to achieve them, etc. By virtue of being a man, he must use his mind to adopt ends and means.[26]

The second axiom pertains to the principle of property, which follows from and reinforces the axiom of self-ownership. The axiom of the right to property is based on the idea that if individuals have the right to their own person, they also have the right to the results of their own labor and the property that they create. If human individuals must use and transform nature in order to live and prosper, they have the absolute right to own the product created by their energy and effort, since it exists as a "veritable extension" of their personality, identity, and being.[27]

STATE POWER AND SOCIAL POWER

The third axiom, the core principle of nonaggression, is again derived from the axioms of self-ownership and right to property. Following the formulation first outlined by the nineteenth-century German sociologist Franz Oppenheimer and later adopted by Mises and other libertarian writers, Rothbard argues in *Man, Economy, and State* that there are only two paths to acquire property and wealth: the economic and the political. The first method, what Oppenheimer calls the "economic means," is *production* in which individuals freely utilize their energy and talent to create and make products that are exchanged in a voluntary manner. The second method, what Oppenheimer calls the "political means," is *coercive expropriation* in which property of an individual is seized unilaterally and forcibly, or with the threat of force, by another individual or group of individuals.[28] The political means is the method of acquiring property, wealth, or economic value through violence or aggression. Rothbard argues that the forcible seizure of the property of one individual by another contradicts natural law and the requisites of social order and economic life. Human beings can only survive and prosper by the production and direct or indirect exchange of products. When property is acquired by aggression or predation, the aggressor is not a producer but a predator and a parasite. Parasitism is a form of the exploitation of labor and a dynamic that generates fissures and conflicts in society because it violates every kind of universal ethic based on reciprocity. Parasitism does not contribute to, but ultimately deducts from, the totality of economic value generated in a society. Thus, an axiomatic principle of social theory is nonaggression—no individual or group of individuals has the right to deny an individual's ownership and control of mind, self, and body or to forcibly seize or expropriate the property or value created by the individual.[29]

The opposition between the economic means and the political means, or between production and coercive expropriation, undergirds Rothbard's analysis of more complex social structures, including the market and the state. Following the Austrian tradition best exemplified by Mises, Rothbard argues in favor of a demystified concept of the market and an axiomatic or praxeological approach to its analysis. In *Man, Economy, and State* he describes the explanation of the free market system as a "great architectural edifice" that starts from "human action and its implications, proceeding to individual value scales and a money economy" in which "the quantity of goods produced, the prices of consumers' goods, the prices of productive factors, the interest rate, profits and losses, all can be explained by the same deductive apparatus."[30] The market itself emerges out of the eagerness of individuals to interact and exchange with each other. Ultimately, the market is defined by purposive action of individuals who act on the need to survive and implement their aspirations to improve the material basis of their lives. The primary implication of this definition is that the market is not a physical thing, nor does it entail any mysterious mechanical, supernatural, or supra-individual forces. The market includes only individuals who act consciously as both producers and consumers to the benefit of each. The prices that emerge in the market are understood as the fundamental outcomes of subjective evaluations and objective choices made by those who operate within it.

Of course, the concept of the market as an organized field where individual human beings voluntarily exchange value is true axiomatically on the assumption that the state or, more specifically, coercive expropriation does not intrude in exchange relations. However, Rothbard devotes much of his analysis to the fact and consequences of the intervention of coercion into the economy. While it appears superficially that the market is a "chaotic and anarchic place and that governmental intervention imposes order and community values" on economic life, the praxeological approach to economic life reveals quite the opposite.[31] Directly, the economic means of fulfilling needs and solving problems, which entails voluntary exchange, benefits all parties to the exchange because each receives what he or she voluntarily agrees to. Indirectly, the economic means creates social order, produces a precise and efficient allocation of societal resources, and yields the greatest satisfaction of the greatest number of participants. The political means, or coerced expropriation, directly and always entails exploitation because it benefits some participants at the expense of the others. Indirectly, it cripples production, frustrates prosperity, produces artificial and imprecise resource allocation, and generates economic and social chaos by setting people against each other. To quote Rothbard, the "free market, unhampered, would not be in danger of suffering inflation, deflation, depression, or unemployment. But the intervention of government creates the tightrope for the economy and is constantly, if sometimes unwittingly, pushing the economy into these pitfalls."[32]

With the significant exception of crime, the primary means through which coercion is introduced into economic relations particularly in modern societies is the state. Rothbard rejects any supernatural or organic conceptions of the state and its legitimacy. He understands government and institutionalized political authority as clearly distinct from society, which is merely the process of individuals interacting with each other. Reminiscent of Max Weber, Rothbard defines the state as that "organization in society which attempts to maintain a monopoly of the use of force and violence in a given territorial area."[33] Moreover, the state is the only organization in society "that obtains its revenue not by voluntary contribution or payment for services rendered but by coercion."[34] As such, it is the "systemization of the predatory process over a given territory."[35] Individuals and all social organizations and institutions except the state obtain income or economic value through the peaceful and voluntary production and exchange of goods and services. The state, however, obtains its revenue through coercion and its "legitimacy" through ideology. The social role of the state is to regulate and dictate the actions of its individual and collective subjects, always with the intent of maintaining its power and reinforcing its monopoly on the use of legitimate force. Using Oppenheimer's terms, the state is the organization of the political means of obtaining wealth and imposing some order on society. Rothbard's political perspective, thus, is firmly rooted in the camp of political conflict theorists, such as Oppenheimer, Albert J. Nock, Gaetano Mosca, and Robert Michels, who all deny any contractual or consensual foundation or legitimacy of the state, and all functional attributions to it except for its predatory and exploitative role in society.[36]

The anarcho-capitalist theory of politics entails a conception that the state is conceived in violence and conquest. It envisions an ongoing social struggle or dialectic between a ruling caste which has privileges coercively granted by the state and a caste of subjects who are exploited or who have burdens coercively imposed on them by the state. The social struggle between the two castes proceeds through efforts by the ruling caste to maintain and expand its ability to impose order and expropriate wealth and the efforts of the subject caste to resist these encroachments on individual freedom.

Rothbard's radical individualist conflict analysis of the state has some striking parallels with the radical socialist analysis developed by Marx. Most significantly, both include a dialectical concept of society in which opposing social forces struggle over power, wealth, and other forms of social desiderata. In both theories, political power is maintained and expanded through coercion, the threat of coercion, and an elaborate ideology promulgated by intellectuals that legitimates the rule of some individuals and groups by others. The struggle between the opposing social forces ultimately results in the creation of a new social and political formation.

There are enormous differences between the two approaches as well. In the Marxian analysis, the struggle is between social classes that are defined by their relationship to the technology or means of production. Under capitalism, the main conflict is between owners and workers and the main form of exploitation is the surplus value that owners are able to expropriate from the workers. The theory holds that the workers eventually begin to resist this exploitation, develop their own political parties, and seize state power through a revolution. The state then expropriates property in the name of the totality of society, creates a commonwealth, and eventually withers away or dies out.[37] The anarcho-capitalist position envisions political castes, not social classes, as the primary actors in the struggle. Castes are conceived as more rigid and fixed social groups that are comprised of individuals who may or may not own capital, but are collectively defined by their relationship to the state. The fundamental social divide is whether individuals are members of the group that wields coercive power and has the ability to expropriate wealth, or not. The state, not capital, is the entity that creates the basic fissures in society. Further, the anarcho-capitalists do not envision a revolutionary struggle in which one group becomes victorious with the seizure of state power and uses it to impose its own ideals and to serve its own interests. Instead, the vision is to eliminate the state completely and to reorganize society according to the principle of voluntary exchange. In anarcho-capitalist thought, revolution entails the "death of politics," to use the phrase espoused by Karl Hess, or the transcendence of the state in favor of more individualized and social approaches to meeting needs and addressing problems, including external and internal security. History is the conflict between social power and state power. Liberty is goal of revolution and is defined by the triumph of the economic means over the political means.[38]

Rothbard's revolutionary anarcho-capitalism places much greater reliance on the role of natural law and the free market to structure human relationships than it does any form of political organization. Rothbard, along with David Freidman, is probably the most forceful expositor of the opposition between market, or social power, and the state, or political power, as competing principles of social organization.[39] Unlike the left-oriented anarchists, Rothbard has little regard for egalitarianism. He believed that the search for absolute equality or equality in social outcomes was a form of primitivism that could not be achieved and was undesirable even if it could. Inequalities along all dimensions, including income and wealth. are perfectly legitimate as the natural consequence of human freedom, as long as they are not artificially created by the state. Part of the problem humanity confronts is that state power is based upon, creates, and reinforces a multitude of inequalities.

For Rothbard, racism is generated by the state or becomes patterned behavior in social institutions supported by the state. Racism is a collectivist ideology promulgated by governments or ruling classes that have an interest in social inequalities based on racial and ethnic differences. Thus, Rothbard's critique of racism differs considerably from that offered by Ayn Rand.

Objectivists argue for a state that is limited to the protection of individuals and their private property against physical invasion. They favor a government limited to supplying police, courts, a legal code, and national defense. This normative position on the legitimate scope of state power is similar to Rothbard's laissez-faire economic theory, according to which private property and unregulated competition generally lead to both an efficient allocation of resources and a high rate of economic progress. The difference is that Rothbard promotes the free market as the societal mechanism to provide for all social needs, including the internal and external defense of individual liberty and private property. Rothbard argues that the state can be abolished because these defensive functions can be turned over to the free market. Police and military services can be sold by firms that freely compete, that a court system would emerge to peacefully arbitrate disputes between individuals and firms through a legal code based in custom, precedent, and contract.

In *Power and Market*, Rothbard praises the increasing reliance on private security guards, gated communities, arbitration and mediation, and other market-based defensive and legal services assumed to be the sole province of a governmental monopoly.[40] Market alternatives to the state should assume *all* legitimate security and public services. Market structures might involve individuals or groups subscribing to competing police services; these police services might then set up contracts or networks for peacefully handling disputes between members of each others' agencies. Alternately, police services might be "bundled" with housing services, just as landlords often bundle water and power with rental housing, and gardening and security are today provided to residents in gated communities and apartment complexes. Private security forces would have strong incentives to be peaceful and respect individual rights. Failure to peacefully arbitrate disputes will yield to jointly destructive warfare, which is bad for profits. While he certainly promoted the elimination of the state, Rothbard did not seek to eliminate coercive power altogether from society. Criminals should be punished. Racially motivated crimes and forms of discrimination can also be controlled through market mechanisms. Traditional punishment would be meted out after a conviction by a neutral arbitrator, or a system of monetary restitution might exist instead. Convicted criminals owe their victims compensation, and should be forced to repay these debts. In Rothbard's view, all social needs, including the security of individuals from minority groups, can be met through market mechanisms; the state is both unnecessary and contradictory to the defense of individual liberty. Social power, not state power, is the legitimate and effective means to ensure that individuals are free and that their property is secure from coercive expropriation.[41]

RACISM AS INTERNAL COLONIALISM

The antagonism between state power and social power, or the conflict between state and the market, is at the core of the anarcho-capitalist analysis of race and critique of racism. Rothbard's views on race and racism were derivative of Mises's analysis of racism that appeared in *Omnipotent Government*, which was originally published in 1944.[42] The project Mises set out to accomplish in *Omnipotent Government* included an understanding of the role and importance of both war and racism in the rise of the "total state." Mises's specific animus in this work is appropriately directed toward Nazism and its treatment of Jews. However, he also analyzes anti-Semitism more broadly and uses it as a platform for a more generalized critique of racism. Mises's critique includes the methods governments use to impose racism on society, as well as how they use it to expand systems of direct and ideological social control. While the analysis in *Omnipotent Government* focuses on the racism of German Nazism, Mises is also concerned that humanity has entered a historical period in which the power of governments to control their populations through coercion and ideology is so strong that we should consider it the age of totalitarianism. Racism proves to be an important mechanism of totalitarian control in all forms of government. Mises admonished that even in democracies "the individuals who form the majority are not gods, and their joint conclusions are necessarily not godlike" in part because democracies are also capable of pursuing racist policies and otherwise abrogating individual freedom, the rights of persons, and the form of social power found in the market.[43] The basic political choice confronting humanity in the historical period of omnipotent governments and total war is the transcendence of racism through the pursuit of individual freedom or the acquiescence to the fabricated social divides created by omnipotent governments.

In *Human Action*, Mises attacks what he called the "racial polylogism" of Marxism and the sociology of knowledge for their relativist understandings of cultural and historical diversity. Mises is very concerned that Marxist philosophy and the emerging professional social sciences were exaggerating the differences between peoples and creating a political environment in which governments were to become the absolute purveyors of truth. The discrediting of social knowledge by Marxists and social scientists as "false consciousness" create an opportunity for political and cultural elites to promulgate absolute truth and to mitigate the presumed disorder in the marketplace and in society through the acquisition and exercise of political power.[44] The relativist analysis of Marxism and social science presumes that their philosophic categories represent fundamental and irreconcilable conflicts among people that can only be managed through state power. Moreover, the relativism of social science negates any sense that there are absolute human rights. With the notable exception of Herbert Spencer, the founders of modern social science, such as Auguste Comte, Karl Marx, Ferdinand Toennies, Max Weber, and Emile Durkheim, all believed that historical changes had produced dramatic irrational, social disorganization that needed the external mediation of the state to impose social order. The voluntary exchange of the market, the "economic means," and social power are viewed by social science as the problem that must be solved by the intervention of political power.[45]

While there are many examples of the incipient development of the total state, Soviet Communism is the exemplar of totalitarianism of the modern world because it managed, at least in ideology, to collapse all forms of social power into state power. The market and all other mediating social structures were eliminated in favor of the total administration of social life by the Soviet state. The Nazis, of course, differed from the Soviets in a number of respects and eventually became enemies of the communists, but they did not differ in their chauvinist view of the role of the state in society and history. "The Bolsheviks set the precedent. The success of the Lenin clique encouraged the Mussolini gang and the Hitler troops."[46] Nazism is usually regarded as essentially a theory of racism, particularly in its promulgation of claims regarding the lofty ancestry of the mythic Nordic-Aryan master race and the subhuman status of the rest of humankind. Mises explains that the basic philosophic tenet of Nazism is that the superiority of the so-called master race justified the German claim to global domination. In order to provide the ideological and philosophic foundation for their world hegemony, the Nazis needed to fabricate and assemble elements of pseudoscientific and folk knowledge into a form that could be easily proffered and consumed by millions of people.

Hence, anti-Semitism became the official doctrine that justified much of Nazism's external aggression and its internal interventionism in economy and society. Mises demonstrates in *Omnipotent Government* that anti-Semitism became an all-encompassing ideological system that included many contradictions and factually false notions, but its role was not to communicate any sort of meaning or truth about racial or cultural differences. Jews were held responsible by the Nazis for the presumed evils of both laissez-faire capitalism and communism. Instead, Nazism used anti-Semitism to justify the behavior of the Nazi state. Mises concludes that "(t)he Nazis simply call everything that is contrary to their own doctrines and tenets Jewish and communist. . . . In the Nazi dictionary the terms Jew and communist are synonymous with non-Nazi."[47] An important category of anti-Semitism in Nazi Germany involved the intervention of the state in the economy. Despite decades of anti-Semitic propaganda, so-called Aryans consciously bought goods from Jewish shop owners, sought treatment from Jewish doctors, consulted with Jewish lawyers, and read books and articles written by Jewish authors. Legal discrimination against Jews emerged in Nazi Germany, in part, as a way of eliminating non-Aryan competitors in the market. Business people who wanted to minimize their competition could not rely on the alleged cultural hatred of the Jews in German civil society; they needed legal discrimination that outlawed commerce with them. This form of discrimination cannot be attributed to nationalism or any cultural legacy of race hatred. It is a direct result of governmental interventionism in the economy and an irrational policy that favors the less efficient producers to the disadvantage of consumers and all other producers.

Rothbard pursues an analysis of racism and resistance to it in the United States in the 1960s to the 1990s that continues many of the themes identified by Mises in *Omnipotent Government*. Rothbard analyzed slavery and the revolts against it in his four-volume study of the period before the American Revolution entitled, *Conceived in Liberty*. In his study of early American history, Rothbard envisions racism, and slavery in particular, as a mechanism of governmental control of economy and society. Revolts against slavery and racism are, at root, rebellions against the social divides created by government. Rothbard's more contemporary analyses of race and ethnic relations, particularly that of the tumultuous 1960s, appeared in his journals *Left and Right*, *Libertarian Forum*, and *The Rockwell-Rothbard Report*. In 1968, on the heels of many of the most destructive racial riots in American history, and at the zenith of the student rebellion in the United States, Rothbard published several articles in *Left and Right* that addressed not only the struggle of black Americans, but a wide range of struggles for self-determination based on race and ethnicity, including the Irish Catholics, the French Canadians, and Poles in Chicago. It was during this same period that Rothbard collaborated with the Peace and Freedom Party activists in New York City on a variety of grass roots protests. "The Black Revolution," an essay that appeared in *Left and Right* is a vintage Rothbardian analysis of race, racism, and the interstices at which the rebellion against racism overlapped with the political project of anarcho-capitalism.[48]

Rothbard begins the analysis of racism in the United States in this article by drawing a distinction between the goals and accomplishments of the civil rights movement and those of the new black revolution. Rothbard dismisses the goal of the civil right movement of forcibly integrating blacks and whites in all private and public facilities as a liberal and statist response to prejudice and discrimination. However, he argues that, despite these efforts, the policy goal of integration had not been achieved in the crucial areas of employment, housing, and social power. In fact, despite the activism and protests since the mid-1950s, the country remained significantly segregated and racist. He noted that the new reality was that integration was not likely to occur as an outcome of law, coercion, and public policy, but could only occur as a consequence of a change in culture, philosophy, or "the hearts of men." Moreover, the goal of forced integration itself was "flawed at its root" because people cannot derive satisfaction, joy, or dignity if they are forced to interact with each other.[49] As a result, many blacks began to abandon the ideals of compulsory integration in favor "black nationalism," which he describes as a cultural tradition that had earned considerable disrepute in America, but was nevertheless at the core of the black community and had great appeal to the most marginalized black Americans.

The idea of black nationalism emerged in the United States in the 1920s through the work of Marcus Garvey, who preached a "return to Africa" as the mass action that blacks should take in response to continued racism. The idea largely dropped from public discourse until it reemerged in the 1950s in the program of the Nation of Islam and, separately, in the speeches of Malcolm X. Rothbard reminds us that many conservatives and racists were enthusiastic about black nationalism because of its emphases on "self-help, thrift, dignity, and pride, in contrast to the old ideals of coerced integration from above."[50] While some of the basic goals of black nationalism were highly laudable from an individualist and libertarian perspective, Rothbard argues that it cannot hope to flourish "within the context of the black reality in America: permanent oppression by the "white power structure."[51] The initial task is to free black people from the "white-run" government at the local, state, and federal levels. The virtues of black nationalism are analogous to the virtues of the free market and individual liberty in that they can only be achieved by "liquidating the tyranny of the government of the United States, and all other governments throughout the world."[52] Distinguishing his perspective from that of the "libertarian-conservatives," Rothbard argues that resistance to racism has meaning only if it produces liberty, which is a "profoundly revolutionary concept" that can only be achieved through "the liquidation of the oppressor State."[53]

In his critique of the government's efforts to assert control during and after the urban riots of the summer of 1967, Rothbard says that the great lesson of the "summer rebellion that we all should absorb is that the black population of the United States is a colonized and subject people."[54] The internal colonization of black people in the United States is an *internal* expression of the *external* imperialism that characterized American foreign policy in the late 1960s. It is a reflection of the same political and economic dynamics that propelled the government toward an aggressive and exploitative posture in its relations with other nations. It is also analogous to Mises's argument in *Omnipotent Government* that discrimination against Jews proceeded not from racist cultural prescriptions, but from direct action by the state that obstructed commerce between Jews and others. In the case of the United States, black Americans are internally viewed as an alien population whose neighborhoods are occupied, pacified, and exploited for the economic and political gain of the ruling elite. The internal colonization of black Americans functions to mitigate economic competition, to transfer wealth from black communities to white communities, and to reinforce state power. Black nationalism and anarcho-capitalism are parallel and overlapping political responses to internal colonization in that both seek to liberate black communities from the direct and ideological control of the United States government so that black people can freely determine their own political and cultural futures. As such, black nationalists and anarcho-capitalists have much in common and are similarly differentiated from other perspectives on both the left and the right.

In Rothbard's analysis of racism in the United States, internal colonization is manifest in the operation of four forms of governmental activity: police power, urban and regional planning, education, and the welfare system. Perhaps the most significant critique Rothbard offers of the racism found in the government's response to the urban riots of 1967 was the use of police force and riot control methods by National Guard troops. Rothbard noted significant parallels in the discourse about the riots among politicians and military leaders. Phrases such as "hold and clear" and "search and destroy" were used by both politicians and military strategists to characterize the tactics employed by police and National Guard troops to pacify urban areas and quell the "guerrilla warfare." The spark for "every single case of black rebellion" in 1967 was police brutality. The police, National Guard, the federal troops were responsible, according to Rothbard, for precipitating each riot, for creating the hysteria about sniping and looting, and the "greatest bulk of the crime committed during the riots." The behaviors of the police and the troops "was clearly reminiscent of the behavior of U.S. imperial troops in Vietnam, or, in fact, of military occupiers anywhere."[55]

In addition to the use of direct coercion to maintain order, three other institutional processes function to preserve the racist structure of the internal colonies within the larger society. The first of these "colonial administrators" are the urban renewal planners who were initially expected to assist the poor by creating a higher quality of life in urban environments but who actually functioned to destroy black communities. The radical libertarians agreed with the black nationalists that urban planning and renewal is really a "vast subsidy" of real estate speculators who profit at the expense of taxpayers and the urban poor. Governmental planners implemented projects that proceed by forcibly relocating black families into smaller and more expensive urban renewal housing. The new projects quickly became slums and failed to address the more fundamental causes of poverty, which Rothbard suggests are the powerful state and the absence of a free market.[56]

In his various essays on ethnic nationalism, Rothbard also criticizes education, or, more specifically, the public school system as another important agent of racist, colonial administration. Rothbard objects not only to white bias in the instruction, curriculum, and administration of public schools, but to its compulsory nature. In his view, the public school in colonized communities was a "vast prison-house and chain-gang" operated by teachers and administrators who despised the mores and culture of the students under their charge. Rothbard voices approval of the studies of Jonathan Kozol and Paul Goodman which focused attention on the problems generated by compulsory mass education and its outcomes for the children who suffered the physical, intellectual, and psychological degradations inflicted by the white guardians of the schools. It is no surprise that black youth were embittered by their experience with the public education system! Rothbard was an opponent of all forms of public, compulsory education and, consistent with his libertarian principles, advocated for the complete privatization of schooling at all levels.[57] However, he clearly believed that, in the context of the relations between a colonized population and its oppressors, education became a particularly pernicious form of governmental control.

Rothbard identifies the welfare system as a particularly odious agent of internal colonial administration. Welfare workers and the programs they administer impose public policies that place a premium on the surveillance of the populace by the state and attempt to create and reinforce a dependency-oriented culture. From a pro-capitalist point of view, of course, individuals must not be dependent on the state for their livelihood, but must use their own talents and skills to carve out their own niche in the world. The racism of internal colonialism, however, negates this capitalist ethic in favor of a social welfare system that is geared toward the management and control of restive populations rather than allowing them to create their own solutions to the problems they face in everyday life. From the standpoint of the state, surveillance is an indispensable element of the welfare system once one understands that welfare is a social system that promotes community dependency on the racist state; it is not an organized public approach to societal benevolence.[58]

Rothbard discovered that his internal colonialist critique of police power, planning, schooling and welfare was virtually identical to the critique of racism advanced by black nationalists.

> (The) ghettoes are enmeshed in a network of white-run and white-operated despotic control agencies. Hence the black revolution. Hence the cry for black power. It is a call for black power in black areas, it is a call for allowing the Negro people at last to run their own lives as they see fit. It is a call for an end to white race rule over the Negro.[59]

The political goals of the "black revolution" are entirely feasible if the movement focuses on overthrowing federal and local government rule in black areas of the country and not the government in its totality. Assuming that black areas could be identified as territories where black Americans are concentrated, the intent was to challenge, confront, and disintegrate white rule over these areas. However, the "black revolution" has a broader significance as a model for the struggle of oppressed people globally since many of the people in the underdeveloped world saw themselves in conflict with either American or Soviet imperialism. Thus, the activists in civil rights organizations began to interpret their struggle in more global terms in the late 1960s, consciously linking themselves with anti-imperialist forces abroad. Rothbard argued that the more global rhetoric of anti-imperialist activists such as H. Rap Brown, Stokely Carmichael, and Malcolm X reflected a broader interpretation of the experience of black people in the United States. The social and political dynamics that underlay the internal colonialism at home, particularly the role of state power as the negation of the social power of people acting voluntarily within their communities, were apparent in the external forms of colonialism.

Thus, anarcho-capitalism and black nationalism are parallel and compatible philosophies of resistance and revolution. The most sensible political option at the time, as far as Rothbard is concerned, was a "coalition of opposition" among those in the far Left and the far Right who are hostile to the "U.S. Liberal-Conservative Establishment."[60] He quotes with enthusiasm a statement from Carl Oglesby, a previous president of the Students for a Democratic Society that called for a fusion of the laissez-faire, individualist, libertarian Old Right with the minority and student activists comprising the New Left. "The Old Right and the New Left are morally and politically coordinate" since both are antiracist, antiwar, and individualist. Both represent the legacy of "American humanist individualism and voluntaristic associational action" in the political and cultural struggles of the 1960s.[61] Consequently, the legacies of American humanism and individualism are at odds with the Establishment that represents the fusion of the worst of the New Right and the Old Left.

Rothbard's endorsement of the black power or black nationalist movement reflected his judgment that the movement away from integration as the goal of the civil rights organizations was completely consistent with his anarcho-capitalist vision for society. Integration, he argued, was essentially a statist and coercive movement since it entailed forcing black Americans into areas where they were likely to encounter significant racial hostility. The black power concept promotes the libertarian critique that blacks had always been an internally colonized people in the United States and that the goal was the elimination of the ability of the government to direct and control the lives of people. He also expressed the heterodoxical thought that black nationalism had tendencies more toward capitalist and libertarian, rather than socialist, prescriptions for economic life.[62]

Rothbard's support of a coalition with the New Left and the black nationalists was not a blanket support of all forms of nationalism. He was clear in his argument that their were qualitative differences in the forms of nationalism apparent in the global crises of the time. He argued that the forms of nationalism that were invasive, statist, racist and imperialist deserved nothing more than an implacable struggle for their demise. On the other hand, those forms of nationalism that promoted liberation from the state and the external control of people's lives deserved the support and endorsement of libertarians. The tendency for social movements to equate ethnic struggles with a critique of the state and capital is a reflection that many people realize that the "vaunted democracy" of the United States prohibits people from organizing and controlling their own lives. The struggles against racism and imperialism have been reduced to a multicultural, political correctness movement that seeks purity in language and culture but fails completely to challenge the more significant and direct forms of racism and statism. The multicultural movement, which Rothbard lampooned as a pathetic surrogate for social change, stood in stark opposition to the antiracist revolutionary perspective he first articulated in the midst of the social upheavals of the 1960s and 1970s.[63]

FUSION AND TRANSCENDENCE:
RACISM AND REVOLUTIONARY CHANGE

Unlike Rand, who appeared content to comment on political processes to her readers and acolytes, Rothbard was fully engaged in the political process as both a theoretician and an activist. He was not content to attack statism merely from the standpoint of academic economic theory. He advocated revolution and founded a theory of revolutionary change on the concepts and problematics that he outlined in his articulation of the history of economic thought. Just as Rothbard envisioned history as a struggle between social power and state power, he argued that this conflict defined the struggles occurring in the post–World War II period across the globe. Thus, the model that contemporary anarchists and libertarians seeking radical and fundamental change should follow was not that of socialists and communists. Indeed, the revolutionary movements based on the classical liberal, or as Rothbard prefers, the *classical radical* ideas of the seventeenth, eighteenth, and early nineteenth centuries constitute the model that contemporary radical movements should follow. Foremost among the ideas in the theories and movements of classical radicalism that overthrew theocracy, feudalism, and mercantile statism were individual liberty and the free market economy.[64]

From Rothbard's perspective, socialism, communism, and the type of collectivist and nationalist philosophies that permeated revolutionary movements during the latter half of the twentieth century are all forms of a reactionary reversion to precapitalist mystifications of the state and an opposition to free trade, the market, and social power. Socialism, even it its most progressive and revolutionary forms, is an enormously self-contradictory philosophy. Even the most humanist, decentralist, and radical among the socialists and leftists espouse an old-fashioned means of pursuing change, although they may have included some of the nobler goals of anarcho-capitalism or radical libertarianism. It is impossible to reconcile the political strategy of economic collectivism and the pursuit of state power with the goals of material progress, individual liberty, and the dissolution or withering away of the state. Rothbard does not envision an effective challenge to racism that did not work to extend market and libertarian ideals to the life circumstances of all people. The socialist and communist concept that a state is necessary to eliminate racism is a fantasy that only served to perpetuate impoverishment and to reinforce the domination of individuals, groups, and society by governments.[65]

The political critique of socialism and communism that Rothbard advanced in the late 1960s and early 1970s occurred in the context of the dissolution of the New Left, which was heralded by the ideological split in 1968 in the Students for a Democratic Society (SDS). In *Egalitarianism as a Revolt Against Nature*, Rothbard applauds the loose and flexible anti-ideological position the New Left promulgated prior to 1968 primarily because the philosophic ambiguity provided an opportunity for youth, minorities, and other disaffected groups to articulate a genuinely libertarian analysis and critique of the Vietnam War, racism, and other important political trends of the period. It also provided a tactical opportunity for radical libertarians to seek and develop allies with those who sought more decentralist and voluntaristic approaches to the reorganization of society. When SDS became dominated by "Marxist-Stalinist" factions and expunged the more anarchistic oriented leftists, Rothbard thought that libertarians needed to become more circumspect in the defense of their principles and work to distinguish their ideas from the communist variants of anarchism that emerged out of the dissolution of SDS.

The form of anarcho-communism or libertarian socialism propounded by the New Left through such theorists as Murray Bookchin, Noam Chomsky, and Norman O. Brown was significantly different from its original expressions in the writing and political activism of the Russian anarchists Mikhail Bakunin and Peter Kropotkin.[66] For one thing, the type of "post-scarcity" drug-rock youth culture anarchism advocated by Bookchin and Brown was irrationalist, primitivist, and tribalist, a far cry from the internationalist and more scientific form advocated by both Bakunin and Kropotkin. However, all forms of anarcho-communist thought and practice that emphasize an allocation system based on "need," not voluntary exchange, share features that radically distinguished them from the market-oriented forms of anarchism. Philosophically, anarcho-communism is an all-out assault on individuality and reason since the end-game is to coerce everyone to live in communes sharing meager possessions, allocate resources according to some mythical centralist determination of needs, and homogenize all so that no individual advances beyond communal norms.

At the root of all forms of communism, compulsory or voluntary, lies a profound hatred of individual excellence, a denial of the natural or intellectual superiority of some men over others, and a desire to tear down every individual to the level of a communal ant-heap. In the name of a phony "humanism," an irrational and profoundly antihuman egalitarianism is to rob every individual of his specific and precious humanity.[67]

The classical and post-scarcity forms of anarcho-communism had little in common with Rothbard's type of radical libertarianism, which places a premium on economic analysis and the importance of a money economy to transcend primitive levels of subsistence. Rothbard does not accept the anarcho-communist notion that the abolition of both the state and private property would be the catalyst for an incipient Garden of Eden in which prices fall to zero and that all goods and services will be available to all without work, without effort, and without using any scarce resources. The "freedom" offered by Bakunin, Kropotkin, Bookchin, and the rock-drug culture ultimately meant only "enslavement to unreason, to unexamined whim and to childish caprice." In Rothbard's critique of anarcho-communism, racial stratification and domination can be effectively challenged only by the absence of interpersonal invasion and not through the primitivist elimination of both the state and private property.

Rothbard's anarcho-capitalist vision of individuality and society is a unique revolutionary alternative to the forms of state capitalism that characterize the sociopolitical formations that dominate nations today. Rothbard differentiated himself from all positions on the left and the right, and drew parallels between his political orientation and the revolutionary abolitionist philosophy and practice of William Lloyd Garrison, who offers a realistic and idealistic model for the political practice of libertarians. Garrison's agitation against slavery included the "proper and libertarian" goal of an immediate and uncompromising abolition of slavery. Garrison also knew that slavery would not end immediately nor would the emancipation occur with a "single blow," but he argued against gradualism in theory because it resulted in "perpetuity in practice." There are important parallels between the abolition of slavery and the abolition of the state not only in terms of the goal of eliminating invasions into interpersonal freedom, but also in terms of the revolutionary practice required for abolishing the two institutions.[68]

Rothbard favors the most immediate and expeditious means of eliminating the state as long as these means do not contradict the goal of achieving liberty or elevating the market principle in society. However, anarcho-capitalists do not need to limit themselves to advocating the immediate abolition of the state. They can also participate in forms of practice that are transitional in nature as long as these do not lose sight of the goal of liberty. Transitional or reformist forms of practice, therefore, must always hold up "the ultimate goal

of liberty as the desired end of the transitional process" and never explicitly
or implicitly contradict that goal. All transitional or reformist opportunities
cannot be categorically accepted or rejected but must be interpreted in light
of the vision of a society that elevates the principles of individual liberty and
the free market.[69] Hence, Rothbard understood much of his political practice,
including the coalitions he built with black nationalists, New Leftists, and the
Libertarian Party, as a transitional phase in a broader, longer-term, market-
oriented anarchist strategy to eliminate the state and its pernicious impacts on
society.

Rothbard's enthusiasm for black nationalism is based on the parallels he
envisions with anarcho-capitalism: It is part of a transition to a qualitatively
different type of society with a qualitatively different configuration of relations among racial and ethnic groups. Rothbard's support for black nationalism in the context of the struggles of the 1960s and early 1970s can also
be understood as a logical and consistent outcome of his emphases on self-
ownership, voluntary exchange, social power, and critique of imperialism.
Certainly, the critique of racism is an important feature of the anarcho-
capitalist vision of society since racism represents one of the most abhorrent uses of state power.

It is also clear that the liberal goal of forced integration in the 1960s generated considerable opposition among both black and white Americans.
Forced integration probably had mixed results with some successes and some
failures when measured against the standards of equity and absence of prejudice and discrimination. Thus, Rothbard was completely justified in his
search for alternative approaches to the critique of and opposition to racial
domination. Furthermore, the internal colonialist thesis had considerable potential to explain the origins and perpetuation of racism in American society
since the political and economic dynamics of exploitation and domination of
groups based on race or territory seem very similar. It is not quite as clear that
Rothbard's support for black nationalism, or any other form of ethnic nationalism, is either a laudable philosophic critique of racism or a viable political
challenge to it.

Rothbard's support of black and ethnic nationalism was a component of
the "transitionalist" strategy that he espoused in a number of venues, including the alliances he sought at various times with the Old Right, the New
Left, the Objectivists, and the Libertarians. He was well aware that the chief
danger of a transitional political strategy was that the important or ultimate
goals or principles of a revolutionary philosophy would be compromised. In
this case, the anarcho-capitalist vision of a society based on the qualities and
accomplishments of individuals, not races or ethnic groups, is the ultimate
goal. The overarching political question is whether an alliance with or sup-

port for ethnic nationalist philosophies and movements advances or frustrates the goal of Rothbard's version of libertarianism. Rothbard identified black nationalism, and all other forms of ethnic nationalism, as allies in the critique and opposition to racism and the state, but he did not develop how the ideas of ethnic nationalism advance the goal of a market anarchist society. How does an ethnic nationalist or monocultural community contribute to the formation of an individualist or market-based social system? Does ethnic nationalism equate with tribalism and, therefore, frustrate and negate the goals of individualism and libertarianism? What are the exemplars from the history of ethnic nationalism that provide evidence that racial and cultural separatism, in any form, can lead to a social system that values and defends individual liberty? Are not the prevailing historical examples we have of racial and ethnic nationalism evidence to the contrary? Don't social regimes based on racial or cultural separatism also tend to foster collectivism and authoritarianism?

Rothbard's understood his support of ethnic nationalism to be an element of a transitional strategy in a revolutionary philosophy for social change. The idea of a transitional strategy is that revolutionaries and revolutionary movements may have to develop temporary alliances or adopt temporary positions that are not fully consistent with their ultimate goals as a means of achieving the vision they have for society and individuals. From Rothbard's point of view, support for black nationalism was a temporary strategic alliance important for the anarcho-capitalist critique of society and its ultimate victory over the collectivist state. Rothbard ridiculed the Marxists for promoting transitional strategy of acquiring and maximizing state power en route to a classless, stateless society. If Rothbard and his anarcho-capitalist comrades are justified in supporting nationalist and tribalist ideas and movements en route to a better society, why aren't Marxists justified in doing the political equivalent? It is significant to note that Rothbard was consistent in this view of political tactics since he articulated the same argument in his discussion of his relationship with the Libertarian Party, an organization that does not promote anarchism, although it does seek to restructure politics along the lines of the minimalist state.[70] At issue is Rothbard's philosophic and political stance on the relationship between ends and means: At what point, or in what ways, does the estrangement of political practice from political theory result in an unacceptable compromise of principle and a distortion of the vision for a new society? It is difficult to understand how philosophic and political support for racial and ethnic nationalism amounts to anything other than a tribalist justification for a racially and ethnically divided society.

From start to finish, Murray Rothbard was a social scientist who sought to fuse elements of different and, at times, divergent philosophical and political positions into an original and unified philosophy of economy and society. Politically, Rothbard was a revolutionary anarchist who sought fundamental change in social institutions and in how people interact with each other in everyday life. His view of racism was clearly intended to be an important part of his analysis and critique of American politics and culture in the latter half of the twentieth century. Despite the varied strengths and contributions of his prolific writings, including and, perhaps, especially the internal colonialist critique of racism, Rothbard's analysis of racism falls somewhat short of individualist ideals because of its uncritical support of racial and ethnic nationalism. At the social and cultural level, nationalism militates against universality and inevitably promotes fissures and conflicts within and among communities. At the individual level, nationalism reduces personal identity to the ascribed, not achieved, characteristics of a collectivity. Unlike the internal colonialist critique of racism, Rothbard's effort to fuse black nationalism, Irish nationalism, and French Canadian nationalism onto his market anarchism was the outcome of his consistent desire to cultivate alliances, but it does not appear to provide an adequate philosophic ground for either a societal transcendence of racism or the promotion of individual liberty. The market anarchist analysis of racism would be improved by an increased focus on internal colonialism as a critique of the status quo and a decreased emphasis on the interest in fusing its philosophy for the sake of temporary political tactics.

Ayn Rand's political detachment enabled her to develop a perspective on race and racism that entailed a real philosophic transcendence of traditional American political ideas on the racial divide. Rothbard's efforts to fuse otherwise disparate political tendencies forced him into positions that deny the universality of his own principles of self-ownership and individual liberty. This problem in his political practice is apparent not only in his efforts to fuse his ideas onto racial and ethnic nationalism, but in his efforts to merge ideas and tactics with Libertarianism, which is the focus of chapter 4.

NOTES

1. A complete listing of Murray Rothbard's scholarly output and a bibliographic essay by David Gordon are available at the website of the Ludwig von Mises Institute, http://www.mises.org/content/mnr.asp.

2. See the following essays on Rothbard's life: Walter Block, "Living a Life of Principle," http://www.mises.org/content/blockonmnr.asp; Hans Herman Hoppe, "Murray Rothbard: Economics, Science and Liberty," http://www.mises.org/etexts/hhhonmnr.asp. Wendy McElroy, "Murray N. Rothbard: Mr. Libertarian," http://zetetics.com/mac/rockwell/mcelroy000706.html. Important commentaries on Rothbard also appear in Randall G. Holcomb, ed. *15 Great Austrian Economists* (Auburn, AL: The Ludwig von Mises Institute, 1999) and Murray N. Rothbard, *The Irrepressible Rothbard: The Roth-*

bard-Rockwell Report Essays of Murray N. Rothbard, ed. Llewellyn H. Rockwell (Burlingame, CA: Center for Libertarian Studies, 2000).

3. Murray N. Rothbard, *The Panic of 1819: Reactions and Policies* (New York: Columbia University Press, 1962); *Man, Economy, and State: A Treatise on Economic Principles* (1962; Auburn, AL: The Ludwig von Mises Institute, 2001); *America's Great Depression* (Princeton, NJ: D. Van Nostrand Co., 1963); *The Case Against the Fed* (Auburn, AL: The Ludwig von Mises Institute, 1994); *The Mystery of Banking* (New York: Richardson and Snyder, 1983); *For a New Liberty: The Libertarian Manifesto* (New York: The Macmillan Company, 1973); *The Ethics of Liberty* (Atlantic Highlands, NJ: Humanities Press, 1982); *The Sociology of the Ayn Rand Cult* (Port Townsend, WA: Liberty Publishing, 1987).

4. Justin Raimondo, *An Enemy of the State: The Life of Murray N. Rothbard* (Amherst, NY: Prometheus Books, 2000).

5. For a sampling of the individualist, libertarian, and isolationist thought of the Old Right, see H. L. Mencken, *A Mencken Chrestomathy* (New York: Alfred A. Knopf, 1949); Frank Chodorow, *Fugitive Essays: Selected Writings of Frank Chodorow*, ed. Charles Hamilton (Indianapolis: Liberty Press, 1980); Garet Garrett, *Insatiable Government and Other Old Right Commentaries, 1923–1950* (New York: Liberty Cap Press, 2005); Isabel Patterson, *The God of the Machine* (Somerset, NJ: Transaction Publishers, 1993); Rose Wilder Lane, *The Discovery of Freedom* (1934; San Francisco: Fox and Wilkes, 1984); Albert J. Nock, *Our Enemy the State* (1935; Auburn, AL: The Ludwig von Mises Institute, 2006).

6. Franz Oppenheimer, *The State: Its History and Development Viewed Sociologically* (1908; Somerset, NJ: Transaction Publishers, 1999).

7. Raimondo, *An Enemy of the State*, 99–109. Rothbard wrote many book reviews for *National Review*, but by the late 1950s his libertarian and isolationist ideas became increasingly out of place with the New Right philosophy articulated by Buckley and his associates.

8. Raimondo, *An Enemy of the State*, 49; Ludwig von Mises, *Human Action: A Treatise on Economics* (1949; San Francisco: Fox and Wilkes, 1963).

9. Murray Rothbard, *Ludwig von Mises: Scholar, Creator, Hero* (Auburn, AL: The Ludwig von Mises Institute, 1988), 65.

10. Rothbard, *Ludwig von Mises*, 64.

11. Rothbard, *Ludwig von Mises*, 49.

12. Rothbard, *Ludwig von Mises*, 7.

13. Raimondo, *An Enemy of the State*, 111.

14. Rothbard, *For a New Liberty*, 297–321.

15. Raimondo, *An Enemy of the State*, 151–209; also see Jerome Tucille, *It Usually Begins with Ayn Rand* (San Francisco: Fox and Wilkes, 1972) and McElroy, "Murray N. Rothbard: Mr. Libertarian."

16. Rothbard, *The Ethics of Liberty*, 35–50; Rothbard, *Man, Economy and State*, 879–881; Rothbard, *Power and Market: Government and the Economy*, 262–66; Rothbard, *For a New Liberty*, 23–26.

17. Rothbard's major statement on the methodology of the social sciences, including economics, appears in *Individualism and the Philosophy of the Social Sciences* (San Francisco: The Cato Institute, 1979).

18. Rothbard, *Individualism and the Philosophy of the Social Sciences*, 3.

19. Rothbard, *Individualism and the Philosophy of the Social Sciences*, 6.

20. Rothbard, *Individualism and the Philosophy of the Social Sciences*, 8–10.

21. Rothbard, *Individualism and the Philosophy of the Social Sciences*, 15.

22. Carl Menger, *Principles of Economics* (1871; Glencoe, IL: Free Press, 1950), 114–74.

23. Rothbard, *Individualism and the Philosophy of the Social Sciences*, 31–61.

24. Rothbard, *Individualism and the Philosophy of the Social Sciences*, 37; Rothbard, *Egalitarianism as a Revolt Against Nature* (1974; Auburn, AL: The Ludwig von Mises Institute, 2000), 219–38.

25. Rothbard, *Power and Market: Government and the Economy*, 262–66.

26. Rothbard, *The Ethics of Liberty*, 46.

27. Rothbard, *The Ethics of Liberty*, 48; *Egalitarianism as a Revolt Against Nature*, 104–5.

28. See Oppenheimer, *The State*; Rothbard, *Egalitarianism as a Revolt Against Nature*, 55–88.

29. Rothbard, *The Ethics of Liberty*, 50.

30. Rothbard, *Man, Economy, and State*, 56.

31. Rothbard, *Man, Economy, and State*, 890.

32. Rothbard, *Man, Economy, and State*, 879.

33. Rothbard, *Egalitarianism as a Revolt Against Nature*, 57.

34. Rothbard, *Egalitarianism as a Revolt Against Nature*, 57.

35. Rothbard, *Egalitarianism as a Revolt Against Nature*, 59.

36. Gaetano Mosca, *The Ruling Class* (1896; New York: McGraw-Hill, 1939); Robert Michels, *Political Parties* (1911; New York: The Free Press, 1966).

37. Karl Marx and Frederick Engels, *The Communist Manifesto* (1848; New York: Verso, 1998).

38. Rothbard, *Egalitarianism as a Revolt Against Nature*, 58–61; Karl Hess, "The Death of Politics," http://fare.tunes.org/books/Hess/dop.html.

39. Rothbard, *Egalitarianism as a Revolt Against Nature*, 86–87. Also see David Friedman, *The Machinery of Freedom: Guide to Radical Capitalism* (1973; Chicago: Open Court Publishing, 1995).

40. Rothbard, *Power and Market: Government and the Economy*, 1–9.

41. Rothbard, *Power and Market: Government and the Economy*, 262–66; Rothbard, *The Ethics of Liberty,* 161–74.

42. Ludwig von Mises, *Omnipotent Government: The Rise of the Total State and Total War* (1944; Grove City, PA: Libertarian Press, Inc., 1985), 176–201.

43. Mises, *Omnipotent Government*, 50.

44. Mises, *Human Action: A Treatise on Economics* (1949; San Francisco: Fox and Wilkes, 1996), 75–89.

45. Don Martindale, *The Nature and Types of Sociological Theory* (Boston: Houghton-Mifflin, 1960); Irving Zeitlin, *Ideology and the Development of Sociological Theory* (Englewood Cliffs, NJ: Prentice-Hall, 1968).

46. Mises, *Omnipotent Government: The Rise of the Total State and Total War*, 186.

47. Mises, *Omnipotent Government: The Rise of the Total State and Total War*, 188.

48. Murray Rothbard, "The Black Revolution," *Left and Right* 3, no. 3 (Spring–Autumn 1967): 7–17; Murray Rothbard, "Black, White, and 'Polish': The Cry for Power," *Left and Right* 2, no. 3 (Autumn 1966): 11–14; Murray Rothbard, "The Irish Revolution," *Left and Right* 2, no. 2 (Spring 1966): 3–7; Murray Rothbard, "Principles of Secession," *Pine Tree Features* (June–August 1967). See also Raimondo, *An Enemy of the State*, 165.

49. Rothbard, "The Black Revolution," 7–8.

50. Rothbard, "The Black Revolution," 8.

51. Rothbard, "The Black Revolution," 8.

52. Rothbard, "The Black Revolution," 8.

53. Rothbard, "The Black Revolution," 8.

54. Rothbard, "The Black Revolution," 9.

55. Rothbard, "The Black Revolution," 9.

56. Rothbard, "The Black Revolution," 12.

57. Rothbard, "The Black Revolution," 12–13; also see Murray Rothbard, *Education: Free and Compulsory* (1971; Auburn, AL: The Ludwig von Mises Institute, 1999).

58. Rothbard, "The Black Revolution," 13.

59. Rothbard, "The Black Revolution," 13.

60. Rothbard, "The Black Revolution," 14.

61. Rothbard, "The Black Revolution," 16; also see Carl Oglesby, "Vietnamese Crucible," in Carl Oglesby and Richard Shaull, *Containment and Change* (New York: MacMillan, 1967), 165–67.

62. Murray Rothbard, *The Irrepressible Rothbard*, 377.

63. Rothbard developed these themes in an array of articles on the antiwar and student rebellions that appeared in the *Libertarian Forum*. In his later years, Rothbard commented on a wide range of racial and culture topics, including politically incorrect language, the Spike Lee film about Malcolm X, affirmative action, and academic studies on the racial divide. In each essay, Rothbard maintained a consistent posture that reformist efforts such as affirmative action and initiatives to purify the culture of racist ideas failed to attack the economic and political foundations of racism and, thus, were unlikely to promote fundamental changes in the relations among different racial and ethnic groups in American society. See Rothbard, *The Irrepressible Rothbard*, for examples of his commentary during the 1980s and 1990s.

64. Rothbard outlined his analysis of the history and political thought of the American Revolution in *Conceived in Liberty, Volume I—A New Land, A New People: The American Colonies in the Seventeenth Century* (1975; Auburn, AL: The Ludwig von Mises Institute, 1999); *Conceived in Liberty, Volume II—Salutory Neglect: The American Colonies in the First Half of the Eighteenth Century* (1975; Auburn, AL: The Ludwig von Mises Institute, 1999); *Conceived in Liberty, Volume III—Advance to Revolution, 1760–1784* (1976; Auburn, AL: The Ludwig von Mises Institute, 1999); *Conceived in Liberty, Volume IV—The Revolutionary War, 1775–1784* (1979; Auburn, AL: The Ludwig von Mises Institute, 1999).

65. Rothbard, *Egalitarianism as a Revolt Against Nature*, 191–98.

66. Rothbard, *Egalitarianism as a Revolt Against Nature*, 199–204.

67. Rothbard, *Egalitarianism as a Revolt Against Nature*, 201.
68. Rothbard, *Egalitarianism as a Revolt Against Nature*, 243–45.
69. Rothbard, *Egalitarianism as a Revolt Against Nature*, 239–45; Rothbard, *The Ethics of Liberty*, 257–73; Rothbard, *For a New Liberty*, 297–321.
70. Rothbard was severely criticized in some anarchist periodicals for his collaboration with Marxist organizations and the Libertarian Party at different points during his career. The critique that appeared in the pages of *The Match!* during the early 1970s was insightful but also very hostile toward Rothbard's support of capitalism and his gradualist and collaborationist view of change. Back issues of this anarchist newspaper are very difficult to find, even within research libraries. However, there are some web references to *The Match!* and its editor Fred Woodworth, who argued for a non-hyphenated strand of anarchism in opposition to both anarcho-capitalism and anarcho-communism. For a sample of Woodworth's perspective on anarchism see http://members.tripod.com/~dashitzine/issue00/anarchy.html.

Chapter Four

The Old Racism and the New

The Libertarian Analysis and Critique of State Intervention in Society

LIBERTARIANISM AS A PHILOSOPHY
AND SOCIAL MOVEMENT

Although the word "libertarian" has much older roots, contemporary usage of the term has been traced back to the early writings of Murray Rothbard as he attempted to differentiate his emerging concept of anarcho-capitalism from the conservatism of the New Right and the Marxism and communist anarchism of the New Left.[1] Today, the term is a general referent to support for civil liberties, but, when it is preceded by a capital "L," it is more specifically a reference to the philosophy and platform of the Libertarian Party, a national political organization that Rothbard helped to create, but which later marginalized and expelled him for his anarchist philosophy.

Libertarianism emerged as a movement and political force in the early 1970s in the United States through the confluence of disaffected "paleoconservatives," Objectivists, and antiwar, antidraft New Leftists who sought an alternative to leftist and conservative approaches to the conflicts and crises of the 1960s and early 1970s. While many of the early Libertarians in the United States owe much of their philosophic development to Ayn Rand, the theatricality and cult-like environment of Objectivism suggested to many in the 1970s and 1980s, that a separate movement and political party was needed to advance the goals of individualist, pro-capitalist, and antistatist activists in the United States. Rand remained an important thinker and source of inspiration for many Libertarians, but the limited government philosophies of John Locke and Thomas Jefferson, and the laissez-faire economic philosophies of Fredrick A. Hayek, Ludwig von Mises, and Murray Rothbard emerged as the primary sources of theoretical inspiration for the emerging Libertarian Party and movement in the United States.[2]

Libertarianism is a visible, although still minor, feature of the political landscape in the United States, primarily because of the activism of the Libertarian Party. The Libertarian Party was formed in 1971 and began nominating candidates for federal, state and local political offices in 1972. Libertarians basically describe their philosophy as "the right to live your life as you wish, without the government interfering—as long as you don't violate the rights of others. Politically, this means Libertarians favor rolling back the size and cost of government, and eliminating laws that stifle the economy and control people's personal choices."[3] Identifying itself as the "Party of Principle" and the "new choice in American Politics," the Libertarian Party claims to be the largest third political party in the United States. The Libertarian Party claims to have active organizations in all 50 states with a membership of over 200,000 registered voters. Moreover, it also claims that its candidates received over a million combined votes in the 2004 election, although this appears to be a decline from the 3,700,000 total votes cast for Libertarians in the 1992 election.[4] The Party targets voters who are disaffected Democrats, Republicans, and Independents who believe that the federal government has become too large and costly, and far too intrusive into the everyday lives of Americans.

However, the Libertarian movement is not limited to the activities of the Libertarian Party. Philosophically, the movement is supported by the Cato Institute, the Independent Institute, Advocates for Self-Government, and the Reason Foundation, all of which publish the studies of Libertarian writers and scholars. Libertarians also claim that a variety of celebrities and public figures, including actors Clint Eastwood and Kurt Russell, the comedian Drew Carey, the journalist John Stossel, and civil rights activist Roy Innis, are members of the Party or otherwise support the philosophy and the movement.

In 2005, the platform of the Libertarian Party addressed racial and ethnic issues directly by stating that Libertarians do not advocate for either public or private discrimination, since both are anti-individualist, but they do not support laws or public policies that attempt to ban or rectify private discrimination.[5] By 2006, however, the Party's platform had been revised so that it no longer addresses racial and ethnic issues directly. Instead, the revised Libertarian platform focuses on categories of individual rights and how they might be applied to a variety of contemporary social issues, including crime and drugs, sex and gender, the economy, and public services. A clear implication of the principles articulated in the 2006 platform is that the philosophy has not changed; the Party opposes both officially imposed prejudice and discrimination as well as governmental or public efforts to ameliorate the consequences of racism exhibited by individuals.

Beyond the platform of the Libertarian Party, there is a considerable amount of libertarian literature that directly addresses or has important implications for multiculturalism, race, and ethnicity. Some of this literature is published by the Libertarian think tanks, such as the Cato Institute. Other literature appears in scholarly journals, such as *Inquiry* and the *Journal of Libertarian Studies*. This is also a broad array of scholarly literature espousing a Libertarian point of view that has been published in book form, including attempts at comprehensive statements of Libertarianism as a political philosophy by John Hospers, David Bergland, and Tibor Machan.[6] Much of the libertarian analysis of race, or the analysis that has implications for race, is best described as public policy analysis that poses a critique of the positive harm that the government does to individuals and social relations as it attempts to assist the poor and disadvantaged, especially through affirmative action and welfare programs.

Unlike the works of more radical individualists, such as Rand and Rothbard, Libertarians are focused on the implications of their small government, free market thought for public policy issues. Although many of the themes that appear in the work of Rand and Rothbard, such as self-ownership, individual rights, and free markets, also appear in the literature of Libertarianism, Libertarians generally do not envision the same type of fundamental change in self and society promoted by Rand and Rothbard. As one prominent Libertarian policy analyst said,

> Libertarianism is a political philosophy, not a complete moral code. It prescribes certain minimal rules for living together in a peaceful, productive society — property, contract, and freedom — and leaves further moral teaching to civil society.[7]

Libertarian writings are largely oriented toward public policy and political practice. Its politics is electoral, not revolutionary. Even with the notable exception of the work of Robert Nozick, its form of argumentation is public policy analysis, not philosophic critique. What unites all Libertarians with other thinkers such as Rand and Rothbard is a strong belief that the intervention of the state into civil society, regardless of the intent, tends to produce inequities and social disorganization.

This chapter addresses three questions pertaining to the Libertarian analysis and critique of racism and multiculturalism: First, what have major Libertarian writers said directly and indirectly about multiculturalism, race, and ethnicity? Second, how do their ideas about race and racism fit within the broader context of their writings on society and social organization? Third, how should their ideas about race and racism be assessed? Do they offer analyses and critiques of racism, in particular, that provide a vision for a world free of forms of racial stratification and domination? The chapter provides an overview and analysis of Libertarian perspectives on race and racism by drawing from the writings of the David Boaz, Robert Nozick, James Bovard, and Charles Murray.

DAVID BOAZ: RACE AS CONTEMPORARY SOCIAL ISSUE

David Boaz is the Executive Vice President and a "policy scholar" for the Cato Institute. He has written *Libertarianism: A Primer* and edited and introduced *The Libertarian Reader: Classic and Contemporary Writings from Lao-Tzu to Milton Friedman* and *Toward Liberty: The Idea that is Changing the World*. He also writes articles that have been published in a variety of journalistic and scholarly venues. He is also a highly visible spokesperson for the Cato Institute and Libertarian ideas. In *Libertarianism: A Primer*, David Boaz argues that because racism and individualism clearly clash, Libertarianism is a philosophy that strongly opposes any form of racism and seeks to liberate the poor, particularly when poverty is a result of prejudice and discrimination promoted by the government.[8] Boaz is clear that Libertarianism is a philosophy that is critical of racism in all forms. "White Americans have denied the individuality of black Americans and treated them as a special class for some 380 years. It's time to try individual dignity, individual rights, and individual responsibility for all Americans."[9]

Boaz bases his argument against racism on what he termed the key concepts of Libertarianism, which include (a) individual rights to life, liberty, and property, (b) the rule of law, (c) free markets, and (d) limited government. He argued that the libertarian and individualist dimensions of the American Revolution gave rise to the Abolitionist movement and served as an important philosophic and inspirational sources of the Civil Rights movement. Thus, the values inherent in the founding of American society are explicitly antiracist because they are pro-libertarian and pro-individualist. Historically, these values have been contradicted by the racist practices of American institutions.

The periods of slavery and racial segregation were prominent examples of the contradiction between fundamental American values toward liberty and individuality and its social practice. However, Boaz suggests that the contemporary period, characterized by equal voting rights, welfare, and affirmative action, has commonalities with the previous historical periods in American society in that African Americans are still denied their basic individuality and humanity. The Libertarian critique interprets contemporary racism as similar to both slavery and segregation in that it attempts to deprive individuals of their dignity, liberty, and sense of self. The early abolitionists were also libertarians who castigated slavery as "man-stealing" since it deprived persons of their basic human capacity to make decisions and determine the course of their own lives. Although Boaz does not equate slavery, segregation, and contemporary racism, he argues that the three periods in American history have definite parallels in that they all entail a denial of the individual "personhood" of African Americans.

The inception of the contemporary period of racism in the United States occurred in the 1960s, coterminous with the dismantling of the segregationist Jim Crow statutes and the launching of the War on Poverty and system of affirmative action. Despite the massive attempts by federal and state governments to engineer equality and social justice, "racial relations in America seem more acrimonious than ever."[10] Further, Boaz argues that the welfare state, the system of affirmative action, and the War on Drugs generated what amounts to an assault on minority people and their communities. Culturally, the federal efforts especially created a belief that African Americans cannot succeed in competitive environments without the assistance of the state. Boaz concludes that any public policy that elevates group identification over individual character, ability, and effort promotes dependency and conflict.

Boaz is very critical of government-sponsored racism as well as efforts by the state to achieve some sort of racial parity in hiring and the distribution of other social desiderata. "The libertarian solution starts with renewing our effort to build a society based on the virtues of choice, responsibility, and respect for self and others."[11] Like Rand, Boaz is concerned about the social fragmentation generated by the state in its contemporary efforts to repair the damage it caused by imposing segregation on the races. He argues that public and institutional policies that provide privileges for one group inevitably generate intergroup hostility and discrimination against others. "We can reduce racial tensions by removing more aspects of life from the political arena, letting people work together—or apart—peacefully in the market process."[12]

Following Boaz, libertarianism entails a critique of all forms of discrimination, but especially those imposed by the government. Libertarians argue that individual rights should not be denied, abridged or enhanced at the expense of other people's rights by laws at any level of government based on sex, wealth, race, color, creed, age, national origin, personal habits, political preference, or sexual orientation. They support repealing any law that imposes discrimination by government. Libertarians do not advocate for either public or private discrimination, since both are anti-individualist, but they do not support laws or public policies that attempt to ban or rectify private discrimination. Still, Libertarianism offers a significant critique of racism and it is a philosophy that should attract antiracists. As Boaz says, "Libertarians reject all government-created privileges and entitlements and call for the state to be scrupulously neutral in its enforcement of individual rights."[13]

RACISM AND ROBERT NOZICK'S ENTITLEMENT THEORY OF JUSTICE

Arguably the most significant statement of political philosophy published during the formative phase of Libertarianism in the United States was Robert Nozick's *Anarchy, State, and Utopia*.[14] Although Nozick himself reportedly moved away from the Libertarian position he articulated in *Anarchy, State, and Utopia*, his early political philosophy is an important statement on libertarianism not only because of the acclaim and scrutiny the book received since its publication in 1974 but because it identifies the legitimate moral foundations of the state and articulates the limits of state power grounded in a theory of self-ownership, individual rights, and distributive justice. Although Nozick does not directly address issues pertaining to race and racism, *Anarchy, State, and Utopia* has significant implications for these topics and provides considerable intellectual ammunition for those who seek to understand and critique the relationship between the state and racial domination.

In many respects, *Anarchy, State, and Utopia* is a Libertarian response to John Rawls's *A Theory of Justice*, which was published three years before Nozick's political treatise.[15] Rawls argued that justice in any society must be based on two principles that cannot contradict each other: the liberty principle and the difference principle. The idea undergirding the liberty principle is that each individual in a just society should have equal access to the basic rights and liberties available to individuals in the society. The difference principle is the idea that the distribution of social desiderata should be based on equality of opportunity and arranged so that the most disadvantaged are assisted as much as possible. Rawls's position is not exactly egalitarian, but it argues for a social and political system that is optimally committed to minimizing inequalities and the negative consequences of inequalities. Or, inequalities are justified if they benefit all or if they help the most disadvantaged. For Rawls, justice is fairness where fairness is understood as the maximization of equality of opportunity and minimization of inequality in the distribution of desiderata. Thus, Rawls's theory of justice argued for a type of social democracy or welfare system that utilizes the resources of public policy and state power to ensure equality of opportunity and a social safety net that benefits the disadvantaged as much as possible.

Nozick advanced several arguments against Rawls theory of social justice. However, the most significant for the discussion of the Libertarian arguments against racism is that Rawls's theory ignores or contradicts the idea that individuals are separate persons. Nozick based his critique of Rawls on a concept of self-ownership or the idea that individuals legitimately own their own bodies, selves, and the outcomes of their behaviors, including the accumulation of wealth and property. Society, for Nozick, is the result of voluntary mutual cooperation among individuals. The choices of individuals to cooperate with each other should not be constrained by the imposition of a principle of justice, such as that imposed by Rawls. Rawls's principle of difference appears to impose constraints on the abilities and inclinations of individuals who seek to create or acquire material benefits for themselves unless their efforts would improve the life circumstances of the most disadvantaged in society. The principle of difference assumes or entails the idea that talented and energetic individuals are little more than a resource for those who are less talented or less inclined to create and acquire wealth. Rawls's philosophy is an argument that some individuals should be sacrificed for the sake of others. Nozick recreates political philosophy on the basis of a concept of justice that did not require the sacrifice of some persons for others.[16]

The philosophy Nozick's presents in *Anarchy, State, and Utopia* is not anarchism. Therefore, he carefully separates his political position from that of Rothbard and other anarchists. He also distinguishes his point of view, especially on property rights, from that of Ayn Rand. He seeks a justification and role for the state in society, but he wants a middle ground somewhere between anarchy and the types of governments that characterize the contemporary historical period. He settles on the concept of the "minimal state" as a framework for his utopian society. Within this framework he explores a number of topics that have considerable relevance for racism and the restructuring of race relations, including concepts of justice, equality, opportunity, and self-esteem. Nozick bases his theory of the minimal state on an atomistic view of the individual and society. He observes that individuals lead separate lives and concludes that it is wrong to sacrifice one person for the sake of another or for the sake of some public purpose. Nozick's thesis of self-ownership states that one individual cannot be a resource for another, unless there is a voluntary agreement or contractual arrangement to that effect. Further, the state cannot legitimately force an individual to suffer some sort of loss or disadvantage just so another will benefit. Only the individual has the right to determine what happens to his or her life, liberty, body, and the outcomes of his or her behavior. For Nozick, individual rights are absolute and paramount in that they trump all other considerations of need, fairness, and happiness. Individual rights thus comprise the totality of the political vision of Nozick's argument for Libertarianism. The key thesis of self-ownership is that, except for punishment or self-defense, the only things that others may do to an individual are those with which she or he voluntarily consents. Each individual must be protected by a sphere of rights that neither other individuals nor the institutions of society may intrude. By recognizing the right to noninterference, the separateness of the lives of individuals and the legitimate ownership of the self are respected and protected.

Nozick was not the first to articulate this thesis of self-ownership since it appears to be included in the political theories of Thomas Hobbes, John Locke, John Stuart Mill, and Ayn Rand. However, with the possible exception of the writings of Max Stirner, Nozick is somewhat unique in the emphasis he places upon self-ownership. His thesis of self-ownership constitutes one of the two elements of his theory of the minimal state. The other element is expressed in his view of property rights. For Nozick, property rights also fall within the protected sphere of individual rights. Where individuals have a justified right to property, this right is as comprehensive and sacrosanct as are the rights to life, liberty, and body. No individual or societal institution can legitimately interfere with an individual's property without their consent, even for the sake of public purposes or a presumed "greater good." Nozick expands upon the notion that legitimate property rights are based on need or merit by arguing that "entitlement" is key. Individuals may also be entitled to legitimate ownership of property (a) if it has been "justly transferred" from others, (b) in certain circumstances, if it has been appropriated in an unowned form from nature, or (c) if its transfer rectifies past injustices.

Nozick's view of the absolute right to life, liberty and property forms the basic principles of the philosophy of the minimal state. The state is justified inasmuch as it protects people against force, fraud, and theft, and as it enforces contracts between people. The only legitimate role of the state is to safeguard the rights of individuals. Any action or program of the state that goes beyond this function inevitably violates the rights of individuals. Thus, efforts by governments to protect citizens against internal and external aggression are legitimate under Nozick's formulation, but those efforts to provide public services, to take care of those who cannot care for themselves, and to supervise the lives of individuals, are not legitimate governmental activities. To drive home the point about the appropriate role of the minimal state, Nozick argued that people do not have rights to welfare assistance and the state has no business assisting the poor for the very reasons he rejects Rawls's theory of social justice.

Nozick's political philosophy entails clear ideas regarding the critique of racism and multiculturalism in American society. To begin with, his theory of individual rights and entitlement theory of justice provides strong critiques of racism and the domination and exploitation of racial, ethnic and linguistic groups. The thesis of self-ownership and the entitlement theory of justice imply that the state cannot legitimately establish law and policy that includes the political and social domination of racial and ethnic groups. It is clear that any effort by the state to promote discrimination, separation, or the appropriation of life, liberty, and property of individuals from any racial or ethnic group is illegitimate. However, the minimal state has a very limited role in responding to racism. Nozick's minimalist utopia prohibits any official form of racism and prohibits the differential or preferential treatment of people to provide equality of opportunity or outcomes beyond that which is freely agreed to by individuals.

There is one important addendum to this point in Nozick's philosophy. The entitlement theory of justice provides the foundation for the legitimate transfer of property and wealth from some individuals to others in order to rectify past injustices. His view of property rights justifies the redistribution of social desiderata in order to rebalance or correct past discrimination. Since it is clear that Nozick views racism as the depravation of self-ownership through the violence of some individuals against others, there is some basis in his philosophy for the "reparations" perspective in the multiculturalist agenda, not to reallocate social desiderata through public policy, but to repair past injustices through the legal system and the courts. Thus, those who advocate that the descendants of the slave trade in the United States should receive reparations for the violence inflicted on their ancestors may find in Nozick's philosophy of distributive justice elements of an argument in favor of their position as long as that occurs through the courts and does not violate the life, liberty, and property of other individuals.[17]

JAMES BOVARD: DEMOCRACY AGAINST LIBERTY

James Bovard is a Libertarian writer who developed an impressive body of knowledge that challenges the structure and outcomes of the power and authority of the government in the United States. Since 1989, Bovard published nine books on politics in America. Six of these are directly focused on how the power and policies of the government in America are eroding or eradicating the rights of individuals and the expression of freedom. In *Lost Rights: The Destruction of American Liberty*, *Freedom in Chains: The Rise of the State and the Demise of the Citizen*, and *Feeling Your Pain: The Explosion and Abuse of Government Power in the Clinton-Gore Years*, Bovard has a field day identifying and savaging the impacts of federal domestic policies on the individual liberties and property rights of citizens in the United States.[18] Although Bovard includes one chapter on Clinton's war in Kosovo in *Feeling*

Your Pain, his primary animus in these three books is directed toward the "Principle of Government Supremacy" over individual rights, which Clinton, in particular, succeeded in institutionalizing during his presidency. Bovard's next three books, *Terrorism and Tyranny: Trampling Freedom, Justice, and Peace to Rid the World of Evil, The Bush Betrayal,* and *Attention Deficit Democracy,* continue to develop some of the ideas and analyses developed in his books about the Clinton administration, but are more focused on the predations and foibles of the Bush presidency.[19] In addition to his continued interest in illuminating the exercise of state power through domestic policy and programs, the last three books demonstrate how foreign policy, especially in the aftermath of 9/11 and the resulting War on Terror, have helped to reinforce and strengthen the Principle of Government Supremacy.

Bovard argues that the essence of the state in any society is control and coercion. It makes little sense to think about government as something grander than the "threats, bribes, and legislative cattle prods by which some people are made to submit to other people."[20] Differentiating himself from the anarchists, Bovard says that the fundamental problem of politics is not whether the state can and should be abolished, but how the use of force by the state should be minimized.

Bovard's compendia of governmental abuse and destructive incompetence can be categorized into three themes that help illustrate the Principle of Government Supremacy and its impact on race relations. First, the powers of the federal government expanded rapidly during the Clinton and Bush eras, as did the ability of the state to regulate the everyday affairs of American citizens. The growth of state power and its regulatory functions since the 1990s are found in the increase of the government's assertion of "eminent domain," "property seizure," and "asset forfeiture." These processes basically entail the confiscation of the private property of individuals by the state. Bovard contends, and documents, that the volume of the state's appropriation of private property during the Clinton and Bush years constitutes a veritable "war on property rights" perpetrated by a confluence of local, state, and federal entities, including the courts, local zoning boards, state economic development agencies, the Internal Revenue Service, Alcohol, Tobacco and Firearms, and Housing and Urban Development. The seizure of private property by the state occurs for a variety of reasons, but it is consistently legitimated by the state as in the "community interest," "common good," or "economic development."

When the observation that the coercive powers of the state have expanded is applied to the area of race and ethnicity, Bovard argued that a broad array of policies, programs, and agents have been created to manage relationships among groups and relationships between individuals and organizations. Bovard is not convinced that affirmative action, racial quotas in hiring and college admissions, and hate crime legislation are tools for ensuring racial justice. In his view, they are tools that help maximize the control of the state over the citizenry and do little, if anything, to help promote opportunity and equity.

These adoption of these tools required the creation of a cadre of governmental functionaries he calls "the opportunity police" who employ the tactics of characteristic of all police—surveillance and coercion—to identify and sanction those who violate state policy. The Equal Employment Opportunity Commission (EEOC) is one of the best examples of the policing function of the state applied to the management and control of race relations. Bovard argues that the EEOC forced hundreds of thousands of organizations to change their daily operations to comply with "federal agencies' undefined, constantly changing, and basically dishonest concept of social justice."[21] In *Lost Rights* and *Feeling Your Pain*, Bovard catalogs the ludicrous and outrageous actions that the EEOC has taken against employers who it believed violated federal law or its own regulations.

Rooted in the Civil Rights Act of 1964, the EEOC, like other provisions of the Act, was created with basically good intentions: to combat the repression of black Americans, particularly in southern states. However, it inverts the American ideal of equal opportunity by making it a legally enforceable right. Although this right is commonly thought to be enforceable, it is somewhat nebulous and indeterminate, given the policy and procedural controversies over exactly what constitutes affirmative action and acceptable racial preferences. The right of equal opportunity enables the state to assert its own right to monitor, measure, assess, and punish businesspeople and organizations who allegedly fail to offer equal opportunities. But the state cannot identify and punish those who do not offer equal opportunity without also asserting its right to control the distribution of all opportunity in society, implying that opportunity is a type of commodity that the state rightfully owns and controls. Thus, the Equal Employment Opportunity Commission and other governmental entities that police opportunity in society, function not so much to repair race relations or to ensure equal protection under the law, but to assert the state's control over social, cultural, and economic life.

Second, in addition to the increased exercise and legitimation of its coercive powers in everyday life, the state has become morally glorified in the culture and ideology of American society. The Clinton administration was especially effective in its public relations campaigns to sanctify its "social justice" agenda and particular view of the world with the aura of moral superiority. But this attempt at Orwellian doublespeak was not restricted to the Clinton-Gore years. George W. Bush frequently legitimates his policies and strategies to defeat Islamic fascism through a Manichean separation of the world into good and evil. Governmental policies and strategies are legitimated as necessary to prevent "evildoers" from harming Americans. Both Bush and Clinton sanctified their political agendas at home and abroad through messianic and delusional rhetoric about democracy. The only consistency in policy during Clinton's presidency was that each initiative was destined to enable America to fulfill its democratic promise. Bush legitimated his domestic policies and external military adventures through the claim that they were bringing democratic social institutions to the rest of the world.

The glorification of the state has the consequence of sanctifying or legitimating its increased coercion through the symbolic assertion that what it does is "just" or "fair," or that it is pursuing "justice" and "fairness" through the exercise of power in its programs and the implementation of policy. Historically, the state has killed off or driven out everything less powerful than itself.[22] Bovard finds in his study of the abuses of the federal government, from AmeriCorps to the federal Agency for Health Care Policy and Research to the National Labor Relations Board to Housing and Urban Development and to the Department of Agriculture, that the concepts of "justice" and "fairness" have been converted into symbolic weapons that politicians and governmental bureaucrats use to browbeat the public into acquiescing to coercive and destructive policies and programs.

> Contemporary public policy presumes that government agencies are advanced laboratories for the concoction of new, improved concepts of fairness, as if working in a government agency automatically enables a person to perceive the frontiers of moral progress and thus justifies endowing him with a regulatory bayonet to drive everyone else over that frontier.[23]

Despite the state's efforts to transform governmental coercion into a moral crusade, Bovard argues against the idea that submission to governmental edicts is somehow morally uplifting. Obedience to the state is not the highest calling of humankind.

On the other hand, the government certainly cultivates the false impression that state policy and enforcement are essential to fairness, equity, and racial and social justice. The impression is that the government acts to promote these policy goals. The government's impression management is accomplished in large part through public relations campaigns that utilize significant social symbols that sanctify the exertion of state power and demonize opposition and behaviors the state intends to eradicate. "Hate crimes," for example, entail longer or harsher punishments based on the group identity of the victim rather than the act of the criminal offender, which is founded on the notion that the social context and the social definition of crime are more dependent on its presumed effect on groups than its real consequences for individual victims. Clinton frequently referenced "hate" and the "darkness in our hearts" in his descriptions of the biggest challenges facing America. He urged the nation to be "absolutely resolute" in its efforts to rid the country of "old, primitive hatreds" through the expansion of federal hate crime laws. His Justice Department conflated acts that are hateful and those that are hurtful, continually expanding the definition of "hate crime." His social programs set up reporting systems that were practically designed to overestimate the scope of the problem and inflate the statistics. This, in turn, provided the pretext for his declaration of a national crisis in 1999 and his call more expanded federal role. All of which occurred in the absence of data to support any claim that hate crime was increasing.[24] As an ideological construct, Bovard says that the notion of "hate crime" enables prosecutors and politicians to determine which

> perpetrators are truly evil and which are merely greedy robbers, horny rapists, or abused children-turned mass murderers. Prosecuting hate crimes takes government out of the mundane and makes it seem to be an avenging angel. Government rises from merely trying to punish and thus prevent violence to being a judge of souls.[25]

In addition to sanctifying the state through significant symbols such as hate crimes, the cultural and political systems collude to cultivate dependency and political ignorance among the American populace. Bovard is unique among Libertarian writers in his concern with the uses of culture and ideology to legitimate coercion, pacify restive political opponents, and create a docile, politically correct citizenry. Bovard totalizes the modern form of the American state as the "Attention Deficit Democracy," signifying that the modern democratic state functions without the attention, oversight, or informed consent of the governed.

The most prevalent tool that Bovard identifies in the ideological subordination of citizens to the state is the fearmongering associated with the War on Terror. The horrific attacks of 9/11 and the strange anthrax attacks in the fall of 2001 provided a milieu for the government to incessantly remind Americans how vulnerable they are to the many and powerful enemies outside and within the borders of the United States. Preying on the generalized belief that an important role for the state is to protect individuals from foreign and domestic enemies, the Bush administration was extremely effective, at least until its misadventure in Iraq, in cultivating a sense that the government deserved uncritical cooperation in its War on Terror. Never mind that the success or effectiveness of the Administration's policies are questionable, or that individual privacy and other rights might be violated in the process. The important point is that the government is doing what it can to protect Americans from Islamic fascism. Thus, it deserves uncritical support and cooperation. The assumption is that the best way to motivate Americans to rally to defeat the Islamists is to cultivate and promulgate fears about impending terrorist attacks.

Fearmongering is supplemented by what Bovard identifies as political ignorance and a cultural "dumbing down" of the American populace. Bovard
goes to great lengths in his more recent books to document the extent of ignorance of Americans, or their apparent inability to recite basic facts about
the American political system, political candidates, and contemporary political issues and agendas. Although the data on American voters' knowledge of
political life is sufficiently disconcerting, mere "knowledge of names, titles,
or job descriptions do not reveal if they actually comprehend what government is doing. . . . in an era when government policies and interventions are
proliferating like mosquitoes, a few factoids are not enough."[26] Unfortunately, Americans are also ignorant of the theoretical perspectives that enable
people to interpret the facts about the political system. They typically rely on
their feelings, not theories, facts or ideas, to guide their voting behavior. Candidates and incumbents are successful in mobilizing support to the extent that
they are able to communicate that they care about voting blocks that are
swayed by affective dimensions of political rhetoric. Bovard finds it ironic,
on the surface, that political ignorance is mushrooming despite the expansion
of public education, but it is contradictory to expect schools controlled by the
government to enlighten their students about the structure and exercise of political power in American society. In addition to this conflict of interest, Bovard argues that the state works to ensure that the public school system enforces a form of political cretinization. Although the No Child Left Behind
Act was heralded by Republican and Democratic leaders alike as a public effort to raise academic performance, in fact this legislation further dumbed-
down education by harnessing learning and assessment to performance standards and sanctions that almost guarantee student success, regardless of the
proficiency of students in core subject areas.[27] Thus, despite the faith in education, Bovard finds little evidence to suggest that this major social institution will help generate the critical consciousness needed to reverse the political trends toward more coercion and ideological control.

The No Child Left Behind Act purports to eliminate racial disparities in
student performance in standardized math and English tests by 2014. It is
based on the assumption that prejudice and discrimination are the most important factors determining differences in academic performance. Bovard de-
rides the goal of achieving equivalent test scores in education as a "foolish
egalitarian dictate" that is unlikely to succeed because student performance is
affected by a large number of variables, such as parental pressure to perform
well in school, that will not be changed by federal intervention. The more significant concern is the achievement gap between American students and those
from other countries. Data drawn from international tests demonstrate that
American students compare very unfavorably to students in other industrial

nations. Moreover, the longer American students are in school, the worse their learning compares internationally. Bovard reports that international tests reveal a linear decline in the literacy of Americans compared to citizens of other nations as age declines "from a near-top rating for fifty-six- to sixty-five-year-old Americans to a near-bottom rating for sixteen- to twenty-five-year-old Americans."[28] NCLB will never enable the country to improve its academic standards because it uses the wrong benchmark; the critical measure of relative performance of American students should be against that of their counterparts in other nations. The expansion of state power, glorification of the state, and the cultivated dependency of the populace on the state have important ramifications for race and diversity issues. Power today is sanctified through the rhetoric of racial justice and diversity. State intervention in society attempts to engineer the "appropriate" mix of persons and the "appropriate" structure of relationships among the races and ethnic groups.

There is a fundamental tension in Libertarian literature between (a) the impulse to critique state power and its consequences, and (b) the interest to recreate the state through the articulation of the legitimate foundations of political power and authority. Many Libertarians also have a tendency to propose alternative programs and policies as a means of demonstrating how a society restructured along libertarian principles might work. Hence, writers such as Boaz, Nozick, and Murray spend considerable effort in their work to not only critique the existing sources and outcomes of political power and authority, they also struggle to recreate them in their visions of a new social order. Much of Libertarian thought is system-building, or it is the theoretical recreation of American society along the lines of basic Libertarian principles. As a philosophy and political movement, Libertarianism is concerned with gaining converts to its political faith. Thus, the advocates for Libertarianism believe they must offer the electorate a practical program for a reformed government and society.

Bovard departs, at times, from the tendency among Libertarians to reconstruct the state by proposing how it can be done right. He offers very little in the way of a philosophic statement on how to reconstruct the state so that it can function to maximize individual liberty. Bovard is neither a historian nor a sociologist nor a philosopher. His writings are generally not informed by the methods or perspectives of those disciplines. Instead, as a journalist, he methodically catalogs the incompetence and abuses of the government and demonstrates their negative impacts upon the freedom of individuals in American society.

The dialectic in Bovard's political critique of American society is between the democratic state, as it is currently structured and operates, and the liberty of American citizens. The telos of Bovard's critique is that the government of the United States must be reconfigured by restricting where it can legitimately exert force so that it does not act like an enemy of the freedoms of the American people. In *Freedom in Chains*, Bovard outlines "a few thoughts on an ideal political order." It is clear that he sees little use in articulating a political philosophy that "promises the moon." Instead, he is interested in identifying a few principles that can help limit "havoc on Earth. . . . The goal must be to minimize the coercive power that some people hold over other people."[29] Bovard proposed a list of ideas and reforms that seem pretty standard fare for Libertarians, such as eliminating corporate welfare, phasing out welfare to citizens who need assistance in favor of philanthropy, eliminating unnecessary taxation, distinguishing between vice and crimes and working to prevent and control crime, and adopting an isolationist foreign policy. It is clear that an ideal political order would retain coercive power to protect the nation from foreign predators and to protect individuals from internal predators. Bovard's sketch of utopia also includes a call to improve democracy by developing a more critical attitude toward politicians in education and in culture. The hallmark of his reformation of American political life is the repeal of as many laws and regulations as possible in order to reduce and restrict the coercive power of the state.

The consequences of Bovard's Libertarian reformation of the state for race and racism are similar to those proposed by Boaz. The state has no business creating laws or administrative regulations that deny any racial or ethnic group of their freedom, property, or opportunity to earn a living or develop their abilities. This principle includes all of the statutes and bureaucratic regulations that intend to promote affirmative action, racial quotas, and racial preferences. Bovard argued that the state has no right to even identify or classify individuals into racial and ethnic categories since this right also permits the state to control the structure of society and determine legitimate patterns of social desiderata. The right of the government to assign individuals to racial and ethnic categories should be eliminated and part of the elimination of the democratic welfare state. For Bovard, the contradiction between the welfare state and individual liberty must be resolved in favor of individual liberty. The welfare state, in all of its aspects, including its efforts to promote racial justice, is anathema to individual freedom. In his formulation, the critique and elimination of the welfare state is also the critique and elimination of racism because it adumbrates the overcoming of all forms of social domination.

Welfare state freedom is freedom to do what politicians and bureaucrats want you to do. Empowering the State to liberate the individual makes sense only if the State has no incentive to exploit, abuse, or shackle the individual for its own profit.[30]

Bovard provides a powerful and comprehensive critique of the role of the state in American society. He also provides a set of standards that can be used to assess the extent to which the behavior of the government departs from an ideal political order. Thus, he articulates something akin to an immanent critique of American political life. Bovard leaves an impressive catalog of governmental abuse but very little in the way of a theoretical interpretation of that behavior and what the next steps toward a political transformation might be. However, libertarian writers such as Charles Murray have developed some fairly practical ideas about how society can move from a racist welfare state to a more libertarian form.

CHARLES MURRAY: THE LIBERTARIAN
CRITIQUE OF THE NEW RACISM

Charles Murray is a policy analyst and behavioral science researcher who has served as a research fellow at the American Enterprise Institute since 1990 and, prior to that, with the American Institute for Research. He published no fewer than five books on public policy guided by the protocols of empirical social science and public policy analysis.

Murray refers to himself as a "libertarian-conservative" in his book *What it Means to be a Libertarian*, but his credentials as a libertarian thinker are established by two facts. First, he pursued social scientific analyses that demonstrate empirically the negative impacts of governmental programs on the poor and disadvantaged groups. Second, he offers a theoretical interpretation that outlines not only its basic principles of Libertarianism but what it means in terms of a political system that is restructured according to them.[31] Other individualist and libertarian writers, such as Ayn Rand and Murray Rothbard, approach their studies by assuming the a priori status of libertarian principles and then applying those principles to the analysis of the relationship between the individual and the social world. As the development of the entirety of his work is considered, Murray proceeds in a more deductive manner, deriving libertarian principles from his empirical studies of social and psychological phenomena. Like a social scientist, Murray builds libertarian theory on top of his empirical studies.

Murray's credentials as a conservative are also established in two observations about his work. First, Murray's distrust in the government is matched by his trust in the essential fairness and decency of nongovernmental institutions. Murray evinces a fundamentally conservative trust in the existing structure of society. Murray is by no means a radical or revolutionary. He does not seek the same sort of profound social, personal, cultural, and political changes that interest Rand and Rothbard. Although he proposes difficult and significant changes in American public policy, by no means does he argue for fundamental change in the how individuals relate to each other and to the social order. Second, Murray is not an individualist. The types of reforms he advocates are completely consistent with strong familial and community controls over the behaviors of individuals. He does not challenge the authority of the state or society over the individual, but instead seeks a more focused role for the state in society. While his perspective is demonstrably Libertarian, it is not particularly radical, and it is certainly not egoist nor anarchist.

Charles Murray is probably best known as the coauthor with Richard Herrnstein of *The Bell Curve: Intelligence and Class Structure in American Life*, which was one of the most controversial studies of intelligence and social status to emerge from the behavioral sciences in recent decades.[32] *The Bell Curve* became an enormously contentious study immediately upon its publication in 1994 because of its meritocratic thesis that the class structure of American society is undergoing a radical transformation in which a "cognitive elite" is forming at the apex of the social pyramid based on intelligence and accomplishment, while an underclass is also forming based on increasingly low intelligence rather than discrimination or other social and racial disadvantages. The thesis of *The Bell Curve* was the target of hostility from the media and academia because it challenges fundamental assumptions about the nature of the class structure in American society. *The Bell Curve* rejects the idea that class inequality is based upon and reinforces discrimination against social and racial groups. It also rejects the argument that the solution to the problems caused by the class system is a comprehensive governmental approach to promoting equality in the life circumstances and experiences of all Americans. *The Bell Curve* argues that this assumption is no longer applicable to the analysis of inequality in America.

Herrnstein and Murray were savagely criticized by the multicultural left for legitimating racial and ethnic inequality, and the status quo of the American class structure. As far as Murray is concerned, however, it is important to understand the facts pertaining to the transformation of the class system in the United States, especially if the goal is to improve people's lives. The primary philosophic issue that *The Bell Curve* poses for public policy discourse in the United States is how to reconcile the ideal of equality with the reality of differences in human abilities, interests, and achievements. Specifically, should social science and public policy pursue absolute equality of the opportunities, outcomes, and experiences of all Americans? Or, should social science and policy discourse attempt to identify those forms of equality and inequality that make sense from the standpoints of human development and of helping each individual find a "valued place in society" for themselves? The more Libertarian point of view developed by Herrnstein and Murray clearly supports the latter perspective by emphasizing the importance of equality of opportunity to succeed, and minimizing governmental and institutional efforts to impose an abstract equality of outcomes and experiences.

By 1994, however, Murray was no stranger to controversy about governmental policy and programs directed toward assisting disadvantaged social and racial groups. In 1984 he published *Losing Ground: American Social Policy, 1950–1980*.[33] *Losing Ground* is a fairly standard quantitative social scientific analysis of the varied social programs initiated during the administration of Lyndon Johnson that were intended to promote and cultivate the Great Society. *Losing Ground* provides an analysis of the impact of the social programs of the Great Society on the lives of poor and disadvantaged Americans, particularly blacks. In this book, Murray examines the longitudinal data from 1950 to 1980 on poverty, labor force participation and wages, education, crime, and family stability. On each of these dimensions, Murray finds that the indicators of social disorganization increased as the number and expansion of social programs increased. *Losing Ground* thus raises the provocative question about the ability of the state to effectively improve the lives of disadvantaged peoples through institutionalized programs that are intended to assist them. He says that the data "make the case that the reforms flowing from the new wisdom of the 1960s were a blunder on purely pragmatic grounds."[34] That is, the reforms did not achieve what they were intended to achieve and functioned to exacerbate the divides between rich and poor, the educated and uneducated, and the employed and unemployed. Murray's conclusion is that a new form of racism emerged as a consequence of the affirmative actions or the Great Society programs implemented in the 1960s.

Murray argues in *Losing Ground* that two public policy principles operated independently prior to the creation of civil rights legislation in 1965: equal treatment and a fair shake. The idea behind equal treatment is that all persons, regardless of race or social background, must play by the same rules as they attempt to acquire social desiderata. The principle of equal treatment negates the idea that individuals should receive preferential treatment because of their race, gender, or any other ascribed social characteristic. The principle of a fair shake means that everyone, regardless of race, gender or any other ascribed social characteristic, has a roughly equal opportunity to acquire social desiderata. Murray says that no one

can watch with complete equanimity when a black child is deprived of a chance to develop his full potential for reasons that may be directly traced to a heritage of exploitation by whites. Neither can anyone, no matter how devoted to Affirmative Action, watch with complete equanimity when a white job applicant is turned down for a job in favor of a black who is less qualified.[35]

According to Murray, prior to 1965, the prevailing wisdom was that these two principles were not in conflict or dynamic tension with one another and, thus, both could be applied to racial policy through the adoption of the meritocratic principle that people should be judged and allocated social desiderata through market mechanisms based on merit. During the mid-1960s, however, the prevailing wisdom changed as a consequence of pressure from racial and political elites. The new approach was that minorities, especially black Americans were to be helped by the government to achieve parity in the receipt of desiderata. The market-based, meritocratic principle was replaced by the state interventionist principle in which public policy would become the significant actor in the distribution of wealth and other forms of desiderata. What were the consequences of this transformation in public policy for individuals in disadvantaged social groups?

Losing Ground attempts to identify the real outcomes of the state's intervention in society to promote parity between blacks and whites largely using data collected by the U.S. government on poverty, wages and employment, education, crime, and family stability from 1950 to 1980. The observations Murray catalogs are databased and fail to support the hypothesis or expectation that intervention by the U.S. government either reduced inequalities or ameliorated the life circumstances of black Americans in these areas. In fact, Murray finds that the life circumstances of the poorest black Americans deteriorated in relative terms during the period he studied. For example, in his analysis of data on poverty in the United States between 1950 and 1980, Murray reveals that the poverty rates of black Americans actually declined during the 1950s into the early 1960 as the civil rights movement effectively challenged forms of discrimination. But the progress of the poorest black Americans stopped with the onset of the Great Society programs of the 1960s. Murray also discovers that for young black males, unemployment rates and labor force participation rates compared very unfavorably to those of their white counterparts from 1965 to 1980, after a period of relative parity during the early 1960s and during a period of intense federal intervention in job training.[36]

Murray concludes that it is a "profound irony" that a growing number of black Americans seemed to give up on earning a living at a time when "more blacks were demonstrating that it was finally possible to do so."[37] In his study of wages and occupations, Murray finds that the period from 1950 to 1980 was characterized by major advances in the wages and occupations of black Americans relative to those of white Americans. Comparing the percentage of black and white workers in white-collar jobs from the late 1950s to 1980, the gap that favored whites closed dramatically. Comparing the ratio of black male income to white male income during the same period, the ratio of black to white income improved consistently, an important indicator that wage discrimination was effectively challenged. Murray finds other successes in his study of disparities in educational access and attainment between blacks and whites. But there were other significant signs of social disorganization as he studied indicators of family stability between blacks and whites.

Given the mixed results of governmental intervention in economy and society during the thirty year period he studied, Murray concludes that American society is experiencing a "bifurcation" in the life circumstances of black Americans in which a significant percentage benefited from the elimination of discrimination imposed by the federal and state governments, while a smaller, but still significant, percentage of black Americans remains trapped in impoverished and marginalized circumstances, not despite, but because of governmental efforts to assist. In effect, the poorest black Americans became acculturated to the poverty and destructive behaviors promoted by the welfare state. Murray argues that a "harsh judgment is warranted" as the history of the welfare state's efforts to promote racial parity are concerned.

> If an impartial observer from another country were shown the data on the black lower class from 1950 to 1980 but given no information about contemporaneous changes in society or public policy, that observer would infer that racial discrimination against the black poor increased dramatically during the late 1960s and 1970s.[38]

In Murray's judgment, the practical explanation for the deteriorating life circumstances of the poorest black Americans is a new form of racism. The old forms of racism toward black Americans were attacked during the civil rights movement with such success that considerable prejudice and official discrimination disappeared from many facets of American life. The example Murray uses is the greater representation of black Americans in the professions that increased the interaction, collegiality, and relationships of whites and blacks. But with the implementation of the War on Poverty during the 1960s, the new form of white racism appeared as a condescension toward the black lower class, particularly poor blacks in all-black communities. The new form of racism or white supremacy was operationalized in the form of public policy that was undergirded by a consciousness among white liberals, moderates, and conservatives that the people to be helped by public policy are "predominantly black, and blacks are owed a debt."[39]

The outcome of the new racist interventionist public policy was a transformation in the social definition of both race and culture by academics, journalists, and policy makers that institutionalized a "condescension" in how the behaviors and social realities of minorities, especially poor blacks, were interpreted and addressed through social programs. In every case, they are sociological and political explanations of dysfunctional behaviors and disorganized environments that argue that minority individuals are always victims of external circumstances or otherwise incapable of making productive decisions or creating different behavioral patterns. The interventionist state is necessary, in these formulations, to correct the problems or rectify the deficiencies in behaviors and circumstances. The welfare system, affirmative action, and other forms of governmentally imposed set-asides and preferences are the most obvious examples of how the new racism is operationalized and institutionalized. The critical point is that the transformation reflects a type of racist condescension or supremacy because "whites began to tolerate and make excuses for behavior among blacks that whites would disdain in themselves or their children."[40] The prevailing ideological consequence is that the "system" or the life circumstances of black Americans are reified and blamed for any perceived problems, deficiencies, or inequities. As individuals, marginalized black Americans were stereotyped by the state, the media, and social science as powerless, inept, and malevolent. The white elite, or the white-dominated interventionist state, simply cannot reconcile the contradiction between the two cultural principles of providing both equal treatment and the fair shake. Equal treatment is subordinate to the white supremacist compulsion to make restitution because of its fit with the emergent form of racism. The cultural and political contradiction is that the group that elicited the most sympathy is the group that is also the most victimized by the interventionist welfare state.

In Our Hands: A Plan to Replace the Welfare State is something of a sequel to Losing Ground in that Murray proposes a plan that will replace most, if not all, of the federal welfare and entitlement programs imposed by the United States government. In Murray's view, the new racism engendered by the creation of the welfare state can be effectively attacked by the dissolution of the welfare and entitlement functions of the government. In Our Hands argues that the two fundamental assumptions that led to the creation of the welfare state in the United States and Europe were the beliefs that resources were scarce and that the government was the only social institution that can effectively allocate resources to those who need them. However, these assumptions have been radically undermined by the political and economic developments of the late twentieth century. For the first time in human history, it was no longer economically necessary for anyone in the western industrialized nations to be poor. At the same time, the United States government spends trillions of dollars each year to provide for retirement, health care, and to alleviate poverty and there are still millions without sufficient retirement resources, adequate health care and living in poverty. The argument that government can effectively provide for these needs is certainly suspect. Therefore, Murray proposes that the money be given directly to the people.

The basic idea of Murray's plan is that each citizen will be provided with a cash grant beginning at age twenty-one that continues annually until the individual's death. Murray suggests the program should begin with $10,000, but the award can be indexed with inflation or other pertinent economic measures. The person would be able to use the cash in any way that he or she sees fit. The grant program would be financed by all of the welfare and entitlement programs that provide benefits to people.[41] Further, a constitutional amendment would be passed to prohibit the creation of any governmental program that provides benefits to some citizens but not to others. Murray argues that the cash grant could be financed by existing welfare and entitlement programs, including Social Security, Medicare, Medicaid, welfare programs, social service programs, and all agricultural and corporate subsidies. Murray also proposes that the cash grant include a surtax schedule graded by income, so that the poorest citizens would be allowed to keep the greatest share of the cash grant. Hence, the size of the grant would vary depending on income, with wealthier individuals receiving smaller grants or possibly being expected to pay into the system.

Murray admits that the proposal is not strictly Libertarian since it would leave the structure of taxation and the resource allocation powers of the state unchallenged. However, the proposal contains many individualist and libertarian elements that immediate positive consequences for the poorest racial and ethnic minorities in the United States. Most significantly, people will cease living at the behest of institutionalized social programs and begin living on their own terms. The principle is that,

> A man who has been living off others and then acquires an income stream will typically find that it has become rational to move out if he works. He has gone from a situation in which he had little incentive to work to a situation in which he has substantial incentive to work.[42]

Hence, the cash grant would function to undermine the culture of poverty that subordinates impoverished individuals to the values and rules of governmentally sponsored welfare and entitlement programs. Although Murray does not believe the cash grant program would be a panacea for racial stratification and racial conflict, it would make significant changes immediately and in the long-term because it would help operationalize the idea that the individual's future is in his or her hands. Murray's expectation is that most recipients in the underclass in American society would use the money to invest in an education or to spend it on other opportunities that would enable them to build a better or different life for themselves and their families. Murray defends the cash grant proposal as not only fiscally sound social policy, but some variant of it is politically and economically inevitable, since the outlays of the state's welfare and entitlement programs will eventually far outstrip the ability of the government to pay for them.

In Our Hands is a proposal to replace, not eliminate, the welfare state. Although it does not respond to some significant elements of racism, it is an attack on institutional racism, particularly that which is generated by the welfare system. It contains some important individualist and libertarian elements. Most significantly it would eliminate many federal welfare and entitlement programs and agencies. If implemented, it would provide the most impoverished and marginalized citizens with some resources to build better lives, if they choose to do so. However, the proposal also has some limitations from individualist and libertarian points of view. Politically, the proposal is essentially an income or wealth redistribution scheme. It would create a national program that empowers and authorizes the state to collect and transfer wealth from some individuals to others. It legitimates a role for the state in social engineering and validates a governmental mission in "distributive justice." Moreover, the proposal does not address taxation, or the process by which the state accumulates the wealth it would redistribute. It does not challenge or question the authority of the state to tax or to appropriate and distribute desiderata.

Another point of critique of Murray's plan concerns the intent to scale the size of the cash award according to the person's income. This differential appears to punish those who produce. It appears to favor those who do not. Murray's proposal poses a significant ethical issue: Does living an authentically human life permit the individual to receive or rely on wealth appropriated coercively from others for the sake of his or her material well being? Stated differently, does the institutionalization of a governmental scheme to appropriate and redistribute wealth enhance or frustrate the ability of persons to live as human beings should? Murray's proposal collectivizes ethics and subordinates the property rights of individuals to the social engineering functions of the government.

Murray's forays into public policy analysis focused on racial and ethnic minorities were enhanced in 1997 by his personal statement on libertarianism, *What it Means to be a Libertarian. What it Means* is a fairly tightly reasoned statement of the basic ideas of libertarianism as Murray sees them, and how they might be applied in the political and cultural environment of the United States, including issues pertaining to racial tolerance and discrimination. At the outset, Murray is clear that he proposes a type of Libertarianism that is perhaps not as rigorous or consistent as others. He envisions a role for government that would be restructured according to Libertarian ideas, but he also says that he is fond of tradition and the "nonrational" elements of human existence. Thus, he does not endorse the anarcho-capitalist perspective of Rothbard and he is very careful to separate his perspective from the atheistic individualism of Ayn Rand. The Libertarianism that emerges in Murray's tract on the topic is a fairly mild and practice-oriented argument for removing government from as many facets of social life as possible. It is not a perspective that calls in any way for a revolutionary transformation of society or a radical reconstruction of the principles by which people live their every day lives. It is a Libertarianism that explores how Americans might infuse some libertarian concepts into their understanding of culture and politics at the beginning of the twenty-first century.

Murray precedes his discussion of the implications of libertarian thought for race and ethnicity with an articulation of what he sees as the basic principles of libertarian governance. The first principle he identifies is the familiar notion in libertarian and individualist literature that individuals may not initiate the use of force against any other individual or group. The principle of nonaggression is rooted in the idea that self-ownership is inalienable and, thus, no individual can deprive another of life, liberty, or pursuit of happiness. Significantly, Murray does not include property rights in his list of the elements of self-ownership. The second principle of libertarian governance is that, absent force and fraud, people in a free society cannot be prevented from engagement in voluntary and informed transactions. This principle is rooted in the ethical ideal of cooperation and that people have the right to choose their own behavior and structure their interactions with others without being defrauded or coerced by a third party.[43]

A consequence of these principles is that the legitimate role of the state in society and the lives of individuals must be severely constrained or limited to police power, which is exerted through criminal and tort law and enforced through police, courts, and corrections. The power of the state, according to Murray, must be limited to three functions. First, the state is responsible for restraining people from injuring one another. Murray argued that the creation of a libertarian society requires that individuals be deprived of the use of force and that the state is the only social entity that has authority to use force to prevent people from victimizing each other. Second, the state is responsible for protecting the right of people to enter into those contracts or voluntary agreements that can be enforced by law. In Murray's formulation, the right to enter into contracts means that a government, a third party with coercive power, must be present to guarantee that each party fulfills its commitments. Third, Murray argued that the state also has a legitimate right to use force or police power to promote the public good.[44]

Murray admits that the third point sets him apart from the "strictest libertarians." Like them, he is concerned about the "slippery slope" of legitimating the state's intervention in society, however restricted it might be at the outset. Nevertheless, he argued that the classical liberal tradition entails the notion that the state can legitimately define and promote important public goods and services as long as a handful of critical criteria are met. The state acts appropriately only if it provides goods or services that (a) cannot be provided by individuals on their own and (b) benefit all of the people who subsidize them. The state must fairly compensate people if their private property has been confiscated for public use.[45]

The basic principles of governance that Murray articulates in *What it Means to be a Libertarian* lay the foundation for a discussion of the practical impact of the implementation of libertarian principles. It is significant to note that despite his relatively mild version of Libertarianism, Murray advocates a radical restructuring of the programs and scope of activities of the United States government. He envisions the elimination, without replacement, of federal programs and offices pertaining to agriculture, energy, transportation, training and employment, welfare, and housing and urban development. He would retain some regulation of employment and workplaces in order to protect workers from force, fraud, and unsafe working conditions.

In the areas pertaining most closely to race and ethnicity, Murray argues for the elimination of all governmental regulations pertaining to discrimination and replace them with a constitutional amendment that prohibits the government from requiring discrimination by race, ethnicity, religion or creed, and inhibiting or limiting freedom of association for private individuals and associations. Murray's argument that racism must be attacked by eliminating the state's intervention in society is based on the notion that individual freedom and tolerance for difference are inevitably bound together, just as intolerance is supported by governmental coercion and favoritism. Without the ability to coerce each other, people find ways to cooperate and interact with each other without intolerance and bigotry.[46]

A libertarian society must allow people and private organizations to freely associate, or not associate, if that is their choice. They must have the right and opportunity to make judgments about others and to act on those judgments. This concept is the societal parallel to the role that individual choice and decisions play in a flourishing market economy. Individuals must be allowed to discriminate and make judgments about the value of objects and behaviors, or society cannot function effectively. The horror of racial bigotry prompted Americans to reject the cultural value of discrimination as a social practice, which is to impose a set of values on individual behaviors and social interactions. He argues that discrimination should be permitted in a wide array of social institutions in order to ensure that positive social behavior is rewarded and that dysfunctional or destructive social behavior is penalized. Although an "unabridged freedom of association" might permit people to engage in bigoted behaviors toward racial and ethnic groups, the use of governmental power to eliminate all forms of bigotry in society instigates enormous disruptions in social processes, including the ability and tendency of social institutions to correct unjust and outmoded values and practices.[47]

Government is the one social institution that must be prevented from discriminating because it cannot act capriciously in the exercise of its police power. It cannot legitimately assign a privileged status to one group over another. Yet, this is exactly what the Civil Rights Act of 1964 and the reams of statutes and jurisprudence following it have accomplished. Although the original intent of the legislation was to prohibit discrimination based on race, it was "inevitable that its reach would evolve and expand as it has." Since the government can know only outcomes and not the intentions of individuals, it was inevitable that "additional steps will be taken to promote equal outcomes" to ensure, for example, that firms employ "sufficient minorities, women, people over fifty, and other protected groups."[48] Furthermore, once a group has been assigned a privileged status by the state, it has an eternal right to complain about its treatment.

> At any moment in history a completely fair system for treating individuals will produce different outcomes for different groups, because groups are hardly ever equally represented in the qualities that go into decisions about whom to hire, admit to law school, put in jail, or live next door to. At this particular moment in history a system that is completely fair in its treatment of individuals, judging each case perfectly on its merits, would produce drastically different proportions of men and women hired by police forces, blacks and whites put in jail, or Jews and gentiles admitted to elite law schools.[49]

The denouement of Murray's argument, and that of all libertarian literature that discusses the issue, is that public policy legislation, in general, and the Civil Rights Act of 1964, in particular, are unnecessary and counterproductive responses to racism. Murray, Bovard, and Boaz all argue that American society responded to the need to eliminate antiblack racism ahead of the government. Prior to 1964 there was ample evidence that the nation was largely renouncing injustice, prejudice, and segregation. "America did not make progress against racism because Congress passed the Civil Rights Act of 1964; Congress passed the Civil Rights Act of 1964 because the nation was so committed to make progress against racism."[50] Among the consequences of the Civil Rights Act of 1964 were the transfer of the "moral crusade" against racism from civil society to governmental bureaucracies, promotion of the tendencies toward confrontation and victimization, and the dissolution of an emerging societal commitment to eliminate prejudice, discrimination, and build common bonds that transcend race. "What had been an evolutionary working out of a complicated set of problems became an us-versus-them resentful battle presided over by the bureaucrats and their statistical guidelines."[51] In Murray's terminology, the government's efforts to resolve the contradiction between freedom of association and a society free of discrimination resulted has eliminated an important hallmark of individual freedom and recast racism into new forms. The statist agenda for eliminating racism only undermined the ability of American society to function on the basis of a consensus of values and voluntary cooperation in favor of continued dependency, domination and conflict.

NOTES

1. Justin Raimondo, *An Enemy of the State: The Life of Murray N. Rothbard* (Amherst, NY: Prometheus Books, 2000).

2. See Jerome Tucille, *It Usually Begins with Ayn Rand* (San Francisco: Fox and Wilkes, 1972) and Brian Doherty, *Radicals for Capitalism: A Freewheeling History of the Modern American Libertarian Movement* (New York: Public Affairs, 2007).

3. The platform of the Libertarian Party is available at http://www.lp.org/article_85.shtml.

4. Accessed on December 27, 2006 at http://www.lp.org/article_85.shtml and http://www.lp.org/organization/history.shtml.

5. Accessed on July 15, 2005 at www.lp.org.

6. John Hospers, *Libertarianism: A Political Philosophy Whose Time Has Come* (Los Angeles: Reason Press, 1971); David Bergland, *Libertarianism in One Lesson: Why Libertarianism is the Best Hope for America's Future*, 9th ed. (Cartersville, GA: Advocates for Self-Government, 2005); and Tibor Machan, *Libertarianism Defended* (Aldershot, UK: Ashgate Publishing, 2006).

7. See David Boaz, *Libertarianism: A Primer* (New York: Simon and Schuster, 1997), 231.

8. In addition to his single author book on Libertarianism, see the two readers that David Boaz edited *The Libertarian Reader: Classic and Contemporary Writings from Lao-Tzu to Milton Friedman* (New York: The Free Press, 1997) and *Toward Liberty: The Idea that is Changing the World* (Washington, DC: The Cato Institute, 2002).

9. Boaz, *Libertarianism*, 233.

10. Boaz, *Libertarianism*, 230.

11. Boaz, *Libertarianism*, 231.

12. Boaz, *Libertarianism*, 231.

13. Boaz, *Libertarianism*, 232–33.

14. Robert Nozick, *Anarchy, State, and Utopia* (New York: Basic Books, 1974). While the commentary on Nozick is voluminous, the following are particularly helpful for the discussion about the implications of Nozick's work for libertarianism and racism: Jonathan Wolff, *Robert Nozick: Property, Justice and the Minimal State* (Stanford, CA: Stanford University Press, 1991); A. R. Lacey, *Robert Nozick* (Prince-

ton, NJ: Princeton University Press, 2001); David Miller, "The Justification of Political Authority," in *Robert Nozick*, ed. David Schmidtz (Cambridge: Cambridge University Press, 2002); and Murray Rothard "Robert Nozick and the Immaculate Conception of the State," *Journal of Libertarian Studies* 1 (Winter 1977): 45–57.

15. John Rawls, *A Theory of Justice* (Cambridge, MA: Harvard University Press, 1971).

16. See Nozick, *Anarchy, State, and Utopia*, 183–89 and Wolff, *Nozick*, 120–23.

17. For more information and perspective, both pro and con, about reparations for slavery see http://www.nationalcenter.org/Reparations.html and http://www.reparationscentral.com/.

18. James Bovard, *Lost Rights: The Destruction of American Liberty* (1994; New York: St. Martin's Press, 1995); *Freedom in Chains: The Rise of the State and the Demise of the Citizen* (New York: St. Martin's Press, 1999); *Feeling Your Pain: The Explosion and Abuse of Government Power in the Clinton-Gore Years* (New York: St. Martin's Press, 2000).

19. James Bovard, *Terrorism and Tyranny: Trampling Freedom, Justice, and Peace to Rid the World of Evil* (New York: Palgrave McMillan, 2003); *The Bush Betrayal* (New York: Palgrave McMillan, 2004); and *Attention Deficit Democracy* (New York: Palgrave McMillan, 2006).

20. Bovard, *Freedom in Chains*, 6.

21. Bovard, *Lost Rights*, 165.

22. Bovard, *Freedom in Chains*, 177.

23. Bovard, *Freedom in Chains*, 176–77.

24. Bovard, *Feeling Your Pain*, 313.

25. Bovard, *Feeling Your Pain*, 314.

26. Bovard, *Attention Deficit Democracy*, 13.

27. Bovard, *Bush Betrayal*, 65.

28. Bovard, *Bush Betrayal*, 75.

29. Bovard, *Freedom in Chains*, 249.

30. Bovard, *Freedom in Chains*, 94.

31. Charles Murray, *What it Means to be Libertarian: A Personal Interpretation* (New York: Broadway Books, 1997).

32. Richard Herrnstein and Charles Murray, *The Bell Curve: Intelligence and Class Structure in American Life* (New York: The Free Press, 1994).

33. Charles Murray, *Losing Ground: American Social Policy, 1950–1980* (1984; New York: Basic Books, 1994).

34. Murray, *Losing Ground*, 219.

35. Murray, *Losing Ground*, 221.

36. Murray, *Losing Ground*, 56–66.

37. Murray, *Losing Ground*, 85.

38. Murray, *Losing Ground*, 221.

39. Murray, *Losing Ground*, 221–22.

40. Murray, *Losing Ground*, 223.

41. Murray, *In Our Hands: A Plan to Replace the Welfare State* (Washington, DC: American Enterprise Institute, 2003), 8–14.

42. Murray, *In Our Hands*, 69.
43. Murray, *What it Means*, 7–13.
44. Murray, *What it Means*, 7–10.
45. Murray, *What it Means*, 11–12.
46. Murray, *What it Means*, 79–81.
47. Murray, *What it Means*, 85.
48. Murray, *What it Means*, 85.
49. Murray, *What it Means*, 86.
50. Murray, *What it Means*, 87.
51. Murray, *What it Means*, 88.

Chapter Five

Our Enemies, Racism and the State

Individualist Anarchism and the Struggle Against Slavery and Racial Violence

THE FOUNDATIONS OF
INDIVIDUALIST ANARCHIST THOUGHT

In her introduction to *The Anarchists*, the historical novel by John Henry Mackay, Sharon Presley argues that one of the distinguishing features of the Individualist Anarchists is that they were able to combine an individualist and antiauthoritarian philosophy with a concern and advocacy for the poor and marginalized people in the developing industrial economies.[1] Presley says that Mackay and the Individualist Anarchists, particularly those in the United States, developed a very different form of egoism than that which is prevalent among contemporary Objectivists, Anarcho-Capitalists, and Libertarians. Contrary to the more modern forms of egoist thought, the Individualist Anarchists embraced a "heart-felt compassion for the wretched, miserable, downtrodden victims of the coercion of the State."[2] While most egoists and libertarians tend to agree that the linchpin to ending poverty and discrimination is the promotion of liberty, advocacy for the victims is much more characteristic of Individualist Anarchism, a philosophy that couples a rejection of the authority of the state with a concern for the other person, a concept of self-ownership that Benjamin Tucker would call "equal liberty." In the writings of the Individualist Anarchists, there is consequently a pronounced focus on the ways in which the state and capital collude to exploit and dominate. The collusion of the state and capital generates racism and class stratification.

The nineteenth-century American Individualist Anarchists Benjamin R. Tucker and Lysander Spooner were radical Abolitionists and advocates for resistance to authority, racial domination, and political and economic monopolies. Unlike Rand and Rothbard, Tucker and Spooner were opposed to the capitalist system of wage labor, although both advocated for free trade and against governmental monopolies and intrusion into economic life. Tucker edited the influential individualist journal *Liberty* from 1883 to 1907, and introduced the egoist philosophy of Max Stirner in the United States. Spooner was a radical Abolitionist lawyer whose writings ultimately challenged the legal foundations of the *Constitution of the United States* and the postal, banking, and currency monopolies of the United States government. Spooner was a theorist of guerilla warfare and advocated armed resistance against institutionalized racism in the American South and in other colonized parts of the world. A generation after the heyday of Tucker, Spooner, and their associates, Albert Jay Nock became a popular American essayist and journalist in the early twentieth century who articulated another Individualist Anarchist perspective against racism and racial violence. Although he was not anticapitalist, Nock was also critical of the ruling class and the collusion of the state with big business. Nock argued for the transformation of the class structure of American society. This chapter discusses the antiracist thought of Tucker, Spooner, and Nock. It identifies the basic elements of Individualist Anarchism as a body of thought and provides examples of how Individualist Anarchists promoted resistance to racism distinguished from Objectivist, Anarcho-Capitalist, and Libertarian approaches.

Tucker is known not only through his own writings, but by editing and publishing the periodical *Liberty*, which became the main venue of egoist and individualist anarchism in the United States. Tucker was an Abolitionist and expressed a sharp disdain for religiously-based legislation or constraints on what he called "noninvasive behaviors." He expressed his vision of Individualist Anarchism through editorials in *Liberty* which were later compiled into a collection entitled, *Instead of a Book By a Man Too Busy to Write One*. The most important essay Tucker wrote on anarchist theory is "State Socialism and Anarchism: How Far They Agree and Wherein They Differ," which originally appeared in the *North American Review* shortly after the Haymarket riot in Chicago in 1886. The purpose of this essay was to convey the central ideas of Individualist Anarchism to a broad audience by focusing on the "antitheses" between anarchism and socialism. Tucker's primary importance is the distillation and summation of Individualist Anarchist thought that he developed in his writings and editorship of *Liberty*. Tucker became the central figure in Individualist Anarchism in America because of his association with other radical individualists and his analytic ability to identify and articulate the core elements of this strand of thought. At zenith of *Liberty*'s popularity, Tucker was very influential among individualist intellectuals, including the sociologist Victor S. Yarros, who was an important scholar of the work of Herbert Spencer.[3]

Tucker was born in South Dartmouth, Massachusetts in 1854 in a fairly af-
fluent family. He attended the Massachusetts Institute of Technology and later
became an editor for *Engineering Magazine*. His primary career, however,
was advocacy for the individualist version of anarchism. Prior to the founding of *Liberty* in 1881, Tucker participated in the New England Labor Reform
League where he met Spooner and other individualist and antistatist activists,
including Josiah Warren, Ezra Heywood, and William B. Greene. He also
heard the Abolitionists activists Wendell Phillips and William Lloyd Garrison
speak passionately about the corruption of the American government and the
need for racial justice. He read and absorbed the works of Herbert Spencer,
John Stuart Mill, and the French proto-anarchist Pierre-Joseph Proudhon. The
confluence of these strong personalities encouraged Tucker to adopt Individualist Anarchism as a philosophy late in his teens. He never renounced it, although he became very pessimistic about the possibilities of political liberty
prior to his death in 1939.

The individualist position that Tucker developed was based on three important precepts: the law of equal liberty, the labor theory of value, and the right
of passive resistance to authority.[4] The first precept was a concept of self-
ownership or sovereignty of the individual which Tucker referred to as "the
law of equal liberty." Tucker's concept of self-ownership was rooted in Garrison's abolitionist philosophy that every person, regardless of race or any other
fact, has an inalienable right to control his or her own body, behavior, and the
results of his or her labor. The law of equal liberty is defined as "the largest
amount of liberty compatible with equality and mutuality of respect, on the
part of individual's living in society, for their respective spheres of action."[5]
Thus, each individual is equally free to pursue self-interest, and the pursuit of
self-interest is bound only by "a mutuality of respect." Equal liberty implies a
universal moral or political claim that individuals have a right to as much liberty as that which does not contradict the liberty of others. Equal liberty, therefore, is a universal or generalizable form of self-ownership. It also has an objective form since no individual can be excluded from it. Equal liberty is a
concept of self-ownership that always implies an other; the other's liberty provides the boundary of the individual's freedom and helps define the meaning
of self-ownership or the sovereignty of the individual. The notion of equal liberty was a first principle for Tucker since it is the core concept in all of his
writings.

The second precept of Tucker's Individualist Anarchism is economic in nature but it follows from the philosophic notion of self-ownership or equal liberty. Tucker, and the other Individualist Anarchists Warren, Greene, and Heywood, espoused a type of labor theory of economic value that they used to

define legitimate property and wealth. Tucker claimed that all forms of wealth are created by human effort or the labor of individuals. Therefore, labor, or the persons who create economic value, have an inalienable right to own and control the entire value that they create. Surplus value or surplus wealth can only be appropriated from them by force. The legitimate ownership of property refers solely to the products of human labor. Individuals may not assert ownership over land or natural resources except that which they directly occupy and use. In the Individualist Anarchist formulation, unlike that of the Objectivists and Anarcho-Capitalists, property rights are not absolute, but are dependent upon their use by human beings.

The third precept was the right of passive resistance to authority. Since equal liberty and the right to own and control one's product are fundamental precepts of social life, Tucker also believed that individuals have the right or the freedom to resist invasion of their liberty. Political authority or government is inherently invasive of equal liberty and the right to one's product. Individuals have a right to resist invasion of their equal liberty and product of their labor. Thus, they have a right to resist the state. Tucker argues in an essay entitled, "Passive Resistance," published in 1884, that passive resistance is the only form of political opposition that makes sense in an era of rampant statism and militarism. He argues that neither revolution nor terrorism are viable political strategies since the former only recreates the state in a new form, while the latter is invasive of the rights of individuals and never produces meaningful results. Passive resistance pursues bloodless political change through the refusal to obey. The methods of passive resistance include the refusal to pay taxes, rent, or interest, to participate in electoral politics, and to cooperate with authorities in any aspect of daily life. Tucker suggests that no government could withstand the determined passive resistance to authority by even one-fifth of the population, since the other four-fifths would not want to pay what it would cost to get the one-fifth to cooperate.[6]

A major part of Tucker's work during the late nineteenth century and early twentieth century was to explain how the state could control the economy and commerce. He was also interested in the impact this control had on individuals and society. He believed that interest earned on money loaned, rent paid on land occupied, and profits made on exchanges, particularly the exchange of labor for wages, were forms of exploitation or usury that explained the functions of the state and the formation of social classes.[7]

The principle of equal liberty and the labor theory of value imply a critique of behaviors, processes, and social structures that invade the space that is only legitimately controlled by the individual. For example, if persons are forced to pay rent on land they occupy and use to a landowner, this surplus wealth is a form of exploitation because the landowner has not earned it through his or her labor. Instead, rent is a form of the transfer of economic value from some individuals to others that is sanctioned or supported by the state through the landowner's title, an entitlement to appropriate the surplus wealth that legitimately belongs to the laborer. Similar dynamics occur through interest and profit. Interest, rent, and profit are examples of coercion that are enforced by the state-sponsored banking monopoly, which is also maintained by coercion. Tucker believed that any form of state-supported interest, rent, and profit differentiated people into social classes and function as the basis for the oppression of labor, minorities, and women.

In his classic 1886 essay, "State Socialism and Anarchism: How Far They Agree and Wherein They Differ," Tucker interprets the oppression and poverty of workers and other marginalized groups as the result of four monopolies maintained by governments: (a) the money monopoly, or the state's power to determine and control legitimate currency on the basis of trade and commerce; (b) the land monopoly, or the power of the state to determine legitimate access, ownership, and control of nature; (c) tariffs, or the power to artificially set prices and control exchange; and (d) patents, or the power to determine ownership of knowledge and intellect. From Tucker's perspective, all forms of domination, including the domination of racial and ethnic groups, are generated and maintained by the state's creation of monopolies of economic activities at very fundamental levels. State power produces monopolies that conspire against free trade and prohibit individuals from pursuing their own interests and controlling their lives, labor and property. As a consequence, neither capitalism nor state socialism offer a path to freedom, but only different types of monopoly, domination, and exploitation. Human freedom will not be possible until equal liberty and free trade become absolute. Tucker's definition of anarchism is "all the affairs of men should be managed by individuals or voluntary associations, and that the State should be abolished."[8]

Tucker and the writers associated with *Liberty* extend the concepts of self-ownership and the labor theory of value to their discussion of abolitionism, race, and the struggles of ethnic minorities. The discussions in *Liberty* that pertain to race demonstrate that the radical individualists who wrote for it consistently based a critique of racism on the precepts of self-ownership and the labor theory of value, for better or worse. Abolitionism and the struggle against slavery were the models for the Individualist Anarchist analysis of the role of the state in society, the problems associated with wage labor, and the role of violence in political change. In the pages of *Liberty*, Tucker and his associates apply the methods and ideas of Individualist Anarchism to their analysis of bigotry and racism, the status of black Americans after the Civil War, Jews and Judaism, and the crisis in Ireland in the 1880s. Although

Tucker contributed to the discussion in many of these topics, his primary theoretical importance lies in his articulation of Individualist Anarchism as a
broad philosophy that encompasses the struggles of racial and ethnic groups
against racism as a form of "invasion" or attack on equal liberty.[9]

Among Tucker's commentaries on the struggles of ethnic minorities was
the conflict between the British and the Irish. Tucker outlines in an editorial
that appeared in *Liberty* in October 1881 a critique of the domination of Ireland by Britain, a vision of an alternative future for Ireland, and a strategy for
achieving it.[10] "The Irish Situation in 1881" is vintage Tuckerian anarchism:
brief, direct, clear, and uncompromising in the political position it articulates.
Tucker argues that the tragedy that confronts Ireland has two sources. The
first is the Catholic Church. The second is the government of Britain. Together, these two institutions ensure that the Irish were "besotted with super-
stition; trampled on by tyranny; ground into the dust." Tucker says the Irish
Land League is an organization that can successfully defeat British colonialism and prefigure the birth of a new society out of the struggle against Britain.
The Land League was the "nearest approach, on a large scale, to perfect Anarchistic organization that the world has yet seen." The Land League was
comprised of many autonomous local groups, each in turn comprised of individuals of all ages, sexes, and races, who were inspired by a common purpose
to eliminate British rule and redistribute the ownership and control of land to
those who actually worked it.

Tucker applies his model of the three alternative political strategies available to the Irish situation: revolution, terrorism, and passive resistance.
Tucker urges the Land League to adopt the methods of passive resistance and
avoid revolutionary and terrorist tactics in its struggle against Britain. Tucker
specifically recommends that the members of the Land League stop the payment of rent and taxes, ignore the laws and policies created by the British Par-
liament, boycott elections and polls of any kind, ostracize "deserters, cow-
ards, traitors, and oppressors," and resist British policing and military
authority at every opportunity. He emphasizes that the strategy of passive resistance means that those who would transform social relationships under
colonial rule must prepare themselves to go to prison and continue the work
of those who are sent to prison. Passive resistance is a superior strategy to
revolution or terrorism since the former means certain defeat for the Irish on
the battlefield while the latter means years of demoralizing intrigue with a dubious outcome. Passive resistance is more consistent with the decentralist, anarchistic philosophy of the Land League. It is a strategy for change that would
give birth to a new society based on the principle of equal liberty since it ex-
emplifies resistance to authority without compromising any important element of anarchist thought. "Liberty means certain, unhalting, and compara-

tively bloodless victory, the dawn of the sun of justice, and perpetual peace and justice for a hitherto blighted land."[11] Tucker's advocacy of passive resistance foreshadows the methodology of later ethnic struggles against British colonialism, most notably in India, but his approach to the critique of racism and his strategy for change departs significantly from the more revolutionary position advocated by his colleague and predecessor in Individualist Anarchist thought, Lsyander Spooner.

LYSANDER SPOONER: ANARCHISM AND THE CRITIQUE OF SLAVERY

Liberty was not only the main literary vehicle for Tucker's economics and egoist philosophy. It was also an important journal for the publication of American individualist thought based on natural law theory. This strand of thought within individualist anarchism in America during the latter part of the nineteenth century was most closely associated with the legal and social theorist, Lysander Spooner (1808–1887). Tucker and the egoists who wrote for *Liberty* eventually migrated away from a natural law position that based anarchism on the notion of an individual's natural right to be free from coercion. The egoists believed that natural laws were superstitions and they rejected moral philosophy in its entirety. From an egoistic point of view, freedom is not based on natural right but on a pragmatic compromise where each individual pursues his or her self-interest. The natural law position was probably espoused most effectively among the Individualist Anarchists by Lysander Spooner.

The primary thread that runs throughout Spooner's political philosophy is the idea that government is the enemy of the freedoms individuals enjoy in nature, or the rights that individuals are entitled to by nature or natural law. Unlike Rand, Rothbard, and the Libertarians, Spooner is not enamored with the idea that capitalism best represents society in its natural state. In fact, the capitalism that he observed during his lifetime was the sort in which the prevailing economic interests were inextricably bound with those of the state. One of the primary reasons for his opposition to the state was the positive harm the government's collaboration with powerful capitalists does to individuals and society. The practical consequences of the violations of natural law perpetrated by the collusion of the state and capital include the social production of slavery and poverty. Spooner's development as a political philosopher was marked by a progressive transformation from a radical Abolitionist who advocated political activism within a constitutional framework to an individualist anarchist who challenged even the authority of the *Constitution of the United States*. In his later years, Spooner advocated for an Individualist Anarchist global revolution against the state and finance capital.

Spooner's career as a lawyer and entrepreneur pale in significance to his career as a radical legal theorist. In 1845, Spooner published a critique of legal arguments that slavery was protected by the *Constitution of the United States*.[12] Although he was not yet an anarchist, Spooner's analysis in this early publication reflects the type of legal reasoning that he would later employ to attack the authority of the *Constitution*. *The Unconstitutionality of Slavery* also foreshadows the relationship Spooner would later establish between his legal critique of slavery and political authority itself. Spooner's primary intent in *The Unconstitutionality of Slavery* is to refute the arguments of those abolitionists, especially William Lloyd Garrison and Wendell Phillips, who argued that the *Constitution* was to be condemned because it legitimated slavery. Garrison and Phillips believed that the *Constitution* was part of the social and political system that made slavery possible. For slavery to be abolished, Garrison and Phillips argued that the entire social order needed to be transformed. They believed that this could not be accomplished through incremental reforms that occurred within legitimate political processes. Thus, both Garrison and Phillips opposed voting and political activity by Abolitionists.[13]

Spooner argues in *The Unconstitutionality of Slavery* that those who fight for the abolition of slavery must establish that slavery is unconstitutional as an important initial step. Radical abolitionists, like Spooner, rejected the arguments of Garrison and Phillips as political quietism since their antipolitical stance left the slave states to continue their oppression and torture of black Americans without a meaningful political challenge.[14] Spooner reasoned that if the unconstitutionality of slavery can be established, the antislavery forces have an important lever for pursuing change in the North and in the South.

Spooner's argument that slavery is unconstitutional is initially based on a discussion of natural law, natural rights, natural justice, and the appropriate rules for the interpretation of the *Constitution*. Spooner says that "there is, and can be, correctly speaking, *no law but natural law*" because governments cannot legitimately create rules or principles that contravene the rights that individuals have in nature.[15] Natural law emanates from the nature of human beings, and it is therefore absolute and universal. It cannot be changed or destroyed without also changing or destroying the nature or the species-being of humans. Spooner argues that natural law is higher and imposes "more inflexible obligations" than any other arbitrary rule of conduct that individuals or groups of individuals may attempt to create. Moreover, natural law is the only law that is applicable to very possible situation that pertains to the rights of human beings and supersedes every arbitrary and temporary law created by individuals or groups of individuals that conflicts with it. Hence, constitutions, which are simply contracts created by governments, are void and unlawful if they attempt to authorize anything that violates "natural justice" or the rights of individuals or any class of individuals.[16] The only legitimate role for constitutions and law created by human beings is to articulate and support the natural rights of individuals.

Spooner takes great care to define natural law, natural right, and natural justice as concepts because they constitute the foundation for the "ordinary" or legally established rules that are used to interpret the *Constitution*. Spooner examines what is said in the *Constitution* itself, the context of its development, and applies the ordinary rules of interpretation to argue that slavery is unconstitutional. He identifies in constitutional law a total of fourteen rules of interpretation that range from (a) the priority of the intention of the *Constitution* as expressed in its words to (b) the importance of the consistency of the elements in the *Constitution* to (c) the point that the interpretation of the *Constitution* must "give no shelter to fraud," or the use of its elements to manipulate or coerce those who live under it. Spooner then applies each of the rules of interpretation to the question of whether slavery is constitutional or not. He concludes that

> Slavery is inconsistent with nearly everything that is either expressed or legally implied in the *Constitution*. All its express provisions are general, making no exception whatever for slavery. All its legal implications are that the *Constitution* and laws of the United States are for the benefit of the whole "people of the United States," and their posterity.[17]

Spooner says that the *Constitution*'s reference to the "people of the United States" does not exclude any group from the constitutional protections of life, liberty, and property. All available legal evidence that proves that any one individual is included in the "people of the United States" also proves that slaves are equally a part of "the people." All legal evidence that proves that slaveholders are included in "the people" also proves that slaves are equally a part of "the people." The broadest, most inclusive meaning of the phrase "the people of the United States" is necessary if the government is to fulfill its primary responsibility to secure the personal liberty of people, the sine qua non of all other rights.

Spooner was not the only Abolitionist to make the argument that slavery, and any other abridgement of the lives, liberty, and property of individuals, is unconstitutional. However, several scholars argue that Spooner's "attempt was the most thorough and legally grounded."[18] The methodology that he uses in *The Unconstitutionality of Slavery* is arguably a classic example of immanent critique: It is an attack on the social reality of slavery, and the mystifications legitimating it, through a contrast with the society's most fundamental statement on the rights of individuals. Although Spooner does not argue against the authority of the *Constitution* or the federal government in this book, his emphasis on the argument that the only legitimate role of the state is to protect the natural rights of individuals is certainly libertarian. He clearly makes the argument that governments cannot legitimately sanction slavery nor can they create any rule of conduct that deprives individuals of their life, liberty or property on the basis of their race or ethnicity. Thus, the seed of Spooner's individualist anarchism germinates in *The Unconstitutionality of Slavery*. Wendell Phillips commented that the limitations that Spooner's argument places on governments makes it a form of "practical no-governmentalism."[19]

The dual themes of the unconstitutionality of slavery and the very limited authority of governments were developed more deeply by Spooner in *A Defence for Fugitive Slaves*, a pamphlet he published in 1850 that challenges the right of the government to return slaves who escaped from slaveholders and to prosecute Americans who assisted runaway slaves.[20] The Fugitive Slave Laws were passed by Congress in 1793 and 1850 to provide a legal framework and an enforcement mechanism to end the migration of runaway slaves from the South to the North. Spooner argues that these laws are both unconstitutional and illegal because they authorize the return of those arrested without a trial by jury, required the exclusion of evidence from the legal proceedings, and established a system of commissioners and magistrates to adjudicate these cases in an unconstitutional, "summary" manner. Once again, Spooner uses constitutional and case law to argue the unconstitutionality and illegality of laws that are intended to perpetuate slavery by repressing resistance to it.

Spooner's major theoretical development in *A Defence for Fugitive Slaves* is the argument he makes in favor of the right of people to resist the "usurpation" by the government of the life, liberty, and property of individuals. Resistance to unconstitutional and illegal laws is "a defence of the natural rights of the people, against robbers and trespassers who attempt to set up their own personal authority and power, in opposition to those of the constitution and people, which they were appointed to administer."[21] He says that it is an absurd contradiction to argue that people have a right to institute government to protect their lives, liberty, and property, but that they have no right to preserve their freedoms by resisting the usurpation of their natural rights by governments. "The right and the physical power of the people to resist injustice are really the only securities that any people ever can have for their liberties. Practically no government knows any limit to its power but the endurance of the people." Though not quite an anarchist and not quite advocating the legitimacy of revolution, positions he would soon take, Spooner argues that nothing but the strength of the people and the knowledge that they will resist deters the state from plundering and enslaving. "Nothing but the fear of popular resistance is adequate to contain them."[22]

Thus, by 1850 Spooner articulated a conflict or dialectical foundation for political order in his critique of slavery and the legal and political support for it. His social theory is a rejection of the social contract theory of order. He envisions society to be an ongoing struggle between the forces of political institutions, whose tendency is to usurp the life, liberty, and property of individuals, and the general population, who always threaten resistance to the usurpation by the government. Natural law, natural right, and natural justice emerge as transcendent principles in Spooner's critique of slavery and any governmental action that infringes the rights of individuals.

In *Poverty: Its Illegal Causes and Legal Cure*, Spooner argues that poverty is a social problem that is manufactured by governmental constraints on trade, banking, and currency.[23] He advocates for an economic system, rooted in natural right, in which each individual is allowed to own and control "all of the fruits of his own labor," work directly for himself, and have fair access to capital obtained on credit. Spooner assails the system of wage labor since "a part of the fruits of his labor go to his employer, instead of coming to himself." He also challenges the governmental control of banking and credit because it denies individuals the right to enter into contracts freely and because it guarantees inappropriately high interest rates favoring creditors. "If free competition in banking were allowed, the rate of interest would be very low, and bank loans would be within the reach of everybody whose business and character should make him a reasonably safe person to loan to."[24] The system of regulated banking ensures the centralization of the control of finance capital and the concentration of productive capital within the hands of a small proportion of the population. Poverty and class inequality are the outcomes of a political and economic system that restricts access to capital in order to maintain artificially high interest rates. Spooner's analysis of the social class system, like his analysis of slavery, is therefore based on an examination of the interstices where the interests of political domination and economic exploitation overlap. His emerging anarchist critique is not only an attack on slavery and poverty, but on their institutional support in political authority.

SPOONER'S ANARCHISM AND GLOBAL REVOLUTION

Spooner's constitutional and legal critique of slavery became the foundation for his Individualist Anarchist political theory. Spooner's Individualist Anarchism includes a fairly detailed strategy for pursuing revolutionary warfare against the Southern slaveholders and the government that supported them. It is also an argument for global revolution against all forms of ethno-racial domination. Spooner's revolutionary anarchism appears in his pamphlets "A Plan for the Abolition of Slavery" and "To the Non-Slaveholders of the South," both of which were published in 1858. In these pamphlets, Spooner outlines a strategy for a type of guerilla war against slavery and the political reconstruction of the slaveholding states.[25] The case that Spooner makes for the abolition of slavery is predictably based on his view of natural law and natural rights. The case for revolution is comprised of four parts. First, like all people, slaves have a natural right to their liberty. Second, slaves have a right to be compensated for the injustices they have suffered as "far as the property of the Slaveholders and their abettors can compensate them." Third, slaves have a natural right to take by "stratagem or force" the liberty and compensation that the government denies them. Fourth, those who have the ability to assist the slaves are morally bound to do so. "When a human being is set upon by a robber, ravisher, murderer, or tyrant of any kind, it is the duty of the bystanders to go to his or her rescue, *by force, if need be. . . .* nothing will excuse men in the nonperformance of this duty." Moreover, "governments and laws are of no authority in opposition to (this duty). If they interpose themselves, they must be trampled underfoot without ceremony."[26]

Following the argument he makes that philosophically justifies a social revolution, Spooner outlines the concrete actions that the revolutionary antislavery movement should take. His revolutionary theory includes the hallmark of exemplary and spontaneist approaches to revolutionary activity, such as those articulated by Mikhail Bakunin and Rosa Luxemburg, in which direct action by individuals and small groups that occurs without the external direction of a centralized political authority. The initial actions of the revolution against slavery should include educational efforts to "advocate the enterprise" to non-slaveholders and to "inform the slaves of the plan of emancipation, that they may be prepared to cooperate at the proper time." Spooner also envisions more direct actions toward the abolition of slavery. He advocates the formation of "Vigilance Committees or Leagues of Freedom" whose members pledge to support the enterprise publicly and without reservation, refuse to vote or participate in any political or military activity that supports slavery. The Vigilance Committees should also raise money and acquire military equipment, and form military bands that include the "more bold and resolute slaves" to prepare for actual hostilities against the slaveholders and the government that supports them. He encourages the military bands to collect arms, horses, and supplies that will enable them to carry on their warfare upon the slaveholders.

Spooner does not advise a general insurrection, or the taking of life, until Northerners, such as himself, are able to go to the South in "such numbers as to insure a certain and easy victory." In the meantime, he advocates for the seizure of the property of slaveholders, the public chastisement and flogging of slaveholders and their accomplices. Spooner is especially aware of the propaganda value that the direct actions of the self-organized military bands, especially those comprised of blacks, will have on the resolve of the slave holders and the government.

> A band of ten or twenty determined negroes, well armed, having their rendezvous in the forests, coming out upon plantations by day or night, seizing individual slaveholders, stripping them and flogging them soundly, in the presence of their own slaves, would soon abolish slavery over a large district.[27]

In addition, the military bands should seize the weapons and hunting dogs of slaveholders. The military bands are justified in killing the slave-hunting dogs and their owners if that is essential to their self-defense. In those cases where slaves on a plantation are not sufficiently powerful or resolute, they should be assisted in deserting, especially when and where this would cause economic disruption to any sector of the slave economy of the South.

Spooner emphasizes the political nature of the struggle against slavery as much as he emphasizes its military and economic dimensions. He argues that the Vigilance Committees or Leagues of Freedom should organize resistance to taxation, give no legal assistance of any kind to slaveholders, abandon all military, patrol, or police service to the government, and do anything that can be done "safely and rightfully" to overthrow the government. Spooner concludes his plan for the abolition of slavery with the admission that he is advocating for a type of war—a revolutionary war waged by private individuals. But this revolutionary war is justified and may become necessary because the government will not act on its own to abolish slavery. In struggles of this type, it is always imperative that private individuals and spontaneously formed groups, acting out of a sense of right, take the initial steps to either force the government to abolish slavery or to organize a new political institution that will abolish slavery. The abolition of slavery could be bloodless if enough Americans would join the struggle since "slavery can live only in quiet, and in the sympathy or subjection of all around it."[28]

Of course, history demonstrates that the struggle would not be bloodless. Soon after the publication of Spooner's pamphlet, John Brown, apparently having been encouraged by Spooner's writings, embarked on his attack on Harper's Ferry and, thus, initiated the violent struggle against slavery.[29]

Arguably, Spooner's most important contribution to Individualist Anarchist theory was entitled, *No Treason, No. 6: The Constitution of No Authority*.[30] This publication was part of a series of pamphlets that Spooner wrote soon after the Civil War. The *No Treason* pamphlets signified a clear end of Spooner's belief in the role of the state in the protection of individual rights and the beginning of his career as an individualist anarchist. *No Treason, No. 6*, the last in the series of pamphlets, is a direct attack on the state itself and its foundation in the *Constitution*. This pamphlet "surpassed in extremity and daring any similar document written and published by a native American." [31] *No Treason, No. 6* is a more radical document than Spooner's previous work, in part, because the argument he makes is a summary of the objections he made in earlier publications about the interpretation of the *Constitution* as it applied to blacks, women, children, and the adult males who were disenfranchised by property qualifications. In *No Treason, No. 6*, Spooner's focus is on the authority of the *Constitution* itself.

An important element of democratic forms of government is consent of the governed, which implies a central principle: that the active, free, and voluntary agreement of individuals is necessary for any state that grounds its legitimacy in consent prior to its exertion of any form of control over individuals, including taxation or the appropriation of any form of property or wealth from individuals. Spooner argues that a departure from this principle is merely another way of establishing government on coercion or substituting might for right. The *Constitution* is, at bottom, a contract among the individuals who signed it or who agreed to it at the time of its adoption. It cannot bind or serve as justification for the control of behavior of individuals of successive generations who have not freely and actively agreed to it. The *Constitution of the United States* has no legal or moral authority over anyone because no one living ever signed it.

In the absence of any evidence of consent, the *Constitution* has no basis as a legal document and provides no legitimacy for the behavior of the American government. For Spooner and other Individualist Anarchists, consent or voluntary agreement is essential to any type of contract or any type of social relationship. The idea of an "implied social contract" as the foundation of political authority is particularly abhorrent to Spooner and other Individualist Anarchists because it legitimates the deprivation of the opportunity by individuals to choose. It invades their personal liberty and negates the principle of equal liberty. The state and other forms of political organization cannot be legitimately imposed on individuals. A perpetual or implied social contract contradicts the legitimation of the state based on the consent of the governed. It negates the natural right of human beings to create the social institutions that structure their actions and obligations to each other. Using the concepts of natural law and natural rights, Spooner adumbrates the arguments by later anarchists who founded their criticism of the state on the idea that it unavoidably creates and institutionalizes coerced relationships among people. The Individualist Anarchist vision for the future of society that Spooner articulates is a fluid, voluntary organization based on free agreements among individuals.

No Treason, No. 6 closes with a section on the struggle against slavery, once again revealing the contradiction between the ideological claims the government made about the purpose of the Civil War and the political realities of it. Reminiscent of Marx and the earlier analysis of the class system developed in *Poverty: Its Illegal Causes and Legal Cure*, Spooner argues that the North did not pursue the war against Southern secession "from any love of liberty, or justice." Its primary purpose was not to free the slaves. Instead, the war effort was rooted in the "purely pecuniary considerations" of finance capitalists and their accomplishes in the government in the North who intended to control the markets in the South. The Northern merchants and manufacturers were initially willing to continue their conspiracy with the slaveholders in the South to maintain the feudal form of production in that part of the country. With the secession of the Southern states, however, the Northern capitalists threw their support behind the war effort in order to ensure that the market as a whole was not fragmented, weakened or destroyed. They supported the war effort in order to profit from it. Money was "lent in enormous amounts, and at enormous rates of interest. And it was only by means of these loans that the objects of war were accomplished."[32]

After the Civil War, the finance capitalists in the North demanded the principle and interest on their loans to the government. This repayment was "extorted," to use Spooner's term, from "the enslaved people of both the North and the South." The extortion took several forms, including taxation, tariffs, and the expansion of banking monopolies. The consequence of the Civil War was a societal transformation that meant that black and white people were both subordinated to "the industrial and commercial slavery" and increased governmental control over their lives, labor and property, a deliberate scheme to monopolize the markets and currency of both the North and the South. The abolition of slavery was not a motive or justification for the war, but only a pretense and fraud because the Northern capitalists and politicians needed the support of the slaves to pursue their agenda to expand their control over the economy of the South. The consequence was the abolition of chattel slavery and the imposition of wage slavery, a difference in degree of exploitation, not principle, since both are defined by institutionalized economic and political restraints on the natural liberty of human beings.

Spooner also articulates an international perspective on revolution and individualist anarchism that continued many of the themes that he originally discussed in *Poverty: Its Illegal Cause and Legal Cure*, *No Treason, No. 6*, *The Unconstitutionality of Slavery*, and *A Plan for the Abolition of Slavery*. In 1880, Spooner published a pamphlet that advocated revolution in Ireland and throughout the British Commonwealth as a practical political necessity for the people who suffered under British imperialism.[33] *Revolution: The Only Remedy for the Oppressed Classes of Ireland, England, and Other Parts of the British Empire* is a response to a letter to the editor written by "The Earl of Dunraven," which was likely a nom de plume, and the editorial position of the *New York Herald* that the only realistic solution to the starvation in Ireland is the forced exodus of the "surplus population." Spooner says that if the paper, "threatened to drive (the Irish) out by the bayonet, you could hardly have been more explicit." Spooner is clearly angered and astonished at the callous perspective that the paper promoted by arguing that forced emigration is the best solution to the problem of starvation of the Irish.

The purpose of Spooner's response is to demonstrate that the Irish and "others similarly situated" have the right and the power to drive "you, and all of your abettors, out of both Ireland and England; and also, if need be, from off the face of the earth."[34] Spooner taunts *New York Herald* and the landlord class in Ireland and Britain and predicts that "at no distant day" others who believe that human beings have rights in this world will be ready in sufficient numbers to "try conclusions with you."

The argument that the forced emigration of the Irish from their home is based on the assumption that the landlords in Ireland are the real and rightful owners of the land they control. But this is a false assumption because these lands were originally taken by force, and "robbery gives no better title to lands than it does to any other property." Moreover, there is no statute of limitations on the defect in the original title to the land controlled by the Irish and British landlords; every successive holder of the land only perpetuates the robbery of his predecessors and commits a new theft by withholding the property from its rightful owners or the heirs of the rightful owners. The legitimations of the appropriation of land from its original owners and their heirs does nothing more than tell the dispossessed that "we have taken from you your country, and all your means of living in it."

In contrast to the position of the *New York Herald*, Spooner argues that it would not be a great calamity for either Ireland, Britain or the world if the entire social structure of the United Kingdom were overturned. The social structure of the United Kingdom really amounts to nothing more than a "conspiracy of robbers and tyrants" whose purpose has been to plunder and enslave. The conspiracy exists in an organized form through the State and the Church, but it does not deserve the dignity of the reference to the "whole social structure of the United Kingdom." In reality, it is a very small group of people who comprise this conspiracy and, ultimately, they are weak since their power and privilege rests on an accumulation of crimes that have redistributed land, resources, and wealth from a broad distribution to a very tiny proportion of the population. As wealth is accumulated and concentrated in the hands of a smaller and smaller class of people, the entire social structure of the British Commonwealth becomes more unstable and loses its legitimacy. Why would the *New York Herald* or the British government think the world they dominate is stable and secure when it dispossesses and alienates a growing percentage of the population? Why would they think that the dispossessed will not eventually combine their efforts and, "through a just and lawful" act, overturn the social structure and redistribute the wealth and power that has been taken from them?

The animus of the dispossessed must be focused on the government of England, a "confederacy of villains" that has plundered and enslaved not only the great body of people of England and Ireland, but "peoples in all other parts of the globe." The goal of a revolution in Ireland, England, and throughout the sphere dominated by the ruling class in Britain is entirely just and possible. Spooner points to the examples of the great French Revolution and the smaller revolutions throughout the nineteenth century as evidence that the "existing social structures" are "tottering to their fall." He predicts that the future social and political changes in Europe and its colonies will be to overthrow the existing social structures, not to sustain them. He concludes that the people of England, Ireland, and those "similarly situated" do not need immigration or even modification of their circumstances; they need a revolution that entails overturning the existing social structures and the "retribution, restitution, and, as far as possible, compensation to all the oppressed classes in England, Ireland, and throughout the British Empire."

Immanent critique is at the core of Spooner's assault on the *Constitution* and political authority. His method is to contrast the claims made about the *Constitution* with the realities of government in the United States. As he critiques the power of the state to tax and to legislate, Spooner identifies the principles that are necessary to establish its legitimacy based on its own claims, most importantly that it is founded on the consent of the governed. However, he also employs a transcendental critique by counterposing a concept of natural right and the meaning of human existence against the facts of slavery, exploitation and domination. Both forms of critique enable Spooner to integrate his anarchism with his life-long struggle against the unconstitutionality and illegality of slavery and poverty.

Prior to his death in 1887, Spooner advocated a type of revolutionary individualist anarchism with a pronounced international dimension to it. During his career as a lawyer and a political activist, Spooner progressed from an

Abolitionist position that had room for government and political activism to an Individualist Anarchist position that dismissed any legal ground for political authority over the individual. As an Abolitionist Spooner advocated a revolution and political change to end slavery and poverty. Early in his career, he sought to reconstruct government based on a philosophy of natural rights and a natural law reading of the United States' *Constitution*. As an individualist anarchist, he applied the discourse of natural rights to an argument for the abolition of the state and the revolutionary transformation of society on an international level. Spooner's encounter with the constitutional arguments against slavery laid the foundation for his later adoption of revolutionary anarchism. His immanent critique of the unconstitutionality of slavery, which attacked the legality and legitimacy of slavery using established concepts and legal methods of American jurisprudence, is supplemented by a transcendental critique of racial, ethnic, and class domination that is based on the extension of the same concepts and methods to a global context. Spooner emerges as not only a preeminent individualist thinker and activist, but also one of the most forceful and committed opponents of racism in the history of social thought. He is an important example of a social theorist who achieved the integration of both individualist and antiracist theory.

ALBERT JAY NOCK: ANARCHISM AND
THE CRITIQUE OF RACIAL VIOLENCE

Albert J. Nock (1872–1947) was an American journalist and social critic who is primarily known for his libertarian classic, *Our Enemy, the State*.[35] Nock considered himself to be a philosophical anarchist who popularized in the United States the opposition of the "political" and "economic" means of achieving societal goals, which was originally formulated by the nineteenth century German sociologist, Franz Oppenheimer in his book, *The State*.[36] Nock's career as a journalist spanned from 1910 to his death in 1947. At various points in his career, he was associated with *American Mercury*, *Freeman*, *American Review*, *Harper's*, and *Atlantic Monthly*. He wrote no fewer than seventeen books on literary, cultural, and social criticism. His autobiography, *Memoirs of a Superfluous Man*, was published in 1943 to considerable acclaim at the time, influencing a variety of rightist and individualist intellectuals, including William F. Buckley.[37]

Nock has been referred to as "the superfluous anarchist," "the genteel muckraker," "the forgotten man of the old right," and "the weird uncle" of antistatist thought. Nock carefully cultivated an image of dissidence and eccentricity in his writings and personal behavior. One reviewer differentiates him sharply from conservatives by describing Nock as "a bit anarchist, somewhat bohemian, occasionally blasphemous, and thoroughly misanthropic."[38] Nock's biographer, Michael Wreszin, refers to him as the "superfluous anarchist," arguing that there is a fundamental tension in Nock's thought between an aristocratic elitism and a genuine proletarian anarchism. Nock was certainly a radical libertarian and considered himself to be an anarchist in the individualist and philosophic traditions. Nock's anarchism was a genteel philosophical sort, vastly different from the more violent, communist variety advocated by his contemporaries, Emma Goldman, Alexander Berkman, and Johann Most. Nock was critical of capitalism at times, especially that form of capitalism in which big business conspired with the state against society. He was a strong supporter of labor and enthusiastic about the economic and political protests by trade unions. He believed that the avarice of the industrial class severely undermined traditional values and social bonds in America. His anarchism was a type of Jeffersonian lament for the placid, agrarian, rural social environment that presumably characterized the United States prior to the massive urbanization and industrialization processes of the twentieth century. Wreszin argues that Nock's writings were fundamentally a type of elitist and aristocratic reaction to the agony, blood, and fire exuding from the conflicts and struggles of pre–World War II America. Nock was fundamentally concerned about the historical processes that destroyed traditional American culture and converted social power into state power. Nock was an ardent critic of popular culture because he believed it vulgarized social relationships and conferred too much power to the state and the industrial class.

Unlike Tucker and Spooner, Nock was not a secular progressive, but a religious traditionalist who found anarchism to be most appropriate label for his political ideas and his self-image as an eccentric intellectual, in part because "anarchist" was a particularly inflammatory label at the time. Although he can be challenged on this point, Wreszin concludes that Nock's anarchism, commitment to liberty, and support for the proletariat was really more of a reflection of hatred for popular culture and culture politics than a resolution to improve the life circumstances of the lower rungs of the social stratification system.[39]

This tension within Nock's thought makes him a "less than perfect fit" among the theorists included in this volume. A solid case can be made that Rand, Rothbard, Tucker, and Spooner offer political and social theories and writings that are consistently antiracist. In Nock's case, it is a little more difficult to make this same argument. In his personal papers and in his autobiography, Nock makes a number of prejudicial, hostile, and angry comments about Jews. While most of these comments seem to be critical of claims by Jews of their victimization in America, they must be characterized as racist.

Nock's stature as a consistent theorist of liberty is consequently suspect. Nock's anti-Semitism had its limits because it is also true that Nock's primary intellectual progenitor, Franz Oppenheimer, was himself Jewish and the son of rabbi, facts that Nock was certainly aware of. In addition, Nock was a severe critic of immigration during the early twentieth century. The antipathy he expresses about immigration seems to be focused on a concern about the deteriorating traditional, agrarian culture in the United States, but it must also be criticized as racist, at least in its implications. Thus, Nock's writings are not uniformly supportive of the thesis of this book that individualist and libertarian theorists contribute something important to the critique of both racism and multiculturalism. Why, then, include Nock in this discussion?

Very good arguments can be made for excluding Nock from a discussion about racism and the dialectics of liberty. He has been included in this discussion because his writings are passionately critical of antiblack racism and, particularly, the lynchings that occurred in the United States in the early to mid-twentieth century. Further, he worked with the Association for the Advancement of Colored People (AACP) to seek racial justice. Despite the regrettable and contradictory comments he made about Jews and immigrants, Nock was very critical of the role of governments in the persecution of minorities, both at home and abroad. His view of the role of the state in the social system has considerable value for understanding what Nock calls the "criminality" and "villainy" of governments in their treatment of racial and ethnic minorities. Moreover, Nock's criticism of the record of the state in race and ethnic group relations is intended to "keep down the great American sin of self-righteousness," intending to prompt reflection on the treatment of black Americans, Hispanic Americans, and native Americans.[40] In a 1939 essay on the State that appeared in *The American Mercury*, Nock comments on the "deadly parallels" between the treatment of minorities by the Axis powers, the European democracies, and the government of the United States.

> The German State is persecuting a minority, just as the American State did after 1776; the Italian State breaks into Ethiopia, just as the American State broke into Mexico; the Japanese State kills off the Manchurian tribes in wholesale lots, just as the American State did the Indian tribes; the British State practices large-scale carpetbaggery, like the American state after 1864; the imperialist French State massacres native civilians on their own soil, as the American State did in pursuit of its imperialistic policies in the Pacific.[41]

Nock argues that the treatment of racial and ethnic minorities by governments is nothing new and not really a surprise because the state is "fundamentally an antisocial institution, fundamentally criminal" since it "originated for the purpose of maintaining the division of society into an owning-and-exploiting class and a propertyless dependent class—that is, for a criminal purpose."[42]

Nock's theory of the state and its application to social and cultural issues was rooted in the political sociology of the German social theorist Franz Oppenheimer. Oppenheimer had gained some popularity in Europe and America through his book *The State*, which was originally published in German in 1908 and subsequently published in English in 1915. *The State* had an enormous impact on Nock. The central categories and social antagonisms that Oppenheimer articulates in *The State* constitute the theoretical framework that Nock utilizes in all of his political writings. *The State* is a classic non-Marxian conflict analysis of political institutions in society. In many respects, *The State* is a synthesis of the classic European conflict sociology that developed in the latter part of the nineteenth century and into the twentieth century. Oppenheimer argues that one of the fundamental principles of social life is the pattern in which political institutions and social classes originate and develop. In articulating this principle, Oppenheimer distinguishes between the economic and political means of meeting needs and obtaining wealth. "There are two fundamentally opposed means whereby man, requiring sustenance, is impelled to obtain the necessary means for satisfying his desires. These are work and robbery, one's own labor and the forcible appropriation of the labor of others." The economic means refers to "one's own labor and the equivalent exchange of one's own labor for the labor of others." The political means refers to the "unrequited appropriation of the labor of others." [43]

Oppenheimer defends this sharp differentiation between the "two means toward the same end" as necessary to avoid confusion and "false conclusions" about the nature of government and economic activity. Oppenheimer says that in his otherwise "splendid theory," Marx makes an enormous mistake in failing to differentiate between the two means. Marx's failure to distinguish the economic and the political led him to designate slavery as an "economic category" and political coercion as an "economic force." While Marx argues that purely demographic and economic dynamics produced distinct social classes, Oppenheimer argues that the emergence of an exploitative dominant class and a dispossessed laboring class always results from political, not economic, dynamics. Hence, Marx's analysis of exploitation and conflict results in the disastrous, contradictory conclusion that the acquisition and exercise of state power is essential to the historical process and the emancipation of exploited social classes. Oppenheimer argues that this perspective is a fantasy because the state can never function to liberate; it can only function only to dominate and to assist the exploiting class in its domination.

For Oppenheimer the "sociological idea of the state" is a "social institution, forced by a victorious group of men on a defeated group with the sole purpose of regulating dominion of the victorious group over the vanquished and securing itself against revolt from within and attacks from abroad."[44] Ultimately, the state has no purpose other than the economic exploitation of the "vanquished by the victors."

From the moment when the first conqueror spared his victim in order to permanently exploit him in productive work, was of incomparable historical importance. It gave birth to nation and state, to right and the higher economics, with all the developments and ramifications which have grown and which will hereafter grow out of them.[45]

According to Oppenheimer, no state originated in another fashion and none functions differently, although historically relative circumstances shape the particular form that the state takes and the particular manner in which it operates. History is a process of conflict between a dominant, exploiting class and an ascending class. New forms of political organization arise as one class deposes its nemesis. In Oppenheimer's view, the modern, constitutional state developed through an historical process in which conquest, coercion and exploitation were increasingly institutionalized through the military, policing, and taxation functions of government.

The modern, constitutional state is the most advanced institutional expression of the political means in society since it effectively utilizes not only law and public policy, but behavioral and management science as tools of class warfare. Although he did not describe himself as an anarchist, Oppenheimer argues for the dissolution of the state and the creation of a "freeman's citizenship" which is defined by the elimination of the political means and the ascendance of the economic means. Oppenheimer writes that eventually the state will lose its power to exploit because of technological change and the proliferation of cultural ideas, such as individual autonomy, reason, and free trade that will motivate people to challenge the political means and create a system based on the pure equivalent exchange of labor or commodities for commodities. The state will evolve into a more libertarian "freeman's citizenship."

Oppenheimer's analysis of political change and class warfare was appealing to Nock because it avoided the homogenizing and authoritarian tendencies in Marxist theory and it challenged these consequences that were so apparent in the rise of the Soviet, Nazi, and Fascist states. Oppenheimer was also somewhat optimistic. Oppenheimer's critique ultimately had a happy ending in the creation of the "freeman's citizenship," in which Nock saw the vindication and rescue of the values and social relations of Jeffersonian America.

In *Our Enemy, the State* Nock approvingly restates Oppenheimer's characterization of the state as "the organization of the political means" whose "primary intention is to enable the economic exploitation of one class by another."[46] Nock read and absorbed *The State* by the time that the first issue of *The Freeman*, the libertarian journal he edited, was published in 1920. However, Nock identified himself as an anarchist and had articulated many of the basic elements of his political and cultural critique of America before his encounter with Oppenheimer's book. In 1913, Nock published an article in the *American Magazine* on the lynching of a black man in Coatesville, Pennsylvania in 1911. In "What We All Stand For" Nock uses an example of mob violence against a black man to outline his argument that racial violence is produced by a social system characterized by class hostility that is no longer constrained by a shared culture or sense of civilization.[47]

Nock recounts the story of how the victim of the lynching, Zach Walker, was arrested for allegedly killing an off-duty security guard for a local steel mill in an altercation. Walker was injured in the fight and chained to a bed in the hospital. He was attacked by a mob, shot in the head, dragged a half mile, "thrown upon a pile of wood, drenched with oil, and burned alive."[48] Nock's interest in writing about the lynching is to search for explanations for how and why this type of violence could occur and what it means for the society as a whole. He methodically considers and rejects explanations that suggest that the mob attacked Walker because it feared that he was likely to escape punishment, or that Walker's crime had whipped the town into a frenzy because he killed a leading citizen, or that the lynching was even due to race hatred. Nock says that the crime of lynching did not arise from race hatred. "There is no feverish and sensitive traditional race-feeling in Coatesville which might have brought forth this lynching out of the whole cloth, as it does occasionally in some parts of the South." Certainly, there was a "current accepted commonplace" of prejudice toward blacks, but this did not explain the violence because the prevailing cultural traditions in this Pennsylvania town were Quakerism, not a deliberate racism. There was no cold-blooded, deliberate calculation to exact violence intended to perpetuate the domination of blacks by whites.

In the end, the "crime was without purpose and without fruit. It served no one, appeased no one, consoled no one. It accomplished nothing." Moreover, the official governmental reaction to the lynching was not helpful. The press reacted with indignation, the bars were closed, and the streets were patrolled, fearing black retaliation. But there was not the faintest hint that the lynching was anything other than a "horrible and savage sport" for the mob. None of the instigators or ringleaders of the lynching were arrested. The policeman responsible for Walker's safety were not arrested. The participants who were arrested were exonerated. Subsequent investigations came to nothing. Nock praises the work of the American Association of Colored People for its efforts to investigate the matter. He recounts his work with the AACP and the Governor of Pennsylvania to bring the mob to justice. Ultimately, however, these efforts produced no results.

Unlike the government, the AACP was praiseworthy because its members were willing to promote an unpopular cause, but one that is "fundamental to civilization—equality of opportunity for a great, unprivileged, overborne, unhappy section of our people." Inspired by the actions of the AACP, Nock articulates a basic, transcendent philosophic principle about the nature of civilization, "as long as there are *any* victims of inequality, as long as *any* are exploited or dispossessed, there can be no civilization—and this means negro human beings as well as white."[49] In Nock's view, the lynching and the official reaction to it were indicative of the fundamental problem with government: it is incapable and unwilling to secure the rights of individuals and to promote "the humanizing of men in society."

For an explanation of the lynching and the government's reaction to it, Nock argues that it is necessary to understand the social class system as it appeared in Coatesville. He argues that Coatesville was an industrial "Hellhole" comprised of three distinct social classes. The immense lower stratum was comprised of black, Hungarian, and Slavic workers whose conditions of working and living are exploitive and preclude either "happiness or decency." Above the large working class was a smaller middle stratum that made its living "out of the town, by trading and in other ways." This middle class was continually apprehensive about the effect of the lynching on the "good name" of the town of Coatesville. Nock ridicules this "smug and closed-mouthed" middle stratum for agonizing over the bad publicity associated with the lynching and attempting to hush up such tabooed subjects. At the apex of the stratification system is the small exploiting class that has made "immense fortunes" off of the labor of the workers and their families. Nock sums up the stratification system of Coatesville as a microcosm of the entire country by saying that it has "an upper class materialized, a middle class vulgarized, a lower class brutalized."[50] Nock concludes that the life circumstances of Americans in these conditions depart significantly from the defining characteristics of civilization because of the poverty that is created in the production process and the conflict that it generates within and among the social classes.

The lynching of Zach Walker was a "frightful tragedy" but it was also a "registration" or a measure of the degree of "civilization" in American society. Even if the murderers of Zach Walker had been brought to justice, Nock says nothing has been done for civilization because the industrial class system that produced the brutality and hostility between people in the same social class has been left untouched. The lynching of Zach Walker, thus, was a warning that unless the class system is transformed, and the power of the state curtailed, there will be increased impoverishment, brutality, and conflict among racial and ethnic groups.

Nock frames his discussion of racial violence, as he does many of the social issues he addresses, in term of a concept of "civilization." His writing is a constant quest for the defining characteristics of civilization, or what he called "the humanizing processes in society." He assesses political, social, and cultural dynamics in terms of the defining characteristics of civilization. As the social and cultural realities of communities and societies depart from the defining characteristics of civilization, there is the basis for a transcendent critique of social relations. The two defining characteristics of civilization Nock identifies in "What We All Stand For" are (a) a diffuse, material well-being and (b) homogeneity or shared cultural values.[51] Civilization is what humanizes people. In Nock's view, people are not likely to be humanized unless there are adequate material and cultural conditions for their humanization. The "humanizing processes in society" will be defective until the class system and the state are abolished. Nock provides us with a non-Marxist form of class analysis in which the role of the state is to protect prevailing inequalities and antagonisms, even though these produce dehumanizing social conditions.

The lynching of Zach Walker was an expression of racial and intraclass violence, a social dynamic that the state and exploiting class need in order to maintain their privileged position in society. Nock's Individualist Anarchism provides an important critique of racism and a significant theoretical departure from the analyses of Rand, Rothbard, and the Libertarians. Nock understands that the state, culture, and the class system comprise an integrated societal totality in which each supports and reinforces the other. The three social formations are integrated in fact and must be attacked through an immanent critique that demonstrates the antagonism between the social realities of racial violence and the societal claims of democracy, law, and justice. The primary lesson of Nock's individualist anarchism is that the critique of racial violence must also be a critique of the state and the social class system. The critique of racism is also the search for "civilization," or the humanizing processes in society. In the hands of the Individualist Anarchists, the critique of racism and the search for humanizing processes in society includes the rejection of all forms of external constraints on the individual, except those that the person freely agrees to. The logic of Individualist Anarchism reaches its full expression in the dialectical egoism of Max Stirner, whose thoughts on race and self-ownership are the focus of chapter 6.

NOTES

1. Sharon Presley, "John Henry Mackay's *The Anarchists*: His Message to Libertarians Today," in *The Anarchists*, John Henry Mackay (1981; Brooklyn, NY: Autonomedia, 1999), xxii–xxvii.

2. Presley, "Mackay," xxii.

3. Benjamin R. Tucker, *Instead of a Book by a Man Too Busy to Write One: A Fragmentary Exposition of Philosophical Anarchism* (1897; New York: Haskell House Publishers, 1969). For an example of the writing of Victor Yarros on Tucker and Anarchism, see "Philosophical Anarchism: Its Rise, Decline, and Eclipse." *American Journal of Sociology* 41, no. 4 (January 1936): 470–83. Given the breadth, depth and influence of his work, it is remarkable that Tucker has been given short shrift in the academic literature on him and Individualist Anarchism generally. Fortunately, excellent works on Tucker and Spooner are beginning to appear in academic journals and scholarly books with greater regularity. For examples of the neglect of Tucker's work, see R. B. Fowler, "The Anarchist Tradition of Political Thought." *The Western Political Quarterly* 25, no. 4 (December 1972): 738–52 and George Woodcock, *Anarchism: A History of Libertarian Ideas and Movements* (Cleveland: The World Publishing Company, 1962).

4. I am indebted to Wendy McElroy's fine book, *The Debates of Liberty: An Overview of Individualist Anarchism, 1881–1908* (Lanham, MD: Lexington Books, 2003) for the first two of these precepts. I added the third precept based on the observation that the methodology of passive resistance is a principle that underlies all of his discussions about political activism. Passive resistance also seems to follow directly from the notion of "equal liberty." For another discussion of these concepts and how they interfaced with the ideas of some of Tucker's contemporaries, see James J. Martin, *Men Against the State: The Expositors of Individualist Anarchism in America, 1827–1908*. (Colorado Springs: Ralph Myles, 1970).

5. Tucker, *Instead of a Book*, 65.

6. Tucker, *Instead of a Book*, 411–13.

7. Tucker, *Instead of a Book*, 6.

8. Tucker, *Instead of a Book*, 9. Was Tucker a socialist or a capitalist? Tucker's economics have been analyzed by both his supporters and his critics. I think the answer to this question is that he attempted to outline a third approach that was neither socialist nor capitalist. For different views of this question see Gary Elkin, "Benjamin Tucker: Anarchist or Capitalist?" http://flag.blackened.net/daver/anarchism/tucker/an _or_cap.html (accessed on March 7, 2007) and Murray Rothbard, *Egalitarianism as a Revolt Against Nature* (1974; Auburn, AL: The Ludwig von Mises Institute, 2000), 205–18.

9. Wendy McElroy has compiled an index of the articles that appeared in *Liberty*, http://tmh.floonet.net/articles/ind_intr.html (accessed March 15, 2007).

10. Tucker, *Instead of a Book*, 414–15.

11. Tucker, *Instead of a Book*, 415.

12. Lysander Spooner, *The Unconstitutionality of Slavery* (New York: Burt Franklin, 1860).

13. George Smith, "Introduction," *The Lysander Spooner Reader* (San Francisco: Fox and Wilkes, 1992), vii–xxii.

14. William Weicek, *The Source of Anti-Slavery Constitutionalism in America* (Ithaca, NY: Cornell University Press, 1977).

15. Spooner, *The Unconstitutionality of Slavery*, 7.

16. Spooner, *The Unconstitutionality of Slavery*, 14.

17. Spooner, *The Unconstitutionality of Slavery*, 273.

18. Smith, "Introduction," xiii. Also see the treatments of Spooner's legal thought by James J. Martin, *Men Against the State: The Expositors of Individualist Anarchism in America, 1827–1908* (Colorado Springs: Ralph Myles, 1970), 167–201.

19. Smith, "Introduction," xv.

20. Lsyander Spooner, *A Defence for Fugitive Slaves* (Boston: Bela Marsh, 1850).

21. Spooner, *A Defence for Fugitive Slaves*, 14.

22. Spooner, *A Defence for Fugitive Slaves*, 14.

23. Lysander Spooner, *Poverty: Its Illegal Causes and Legal Cure* (Boston: Bela Marsh, 1846), http://www.lysanderspooner.org/Poverty.htm (accessed March 8, 2007).

24. Spooner, *Poverty*, 6.

25. Lysander Spooner, *A Plan for the Abolition of Slavery* (Boston: Author, 1858) and *To the Non-Slaveholders of the South* (Boston: Author, 1858), http://www.lysander spooner.org/abolitionofslavery.htm (accessed March 8, 2007).

26. Spooner, *A Plan for the Abolition of Slavery*, 5.

27. Spooner, *A Plan for the Abolition of Slavery*, 2.

28. Spooner, *To the Non-Slaveholders of the South*, 6.

29. Smith, "Introduction," xvi. Smith acknowledges that this is a controversial assertion and cites Lewis Perry, *Radical Abolitionism: Anarchy and the Government of God in Antislavery Thought* (Ithaca, NY: Cornell University Press, 1973), 194–208, as a source for it.

30. Spooner, *No Treason, No. 6: The Constitution of No Authority* (1870; Larkspur, CO: Pine Tree Press, 1965).

31. Martin, *Men Against the State*, 191.

32. Spooner, *No Treason*, 51.

33. Lysander Spooner, *Revolution: The Only Remedy for the Oppressed Classes of Ireland, England, and Other Parts of the British Empire* (1880; Boston: Author, 1880), http://www.lysanderspooner.org/Revolution.htm (accessed March 8, 2007).

34. Spooner, *Revolution*, 1.

35. Albert Jay Nock, *Our Enemy, the State* (1935; Caldwell, ID: Caxton Publishers, 1959).

36. Franz Oppenheimer, *The State* (1908; New York: Free Life Editions, 1975).

37. Albert Jay Nock, *Memoirs of a Superfluous Man* (New York: Harper and Brothers, 1943).

38. Franklin Foer, "The Happy Hater," *The New Republic Online*, http://fairuse.1 accesshost.com/news2/happy-hater.html (accessed March 5, 2007).

39. Michael Wreszin, *The Superfluous Anarchist Albert Jay Nock* (Providence, RI: Brown University Press, 1972), ix.

40. Albert Jay Nock, "The Criminality of the State," in *State of the Union: Essays in Social Criticism*, ed. Charles Hamilton (1939; Indianapolis: Liberty Fund, 1991), 269–75.

41. Nock, "The Criminality of the State," 270.

42. Nock, "The Criminality of the State," 270.

43. Oppenheimer, *The State*, 12.

44. Oppenheimer, *The State*, 8.

45. Oppenheimer, *The State*, 27.

46. Nock, *Our Enemy, the State*, 106. Also see Albert Jay Nock, "Anarchist's Progress," in *State of the Union: Essays in Social Criticism*, ed. Charles Hamilton (1927; Indianapolis: Liberty Fund, 1991), 34–51.

47. Albert Jay Nock, "What We All Stand For," in *State of the Union: Essays in Social Criticism*, ed. Charles Hamilton (1913; Indianapolis: Liberty Fund, 1991), 139–48.

48. Nock, "What We All Stand For," 139.

49. Nock, "What We All Stand For," 142.

50. Nock, "What We All Stand For," 146.

51. Nock, "What We All Stand For," 145. Also see Albert Jay Nock, "Our American Upper Class," in *Free Speech and Plain Language* (1931; Freeport, NY: Books for Libraries Press, 1965), 124–44.

Chapter Six

Self-Ownership, the Unique Individual, and the Specter of Race

The Dialectical Egoism of Max Stirner

RACE, ALIENATION, AND THE INDIVIDUAL

Even among individualist and libertarian thinkers, Max Stirner is a unique, idiosyncratic, and somewhat threatening figure in the history of ideas. Born Johann Caspar Schmidt in 1806 in Beyreuth, Germany, Max Stirner is the nom de plume, or perhaps more accurately, the nom de guerre, of a school teacher and writer best known for the uncompromising individualist position articulated in his classic work, *Der Einzige und sein Eigenthum*, which was originally translated in English as *The Ego and Its Own*, although a contemporary scholar suggests that the book might be better titled *The Unique One and His Property*. *The Ego and Its Own* was published in 1844, the same year that Karl Marx articulated his initial critique of alienation in the *Economic and Philosophic Manuscripts of 1844*, and Søren Kierkegaard published his study of alienation in *The Concept of Dread*.[1] Given the profound philosophic interest in alienation at the time, which was largely due to the overwhelming influence in European philosophy of the problematics outlined by Hegel, it is not particularly surprising that Stirner's work has a fundamental interest in alienation, mystification, and reification. Whereas Marx was concerned with alienation as it was generated in the labor process, and Kierkegaard was concerned with the estrangement of human beings from God, Stirner was primarily interested in the individual's alienation from self. *The Ego and Its Own* focused on how the cultural, philosophic, and ideological sources of alienation, especially religion and the state, functioned to separate the individual, the real living person, from self. Although Stirner is not generally considered to be a major nineteenth century philosopher, his dissidence has a durability that rivals that of Marx and Nietzsche. Stirner's critique of alienation has a peculiar, and profound, contribution to the critique of multiculturalism and the struggle against racism.

Stirner was convinced that the speculative or critical philosophy prevailing in the early to mid-nineteenth century, although it attacked right-wing Hegelianism as well as the oppressive and alienative dimensions of monotheistic religions and antidemocratic governments, had simply reconstructed philosophic legitimations for oppression and alienation in new forms. The humanist writings of Ludwig Feuerbach were particularly important stimuli for Stirner's philosophic work. Feuerbach published his most renowned work, *The Essence of Christianity*, in 1841. *The Essence of Christianity* outlined the contradictions and illusory interpretation of religion and history in Hegel's philosophy.[2] Feuerbach promoted a "new philosophy" based on a radical critique of religion and a humanist or anthropological interpretation of human experience.

Feuerbach argues in *The Essence of Christianity* that all religious or mythological thought has a human significance in that it says much more about the thoughts and lives of humans than about God or the object of worship. His study of Christianity led him to conclude that religion is a process in which humanity projects its qualities onto the objective world and then converts those qualities into a subject. Thus, God has a human, not divine, origin. Religion is a means of objectifying humanity's essence in an ideal form. Human knowledge about God is nothing but humanity's knowledge about itself, especially its ideal qualities; religious consciousness is really alienated knowledge about humans that must be returned to them. Humanity must understand itself as the subject, not the object, of its own creations, including its knowledge about God. With the proper controls exerted by the naturalistic and human sciences, Feuerbach believed that the human tendency to externalize and objectify its ideal qualities in religion could be used to promote well-being and community on earth. For Feuerbach, "Man" became the God of the modern world.

The democratic and socialist activists among the left-Hegelians were deeply affected by Feuerbach's humanism, although they transformed it from a philosophic statement into a political program. Marx and Engels were among the left-Hegelians who were greatly influenced by Feuerbach's critique of religion, all of whom were confident that Feuerbach's atheism was the final statement on religion and philosophy. For Marx and Engels this confidence led to the famous eleventh "Thesis on Feuerbach" that advised that philosophers had only interpreted the world, it was time to abandon philosophy and pursue changing the world. Marx, Engels and the other early socialists and communists replaced Feuerbach's "Man" with "Society" as the supreme being in the ideology they sought to impose on the world.[3] Stirner, however, did not believe that Feuerbach had made the final statement on religion or philosophy. He rejected any notion that human essence has any type of metaphysical or objective existence, and vehemently opposed every philosophic or political movement that sought to realize "Man," or any other abstraction, as the new God. Stirner has been characterized as a "total atheist" because he argued strongly against the efforts by Feuerbach and the left-Hegelians, including socialists like Marx and Engels, to enshrine "Humanity" or "Society" as the new organizing principle for society. In Stirner's view, these "fixed ideas" posited by the young or left Hegelians merely recast God in a new way and, thus, adumbrated new forms of domination, alienation, and resistance.

Although he defies easy classification as a philosopher, Stirner's response to Feuerbach and to the nascent socialist and communist philosophers can be called a "dialectical egoism." *The Ego and Its Own* clearly has elements of atheism and anarchism. Yet, it is not merely atheistic and anarchistic. It also has profound elements of psychological and ethical egoism. But, again, it cannot be reduced to egoism. Stirner has been called "the last of the Hegelians."[4] As a student of Hegel, his early writings and *The Ego and Its Own* are thoroughly dialectical. They include much of the terminology familiar to students of Hegel, such as "absolute," "consciousness," "subjectivity," "positivity," and "negativity." In addition, the structure of *The Ego and Its Own* curiously parallels the structure of Hegel's *The Phenomenology of Spirit* and *The Science of Logic*. Most significantly, perhaps, Stirner's mode of argumentation in his early writings and *The Ego and Its Own* include the clash of opposing ideas or forces with the emergence of new, "higher presuppositions" resulting from the struggle of opposites. Stirner was convinced that the critical, idealist philosophy of Hegel and his followers was dissembling, and that it was not a viable negation of the determinist, materialist philosophy that preceded it. Hence, a new presupposition, egoism, emerged from the conflict between materialism and idealism. Since it studies the interplay of complex historical and ideological forces, Stirner's dialectical egoism is rooted in Hegelianism, but it purports to accomplish the original Hegelian "task of freeing the self from its self-inflicted domination of fixed ideas."[5]

Stirner's egoistic critique and his dialectical methodology can be applied to the concept of race as a "fixed idea" and the analysis of multiculturalism as a new form of alienated thought. Despite its many ambiguities and extreme statements, Stirner's thought offers many ideas that contribute to the vision of a post-ethnic or transracial society. The application of the egoist dialectic to the analysis of race and ethnicity suggests that out of the conflict between racism and multiculturalism, a new presupposition, an egoistic transracialism emerged. Stirner does not offer a scientific or historical analysis of the cause or evolution of racism separate from his historical discussion of alienation. Instead, his focus is on a critique of racism and resistance to it as part of the broader egoist response to domination and alienation. This chapter addresses three questions. First, what did Stirner say specifically about racial, ethnic, and cultural dynamics in his writings, particularly *The Ego and Its Own*? Second, how do these ideas fit within the totality of his thought regarding alienation and the egoist resistance to it? Third, what are the implications of Stirner's thought for race as a concept, and multiculturalism as an agenda and analytical tool, in the struggle against racism? The chapter proceeds by first analyzing the content and method of one of Stirner's early essays, *The False Principle of Our Education,* and, then, examines his discussion on race, egoism, and social relations in *The Ego and Its Own.* The chapter concludes with a discussion of the basic elements of the dialectical egoist critique of multiculturalism.

THE FALSE PRINCIPLE OF OUR EDUCATION

In April 1842, Karl Marx published Stirner's essay, *The False Principle of our Education, Or Humanism and Realism*, in his journal *Rheinische Zeitung*. The *False Principle* critiqued the two prevailing philosophical orientations on educational curricula in Germany in the 1840s and articulated Stirner's initial, but defiant, individualist perspective.[6] *The False Principle* is an important essay because it provides a clear means of understanding how Stirner employs dialectics to approach philosophical problems. It is also important because Stirner's conclusions adumbrate some of the critical arguments that appeared two years later in *The Ego and Its Own. The False Principle* is particularly important because it provides some guidance on how Stirner explored race, culture, and ethnicity in *The Ego and Its Own. The False Principle* is very pertinent to contemporary discussions on race and multiculturalism, in part, because it uses slavery and racial domination as a metaphor in his critique of educational theory. This early essay by Stirner assails collectivist and determinist processes of reality construction and identity formation that function to subordinate individuals to fixed patterns of thinking and behaving. It is an argument for reshaping not only education, but all cultural processes of learning and identity formation toward the notion of the free, "self-creating person."

In *The False Principle*, Stirner argues that the two prevailing theories of education at the time—humanism and realism—offered flawed bases for establishing educational curricula because they do not capture or express the spirit of "modern times." The fundamental question he poses is whether these theories cultivate the predisposition of persons to become creators of their natural, social, and cultural environment, or do they assume that human nature can only permit training and adaptation to fixed natural, social and cultural patterns? Both humanism and realism must be challenged and transformed so that pedagogy and all forms of cultural creation can more adequately reflect the principle of modern times, which is "freedom of thought" and its "perfection" or transformation into "freedom of the will."[7]

Stirner's juxtaposition of the "humanist" and the "realist" schools of thought sounds familiar to those engaged in educational theory, policy, or practice because they reflect the different concepts of whether the primary goal of education should be to provide students with detached knowledge of the world they live in or prepare them for practical endeavors, such as citizenship and earning a living. Stirner attacks prior formulations of this problem in the philosophy of education and the philosophy of knowledge that failed to "incur the displeasure" of either camp because they do not articulate the sharp fundamental differences between the two positions. Philosophic problems on critical social issues inevitably entail a struggle between two parties for victory, each seeking to impose its principle of education as the most appropriate for the needs of individuals and society. Stirner's analysis departs from the philosophic legacy of "faint-hearted mediators" and promotes a "sharp decisiveness." The "school question" is a "life question" since the critique of the false principle is broadly applicable to societal and cultural processes of reality construction and identity formation. Ultimately, the stakes are slavery versus freedom. A "faint-hearted" mediation between the two theories offers only a "cowardly expedient."[8]

Stirner constructs a dialectical edifice for his argument by first reviewing the intellectual and historical background of the debate between the "humanists" and the "realists." His analysis is replete with Hegelian concepts and formulations, such as "spirit" and "historical periods." Stirner clearly attempts to understand the historical development of the conflict between the prevailing philosophies of knowledge and education in his historical period. The most significant juncture of the development of the debate between humanism and realism occurs with the emergence of the age of the revolutions of the eighteenth and nineteenth centuries, which destroyed "the master-servant" economy and laid a foundation for a social and cultural formation that allows each individual to be his or her own master. In education as in society, the basic principles of human rights, "equality," and "freedom," gained ascendance as social and cultural constructs that reflected the spirit of the times in the age of revolution. Equality became important because society began to recognize the participation of each individual, and education began to embrace everyone. Freedom became important in both society and education since both promoted the conversation between about the needs, independence and autonomy of each individual.[9]

Stirner then counterposes the basic elements of both humanism and realism as alternative and conflicting pedagogical philosophies. "Humanism" is the philosophy of education and knowledge that has as its goal the understanding of the past with the intent of producing detached, dispassionate scholars. Stirner notes that humanism has a number of strengths. Among other things, humanism helped promote the notion of equality with others and independence from authorities. There are some negative aspects to humanism. These include the lack of any concept of self-determination and a sense of behavior that produces none of the acts of a person who is "free-in-himself." Humanism is an "empty elegance." Stirner applauds "realism" for its clear support for knowledge and learning aimed at the navigation of everyday life, but critiqued it for radiating "the one-sidedness of a special education." Moreover, realism does not promote the ability of the individual to strive to surpass "the equality of others" and "the freedom of others," which refers to the homogenization and conformity that is enforced by modern organizations. Realism yields a "tasteless materialism" and a homogenization of persons by subordinating them to the demands of practical life. Understanding oneself as an autonomous individual is not a concern of the realist school of educational thought.[10]

The opposition between humanism and realism does not exhaust all possibilities for thinking about the basis of social and individual goals for education and identity formation, especially because equality and freedom are subordinated to other priorities. Humanism, for example, focuses on understanding the past; realism focuses on understanding how to navigate the present. Out of the conflict between the two opposing educational philosophies, a new principle for the organization of learning emerges. A new principle for the organization of society also emerges. The "false principle" is the idea that the opposition between humanism and realism adequately expresses the basic choice for the cultural foundation of either education or society.

For Stirner, the antagonism between humanism and realism is a reflection of a society and an educational structure that lacks a philosophical foundation that promotes individual freedom. The conflict between humanism and realism teaches the individual "to reconcile oneself to the positive," or to submit to existing patterns of thinking and behaving by understanding the past and accommodating oneself to the present. "Freedom is not allowed to erupt, the power of the opposition is not allowed to put in a word edgewise; they want submissiveness." Only scholars emerge out of the menageries of the humanists and only "useful citizens" emerge out of the pedagogy of the realists. All are nothing but "subservient people." Stirner asks for a description of the most gifted and educated subjects in Germany. He responds that they are for the most part "scornful, smiling slave-owners and themselves slaves."[11]

For Stirner, the critique of the conflict between humanism and realism is not just an academic or philosophic endeavor because it impacts the thoughts and actions of human individuals. All educational and cultural processes radiate into one center, which he calls "personality."[12] All knowledge remains only a possession of the individual until it vanishes into self-awareness and behaviors reflecting the will or the free choice of the person. The ultimate purpose of knowledge is found in its use, consumption, or expression in the behavior of the individual possessing it. That is, there should be a connection between what the person learns and his or her ability to use it. The problem with education up to the 1840s is that knowledge was not refined or transformed into will. It was not for the individual's behavior. Knowledge must be personal and a reflection of the ego itself. Knowledge itself cannot be taught; instead, the individual must come to self-awareness and self-development. As a social institution, education should not aim toward civilizing persons and training workers, but should be oriented toward the development of "free men, sovereign characters." Education and society do not hinder a person's quest for knowledge. Why, then, should they attempt to limit free will? If education and society attempt to nurture the acquisition of knowledge, should they not also nurture the will? The "old principle" of education was "will-less knowledge." But, the new principle, founded on the cultural ideals of freedom and equality, is not subservience, but freedom of thought that is transformed into freedom of the will. The goal of education is not to produce useful members of society, but to contribute to the development of free, "self-creating" people.

Stirner concludes this essay with the argument that the spirit of the "modern times" is the transformation of freedom of thought into freedom of the will. Modernity is the field for the development of "self-creating" people. Thus, pedagogy must adopt the principle that the goal of learning is the cultivation of the free personality that is self-consciously, self-determining. Humanists and realists were only concerned with disseminating knowledge as a possession of the individual, and, at best, sought to make students into free thinkers. They sought to cultivate an internal freedom. However, outwardly, students remain slaves subject to the control of prevailing cultural norms and political dynamics. The notion of human development offered by modern education, and the theories reflecting it, is one-sided and partial. External freedom, or freedom of the will, is also essential for the cultivation of free, self-creating people. The opportunity to cultivate both internal and external freedom arises only in universal education, where Stirner said we find the true equality of free people. Equality and freedom cannot be alienated. Only in freedom can one find equality. For Stirner, the opposition between the humanists and the realists is superseded by the conflict between the "moralists," who seek to impose convictions and beliefs upon students, and the "personalists," who want the abolition of non-voluntary learning and the rise of the self-assured will. In Stirner's formulation, knowledge must "dissolve," rise again as "will," and establish itself anew as the free, self-creating person.[13]

RACE, MODERNITY, AND THE UNIQUE EGO

Stirner made a break with a number of points he first articulated in *The False Principle of Our Education*, but it is clear that his magnum opus, *The Ego and Its Own*, continued, developed, and expanded upon the emphases on freedom of the will, personal autonomy, and the unique ego that appeared in his early essay. However, other topics, themes, and methodologies appeared in *The Ego and Its Own* that assisted Stirner in the creation of his philosophy of the "Unique One and Its Property." Among other things, Stirner confronts and articulates the meaning and problems of race and modernity. While he can be criticized for adopting a dubious view of sociohistorical development popular at the time, Stirner proves himself to be an insightful critic of ideological social control in the ancient world and the modern, as well as an enemy of historicist conceptions of race and racial explanations of thought and behavior.

Stirner develops and refines his Hegelian methodology in *The Ego and Its Own* by opening his analysis with a section that contrasts the culture and ideology of "the ancients and the moderns." In this discussion, he outlines the stages of historical development that were used by a number of historians and philosophers at the time to understand the fundamental dynamics of sociocultural development. It was common practice at the time to understand history as a series of stages based on the *spirit* or culture and ideology of a city-state, nation, or continent, such as Rome, Greece, China, and Africa. In some cases, particularly those pertaining to Africa and Asia, a stage in historical development was associated with a racial or cultural group. The presumed sociocultural characteristics of many ethnic and cultural groups, including Jews, Moors, Turks, Greeks, Germans, and French were also frequently discussed in this literature.[14]

In the case of the Hegelians of both the right and the left, as well as the early socialists and communists, the discussion of the stages of historical process was intended to elevate, or it had the effect of elevating, the present over the past. Some of these formulations drew parallels between societal development and individual development, following social evolution from childhood to maturity. Or, they argued that one historical period positioned a particular social class for societal leadership and control. These schemas of historical change frequently entailed notions that one historical period was superior to its predecessors. A hierarchy of historical periods was either explicitly stated or implicit in the analysis.

When race was attached to a particular schema, racial superiority became an explicit or implicit feature of this type of analysis. Thus, this type of sociohistorical analysis can and should be criticized as racist. In Stirner's case, it is important to bear in mind that his discussion is critical of both the ancients and the moderns, and suspicious of the facts and the historical method. At the outset, he says that he employed this method to help articulate his critique of "fixed ideas" and identify the unique ego. It is difficult to find in his discussion any assertion or implication that one race, culture or historical period is superior to another, although some of his generalizations about cultures or nations are odd from a modern standpoint. Furthermore, his discussion of the ancients and the moderns leads to ideas that are helpful in the struggle against racism as they promote a critical understanding of the struggle of the individual against cultural practices in all historical periods, the central idea of dialectical egoism.

Stirner draws much of his discussion of historical process from Hegel's *Lectures on the Philosophy of the World* and *The Philosophy of History*, which were originally delivered and published during the 1820s. He also draws from the writings of other scholars writing in this period.[15] The intent and outcome of his discussion of the ancients and the moderns is not to simply reproduce existing scholarly formulations of sociohistorical development. Instead, Stirner is much more interested in developing a critique of this type of analysis and the image that "moderns" have of themselves as spiritually, culturally, and ideologically superior to the "ancients." The primary purpose of Stirner's discussion of historical process is to set the stage for his critique of modernity, especially Feuerbach's modernist deification of "Man" or "Humanity," and to articulate his alternative concepts of dialectical egoism, which include self-ownership and the unique individual. Stirner does not validate or sanctify one culture or historical period over others. Instead, he critiques each as their characteristics and practices depart from the notion of the individual who is free both internally and externally. He is unrelenting in his attack, but he does not discriminate. All cultures, nations and historical periods are subject to his critique of fixed ideas and social processes that alienate the individual from self. His method is the obverse of multiculturalism. Rather than validating all cultural forms, he critiques the fixed ideas of all as antithetical to the unique ego.

The historical schematic that Stirner discusses in the first part of *The Ego and Its Own* includes several broad, pre-Christian historical periods describing the ancients. He begins his discussion with the disclaimer that he does not believe that the writings about any "hierarchy" in historical development is either thorough or sound. However, he describes a schema of the historical development of human thought because it "may contribute towards making the rest clear." Stirner says very little about the cultural dynamics of the early period of antiquity, except that it represents the preeminence of the cultures of Egypt and North Africa. The early period represented a time of dependence of humans on nature and the collectivity, particularly in spirit, culture, and ideology. Stirner is particularly interested in the differentiation of the "me" and the "not-me," or how the sense of self developed historically as an entity autonomous from God and the community. In the initial period of human development, the value of "me" is diminished as the "not-me" of nature and the objective world is too indomitable and immovable to be consumed and absorbed by "me."[16] Thus, individuals are profoundly dependent on the external world, including nature and the social collectivity, both materially and symbolically. The autonomy and resistance of individuals to culture, society, and the state is difficult.

As Stirner's analysis shifted to later periods of antiquity, including the ascendance of the Greek, Roman, Chinese, and Asiatic cultures, he focused on the permanence or immovability of social patterns of thought and behavior. Individuals in these cultures begin to differentiate themselves from others and nature, but societal and cultural mechanisms promoted and enforced habit and routine behaviors. In the later periods of pre-Christianity, for example, conformity and compliance are the critical cultural values and, thus, the primary expectations for individual behavior. In the realms of religion, culture, and ideology, this historical period elevated "moral habituation" above innovation and change. Moral habituation has many functions for society and individuals, but paramount among these is the spiritual function of validating their existence by a supreme being and permitting the person's entry into heaven upon death. Stirner argues that one of the major accomplishments of this historical period is the creation of the concept of heaven that provides the individual in a coercive sociocultural environments with a realm in which "nothing alien regulates and rules him any longer." The person's abnegation by society, alienation from others, and combat against the world ends in heaven. Heaven is the place of the free enjoyment of the self. Thus, Stirner maintains that social and personal change within the latter period of antiquity remained only reformatory and ameliorative, not destructive, consuming or annihilating of prevailing societal and cultural patterns. As he puts it, "[t]he substance, the object, remains," as human beings now have a heaven or a world of spirits, ghosts and specters to find solace and fulfillment.

What distinguishes the world of antiquity from modernity is that, while the former generated and made peace with the existence of spiritual beings, the latter wrestled to understand them. The ancients built the heavens. They do not storm the heavens or challenge the basic constructs inherent in religion, culture, and ideology. The ethic of the modern period is innovation and change or "to wreck all customs in order to put new and better customs in their place."[17] Thus, the moderns are preoccupied with "storming the heavens" and overthrowing old regimes, beliefs, and norms only to install new regimes, beliefs, and norms. Hence, as modernity developed, the Jews overthrew the heaven and gods of the Greeks, the Christians overthrew the supreme being and heaven of the Jews, and the Protestants overthrew the heaven of the Catholics. Each sought to create a realm of freedom, at least in spirit. But Stirner alleges that each only improved and reformed the belief system that already existed: a precept or generalized concept of a supreme being and a heaven that provides refuge from alienation and domination. In the modernist revolutions of religion and philosophy, humans express their enmity to the supreme being and heaven only to reconstruct them. Stirner challenges this tendency by saying, when will humans at last really find themselves? When will they finally annihilate the supreme being and heaven? When will the search for the "immortality of the soul" change to the "mortality of the mind?"[18]

Stirner does not conclude his critique of modernism with his comments on religion. Instead, he extends his critique into a discussion of speculative or critical philosophy, which is clearly directed at Hegel, the Young Hegelians, and, especially, Feuerbach. The speculative philosophy of Hegel, the Young Hegelians, and Feuerbach overthrew the heaven of Protestantism in the effort to create a modernist "heaven on earth," but Stirner was as much of an opponent of this philosophic "realm of spirit" as those created by the ancients in their religions. Among the moderns, both the supreme being and the realm of spirits and ghosts, find their "right standing" in the critical or speculative philosophy of Hegel and Feuerbach. In philosophy, the "freedom of the spirit" and "immortality of the mind" exist in the realm of universal and absolute thoughts, concepts, and ideas, which were taken as the "true reality."[19]

Stirner concludes his discussion of the ancients and the moderns with the observation that humans will never really vanquish shamanism and free themselves from a world inhabited by spooks and ghosts until they reject not only the belief in ghosts or spirits, but also the belief in "spirit" or the prevailing ideas embedded in culture that mediate and regulate the thoughts and behaviors of individuals. This means that it is as important to critique the abstract concepts in the speculative philosophy of Hegel, the Young Hegelians, and Feuerbach as it was to critique the religious and cultural concepts of the ancients. Feuerbach's concept of "Man" or "Humanity" was elevated as the new supreme being governing society, culture, and ideology, with the concomitant idea of fixing eternal and absolute moral laws to serve the new supreme being that no one would ever challenge.

For Stirner, these fixed ideas are as much of a threat to the individual's internal and external freedom as the concepts of "gods" and "heaven" found among the ancients. The Stirnerite dialectical egoist critique of antiquity and modernity provides a vantage point from which all cultures can be challenged. Stirner does not rest with the negative dialectic he formulated in his discussion of the differences between the ancients and the moderns. His discussion in *The Ego and Its Own* moves from this historical account of the rise of the religious, cultural, and ideological concepts of the modernist philosophers to a critique of their politics and his articulation of self-ownership and the unique individual.

THE POLITICAL MEANING OF EGOISM

Stirner's philosophy in *The Ego and Its Own* emerged from the collapse of idealist thought in the philosophy of Hegel, Feuerbach, and the Young Hegelians. Stirner believed that a "higher presupposition" emerged from the conflict between materialism and idealism, which is his dialectical egoism. For Stirner, the key to individuality is the realization that interests and needs are as unique as the person and that society, culture, and the state tend to militate against the individual. Ultimately, it is up to the individual to discover and to fight for what and who he or she is. There is no moral or ideological reference point outside the reality and values chosen by the individual or the Unique One. Hence, Stirner's discussions of race and ethnicity in *The Ego and Its Own* are primarily vehicles for demonstrating that racial and ethnic identities are tools that enable the state and society to control behavior, and that also enable culture to control thought. Stirner's concept of "ownness" or "property" is an oppositional concept that enables and encourages individuals to resist values, beliefs, and identities that the state, society and culture attempt to impose on persons. From Stirner's point of view, the "Ego" or "Unique One" potentially stands outside of, or exists in opposition to, the state and society precisely because of the person's ability to assert ownership over who and what they are. Thus, Stirner's concept of ownership or "ownness" has a clear relationship with the notions of individual freedom and autonomy, just as it entails elements of psychological and ethical egoism. However, "ownness" cannot be reduced to any of them. Certainly, Stirner's concepts of freedom, identity, and reality are rooted in the notion of "ownness," which can be understood as self-conscious self-determination.

The Ego and Its Own is a sharp attack on religion, political authority, and the philosophies of Stirner's contemporaries, especially those who had socialist, communist, or humanist orientations. His attack on the systematic philosophies and religions prevailing during his life entails an opposition to all moral absolutes and a rejection of abstract and generalized philosophies of all types. The human individual is the center of his analysis. In rejecting all of the fixed ideas or artificial constructions of myth, philosophy, and culture, Stirner seeks to identify the elemental self or the "unique one." He argues in *The Ego and Its Own* that we can have certain knowledge only of the unique individual. Moreover, the uniqueness of the individual is the quality that each must cultivate to provide meaning for his or her life. The reality and value of all fixed ideas or generalized concepts, such as "God," "Humanity," "Man," "Class Consciousness," "Social Justice," and "Race Awareness," whether they are found in religion, philosophy, culture, or politics, must be rejected. Politically, this means that the individual owes no obligation to external entities or concepts, including nations, states, classes, races, or ethnic groups. All religious, political, and cultural constructs that seek to impose or promote a commonness or collective identity, are false, irrational, and constraining specters that lack a defensible meaning in the material world. The task of the "unique one" is to resist all efforts to create and impose such specters.

As a student of Hegel, Stirner is acutely aware of both the internal and external dimensions of human existence and freedom. He clearly understands the nature and importance of what philosophers call "negative freedom," a condition in which an individual is rid of external controls or where there is an absence of coercion. But Stirner is much more concerned with "ownness" or the notion that the person possesses or has the ability to obtain those things related to a fulfilling life, especially the ability to be one's own master in thought and behavior. The emphasis on internal or positive freedom is central to Stirner's concept of "ownness." "I am free of what I am rid of, owner of what I have in my power or what I control. I am at all times and under all circumstances, my own, if I know how to possess myself."[20] Ownness is therefore something related to but different from freedom. For Stirner, ownness surpasses freedom, or it at least it surpasses the negative form of freedom." Freedom is usually an "ideal" or a "specter" in political discourse, but "ownness is my whole being and existence, it is I myself."[21] Ownness, therefore, precedes negative freedom as both a value and reality. Ownness, not freedom, is the mover of human action. Speaking of Feuerbach and his atheistic colleagues, Stirner says "it was by this egoism, this ownness, that they got rid of the old world of gods and became free from it. Ownness created a new freedom; for ownness is the creator of everything."[22] Thus, individuals should not only have negative freedom, that is, be free of external constraints, they should be owners or "possess" themselves.

For Stirner, persons who are set free politically or culturally by external actors are really unfree people cloaked in the garment of freedom. Hence, emancipated Jews are nothing different, changed, or improved in themselves. They are only "relieved" as Jews. Emancipated or not, a Jew remains a Jew. That is, they are defined by an artificial cultural category. Persons who are not self-freed are only emancipated. They experience only the negative dimensions of freedom. Similarly, the Protestant state can emancipate Catholics, but unless the individuals make themselves free, they remain simply Catholics. The democratic state can emancipate slaves, but unless slaves make themselves free, they remain only emancipated slaves.[23] The task of the unique one is to experience positive freedom by "possessing self," asserting uniqueness and independence from cultural constructs and societal constraints.

Just as Stirner's concept of ownness, or his egoism, cannot be reduced to negative freedom, it also cannot be reduced to "selfishness" or to psychological or ethical egoism. It is a dialectical egoism, or an egoism that is continually challenged and continually emergent in interaction and conflict with culture, self, and others. Certainly, Stirner's egoist or unique one looks to objects and to others to see if they are any use to him or her as a sensual being. Yet, the individual's sensuality is not the entirety of his or her "ownness." The dialectical egoist is more than a sensual being. When the individual is "given up to sensuality," she or he is not in his or her own. The individual who follows his or her own sensuality, is not self-determining. The individual is in his or her "own" only when the "master of self" or fully self-consciously self-determining, and not when mastered by sensuality or by anything else external to the person's self-conscious self-determination. Thus, while Stirner's concept of ownness is "selfish," it cannot be equated with the form of selfishness concerned with sensuality or material things. The concept of ownness entails much more than sensuality or acquisition; in fact, forms of sensuality and acquisition may contradict "ownness." The dictum that "greed is good" is subordinate to self-ownership in Stirner's egoism.

"Ownness" has no alien, external standard. Stirner does not view it as a fixed idea like God or humanity. It is only intended to be a description of the act of ownership by the person. In sharp contrast to Rand, Stirner would likely ridicule the notion that selfishness is a virtue since "virtue" conjures images of external and fixed strictures on individual thought and behavior.

Stirner argues that his concept of dialectical egoism and the notion of humanity or "humanness" must be equated. However, culture, the state, and the speculative philosophy of Hegel, Feuerbach, and the Young Hegelians elevated the species above the individual making this equation impossible. In the collectivist formulations of these philosophers, the individual can only lift self above his or her individuality, and not above scripture, law, and custom, or the "positive ordinances" of the species. But, for Stirner, the species is nothing but an abstraction, a fixed idea. Life means that individuals cannot remain what they are. They must continually strive to lift themselves above "their individuality," or their existence at any one point in time and space. The cultural, political, and ideological strictures that elevate the species above the individual are, in fact, a form of death in that the individual's innovation, creativity, and survival skills are subordinated to those of the species. "Man" is an ideal. "Humanity" is an ideal. "White" is an ideal. "The African American Man" is an ideal. The "Latina" is an ideal. But to be an individual is not to realize the ideal of "man," "humanity," or any other such abstraction; it is simply to live and appropriate oneself as a unique individual. The individual's task is not to realize the "essence" of man, humanity, a race, or a culture, but to live as a self-conscious, self-determining person. The individual, for Stirner, *is* the species and, as such, is without norm, without law, and without model. All social and cultural categories, including racial and cultural identities, are, thus, abstractions irreducible to the material reality of the real, living individual.[24]

Some of Stirner's detractors accuse him of solipsism, or denying the reality or existence of external forces, in his posture toward the objective world.[25] This is clearly not the case. Again, as a student of Hegel, Stirner understood that the individual thinks and acts within a world that is both external and constraining on individuals. Stirner's fight was not with the *reality* of the external, but its *legitimacy*. He says that it is absurd to argue that there are no external forces that are more powerful than the might of the individual. What matters is the attitude and action that the person takes toward them. While religion, culture, and ideology teach and encourage individuals to reconcile and humble themselves with the external world, Stirner declares that his dialectical egoism is the enemy of every "higher power" or "supreme being."[26]

Stirner's critique is focused on the philosophy of Hegel, Feuerbach, and the Young Hegelians that elevated "Man" to the status of God or the new supreme being, and also elevated the fear of Man to the place of the old fear of God. Ownness or self-conscious self-determination requires that the individual know self as unique. Every supreme being or higher essence above the individual undermines the individual's ownness, might, and self-determination. As long as individuals believe and act on the notion that fixed ideas and "essences" are superior, external, and unalterably constraining on them, or that their task in life is to fulfill an external ideal, they are not egoists or owners. But as individuals no longer serve any ideal or any "higher essence" or "supreme being," they no longer serve any other person either, but are instead their own masters. Ownness refers to an ability on the part of the individual to behave out of truly free or uncoerced choices. When individuals serve themselves in fact, in being, and in consciousness, they are "unique" or "egoists."

THE INDIVIDUAL, SOCIETY, AND THE STATE

Stirner's image of the unique individual who is defined by his or her willed or chosen identity and relations, which constitute his or her property or ownness, suggests the possibility of only very tenuous and precarious forms of social relationships. Stirner is very critical of society, which functions to impose false and irrational beliefs and identities upon individuals. Society subjects individuals to a plethora of constraints that undermine the person's free choice. In concert with many other social theorists, Stirner thus posited a fundamental conflict and opposition between society and the individual. But unlike the social contract theories of Thomas Hobbes, John Locke, and Jean-Jacques Rousseau, Stirner believes that the original state of nature is not an individualistic "bellum omnium contra omnia," but a social existence in which both society and culture predate the birth of the person. "Society is our state of nature." Society also arises through the interaction of individuals, but as relationships and organizations become social institutions with permanent authority structures and patterned relationships and roles, it exists only as a "fixed idea" in which the voluntary union of individuals comes to a "standstill" or degenerates into a "fixidity."[27] Human beings are thus born into a society; they really do not "enter" into it as an equal partner with interactions governed by contracts or norms of reciprocity. Instead, the relationship between the individual and society is a conflict from the beginning. Stirner's primary objection to society is not so much its constraints on liberty, but the efforts by society to appropriate the individual's "ownness" or property. "And ownness is precisely what every society has designs on, precisely what is to succumb to its power."[28]

Thus, Stirner differentiates between those social relationships or organizations that individuals are born into or coerced into and those that they join voluntarily. This distinction provides an opening for him to argue that the egoist or the unique one is not necessarily the insolated, nihilistic misanthrope that some of his harshest critics describe.[29] In opposition to the type of social bond that is eternally external and constraining upon the individual, Stirner proposes the Union of Egoists, which may constrain the liberty of individuals, but is primarily characterized by ownness or the self-ownership of the individuals who belong to it. Whereas society is preexisting and predetermining, the Union of Egoists is the work of its participants; it is their product. The "Union of Egoists" is Stirner's concept of a willed social relationship which is continuously created and renewed by all who own and support it through acts of will.

The Union of Egoists implies that all parties participate in it through a conscious egoism. Ultimately, the most important relationship in this Union of

Egoists is the relationship of the individual to self. Stirner argues that the dialectical egoist participating in a Union of Egoists dissolves society and all coercive relationships by interpreting self as the subject of all of his or her valuing relationships. The relationship of the individual to self, participating in the Union of Egoists, is a "creative nothingness" in which I meet myself as a subject and appropriate and consume myself as my own, for my own enjoyment.

> I, the egoist, have not at heart the welfare of this "human society." I sacrifice nothing to it. I only utilize it; but to be able to utilize it completely I transform it rather into my property and my creature; that is, I annihilate it, and form in its place the Union of Egoists.[30]

Stirner's view of self-ownership structures his understanding and critique of society and social relationships. It also profoundly shapes his view of the state, political parties, and political ideologies. In a number of respects, Stirner's critique of the state and politics is consistent with and, in fact, influenced individualist anarchism in the late nineteenth century. However, Stirner's critique is deeper than the anarchistic opposition between the state and liberty in important respects because of his focus on the state's opposition to ownness and its need to promote fixed ideas.

In opposition to the Union of Egoists, which is founded on voluntary participation and free choice, the state is the enemy and murderer of ownness. "The state and I are enemies."[31] The state demonstrates its enmity and hostility to the egoist by demanding that the person realize a fixed idea of what it means to be human or a citizen in thought and behavior. The human individual within the state is an abstraction, a spirit, and an abstracted essence. The state imposes a duty to do nothing that conflicts with the interests and permanence of the state and to do everything that supports the interests and permanence of the state. The state does not allow individuals to be egoists but only good citizens. It expects humility, respect and, ultimately, impotence before its power and authority. It necessarily entails lordship and bondage. Regardless of its form, the state negates ownness or the will of the individual and it elevates collective identities and interests. There is no possibility of reconciling the egoist and the state since the egoist seeks to annihilate or dissolve the state, while the state seeks to annihilate or dissolve the egoist.

It is significant that Stirner developed his critique of state power in the historical context of the liberal, democratic, and socialist revolutions of the eighteenth and nineteenth centuries, especially since these revolutions all promised to extend human rights and to ensure the full participation of each individual in the political process. Each promised to overcome alienation.

Stirner is a critic of these revolutions, as well as the old regimes they de-stroyed, because they ensured the return of old forms of alienation and re-pression in their attempt to overcome them. Prefiguring Marx, Stirner made the distinction between the bourgeois and the citizen, but he used it to arrive at completely opposite conclusions from the socialists and communists. In *The Ego and Its Own*, Stirner says that it is not the individual or the real per-son who has been liberated by revolution, but only the citizen as a *species*, the political individual. In the French Revolution, for example, it was not the in-dividual who was active as a world-historical figure; only the nation-state of France.[32]

For Stirner, the democracy of the liberal and socialist revolutions is the modern political expression of alienation and repression. Even though liber-alism and socialism entailed philosophies of rights and freedoms, and a re-jection of tyranny and religious mystification, they reconstructed political domination in new forms. The democratic revolutions, for example, freed in-dividuals from the caprice and arbitrary rule of despots, replacing despotism with laws and rational rules that allow individuals access to the state. How-ever, democratic liberalism also strengthens the state's power over individu-als. Political freedom in the democratic republic means that the state has more freedom and power to subjugate individuals. It has a greater ability to anni-hilate and dissolve the egoist.

The socialist revolutions and, later, the communist revolutions elevated "society" as the new fixed idea and the agency of domination. But society is an ideological construct that alienates and dominates people. Thus, the en-forced equality of socialist rule promotes society as the new supreme being demanding the sacrifice of the person's thoughts, loyalties, and resources. The formation of collective social identities is no less oppressive than the freedom of the liberal state or the despotism of predemocratic political struc-tures. This point is the center of the conflict between Stirner and the Marxists who exalt revolution as the political means of achieving collectivist and sta-tist political goals. Stirner argues that societies and communities are abstract fixed ideas that have no essence and negate ownness and the will of the indi-vidual. All legitimate forms of community, union, and association in Stirner's dialectical egoism result from or are the product of the thoughts and behav-iors of individual egoists. They are deliberate constructions by egoists.[33] Thus, the individual becomes a political subject only through opposition to and struggle against collectivities. For Marx, the individual only becomes a political subject and potentially free only as a proletarian uniting with other proletarians within an authoritarian political party to seize state power and to use its technologies of violence and propaganda to suppress political opposi-tion. For Marx, and the socialists and communists, individuals have no political meaning. They become significant actors only as members of a disciplined, authoritarian collectivity.

Stirner's critique of democratic liberalism, socialism, and communism extends to his views on revolution, rebellion, and change. Fundamental to his perspective on political organization and change is the argument that revolution and rebellion are vastly different concepts; revolution contradicts the notion of ownness and the aspirations of the egoist, while rebellion or insurrection is the appropriate form of political expression for the unique one. Revolution aims at the overturning of social and political conditions or the transformation of existing social and political conditions. It involves the coordinated activities of thousands of people acting through political organizations to achieve goals that are fixed in a philosophy of an improved condition of society. Revolution is therefore a political and social act that seeks the rearrangement of society. Designing and fighting over the appropriate constitution for the transformed society occupies the time and talents of revolutionaries, but not that of the egoist.

Rebellion or insurrection also produces the transformation of established social conditions but differs from revolution in that it does not start with that intent. Transformation is not the intention but rather an unavoidable consequence of rebellion, which begins with the discontent of people with themselves. While revolution leads to new arrangements, rebellion leads us "no longer to let ourselves be arranged, but to arrange ourselves."[34] It is not really a fight to replace the established order, since, if it spreads, rebellion ensures that the established order collapses on its own. The objective of rebellion or insurrection is the elevation of the individual above the established order since purposes and deeds are not political nor social, but egoistic. Rebellion is a "standing up" to the state and a "standing with" others who also rebel against the power and authority of the state. Revolution requires the individual to make arrangements for the new social order; rebellion demands that the individual rise up or exalt self. Instead of working to design and implement the ideal political formation, the insurgent strives to become "constitutionless." In rebellion, the individual asserts ownership and discovers uniqueness and his or her own property. "I no longer humble myself before any power, and I recognize that all powers are only my power. All powers that dominate me I then reduce to serving me."[35]

In *The Ego and its Own*, Stirner argues that all political philosophies and formations are artificial constructions. Without foundation in the material world, they become prisons for the mind and the will. They conceal from the individual the existence of his or her own infinite creative powers. All systems and systemizing tendencies must be resisted, and through that resistance, destroyed. The political project of dialectical egoism is not the replacement of one sociopolitical order with another, but the rebellion of individuals against each of them. Only in rebellion against *systems as systems* can individuals evade the submission inherent in idolatry and authority and, thereby, become masters of themselves.[36]

STIRNER AND THE EPISTEMOLOGICAL
BREAK WITH MULTICULTURALISM

The Ego and Its Own generated considerable interest at the time of its publication, mostly among the left Hegelians and other philosophers and activists who were searching for political and philosophic alternatives to the monarchies and the democratic capitalist nations emerging in Europe at the time. With his death in 1856, Stirner was not able to respond to his most important historical critics: the Marxists and the Christians. Stirner influenced two of the philosophic giants of the nineteenth century—Marx and Nietzsche— whose encounters with the philosopher of the "unique one" forced crises in their own thought and generated an "epistemological break" with their early writings.

Stirner's thought may also contribute to an epistemological break with the multiculturalist vision of the struggle against racism. Stirner's dialectical egoism includes at least three important points of criticism of multiculturalism. First, Stirner's attack on "fixed ideas" suggests not only a critique of racism, which is a system of fixed, stereotypical generalizations about people who share similar physical or cultural characteristics, but also a critique of multiculturalism. Stirner's dialectical egoism undermines the notion of validating all cultures, a critical element of multicultural thought. Racism is founded on and evolves from the process by which thought about people is externalized and reified into fixed ideas, thereby structuring behavior and alienating individuals from each other and themselves. The same critique can and should be directed toward multicultural thought, which elevates culture to the status of a fixed idea or a supreme being. In Stirner's thought, "race" and "culture" are fixed ideas or specters that must be dissolved by the egoist in favor of the Union of Egoists.

Second, Stirner's concept of "ownness" or "property" is the core concept of resistance to racism. The notion of ownness means that individuals master themselves, appropriate their own lives, determine their own behavior, and chart their own future. The struggle against racism is an effort on the part of individuals to assert ownership over their beings and their lives. Racism and racist social formations, to greater or lesser degrees, deprive individuals of these desiderata. It is important, then, that theories and movements that oppose racism not deprive individuals of self-ownership. Instead, oppositional theories and movements should nurture and enhance self-ownership. Ownness is devastating to racism and to the fundamental notion of multiculturalism, in which race and ethnicity are assigned primacy in structuring human behavior and experience. Whatever its contributions, multiculturalism cannot generate the negative freedom resulting from the abolition of racism because the positive freedom of ownness or individual self-ownership is antithetical to the core idea that race and ethnicity structure interaction, behavior and experiences. In Stirner's view, racism falls of its own accord as individuals appropriate their own lives and develop the "Union of Egoists."

Third, the critique of the state and revolution in Stirner's thought provides another area where dialectical egoism offers an epistemological break with multiculturalism. The anarchist or antistatist aspects of Stirner's thought directly contradict the statism of both racism and multiculturalism. Multiculturalists are as enthusiastic as racists about the acquisition of state power, as well as its application to fulfill the social agenda of one group over others. Thus, multiculturalists are eager to put like-minded people in positions of power and authority in the state, the corporation, and other complex organizations. They are eager to promote and implement laws, public policies, and social programs that they believe fulfill the multiculturalist agenda. Stirner is opposed to the state and efforts to apply state power because political processes inherently negate the individual's self-ownership. Ownness, not state power, is the telos of dialectical egoism. The dialectical egoist critique of racism focuses on the creation and development of individuals who master their own lives, beings, and futures.

Stirner's dialectical egoism makes an important contribution to the individualist understanding of race and culture. But Stirner has a somewhat contradictory relationship with the other individualist thinkers included in this volume, even though all share an opposition to racism and a strong support of individualism. While there are apparent similarities in their views about religion, the individual, and the state, Ayn Rand and Max Stirner would not likely enjoy each other's company. Rand founded her Objectivism and individualism on a set of philosophic precepts and moral strictures that Stirner would likely reject as "fixed ideas." Stirner would likely ridicule the notion that selfishness is a "virtue." Stirner's concept of ownness directly contradicts Rand's notion that individualism is a moral necessity for human beings to live as human beings.

Stirner is also a likely philosophic antagonist of Robert Nozik and the libertarians who argue for a minimalist state, although all celebrate the notion of self-ownership and are antistatist to some degree. Stirner would never accept the libertarian notion of rights and entitlement as the foundation of the state, property, and individuality. In Stirner's view, these must be taken by the individual. The individual must resist society to assert individuality and reveal ownership. These cannot be not conferred on an individual by a system of laws based on a fictional social contract occurring sometime in antiquity.

Stirner's dialectical egoism also appears to conflict with the concept of natural law and natural right as the basis for the anarchist social orders proposed by Murray Rothbard, Benjamin Tucker, and Lysander Spooner. Despite the influence Stirner had on Tucker and the enthusiasm of both for voluntary social organization, the notion of natural right and law assumes a preferred social and political order that predates individuals, a clear conflict with Stirner's critique of society as an external and constraining entity. Finally, although there has been much discussion about the supposed philosophic connection between Stirner and Friedrich Nietzsche, Stirner would absolutely reject the notion of the Superman as another supreme being and "fixed idea" that robs individuals of their ownness.[37]

While Stirner himself never had a direct personal influence on individualist, anarchist, or libertarian social movements, his philosophy enjoyed at least two major revivals of interest in his work. The first occurred around the beginning of the twentieth century and the second during the 1970s. However, the search for concepts and ideas that can help work through the racial and ethnic antagonism and alienation that human beings confront today needs a similar "epistemological break." The "false principle" Stirner's work illuminates is the notion that the collectivist ideology of multiculturalism, with its uncritical validation of fixed cultural forms, is the only constructive response to racism. Stirner's uncompromising critique of alienated thought, fixed ideas, and collectivized social environments is an enormously valuable tool in rethinking the struggle against racism and the future of the concept of race.

NOTES

1. Søren Kierkegaard, *The Concept of Dread* (1844; Princeton, NJ: Princeton University Press, 1957); Karl Marx, *Economic and Philosophic Manuscripts of 1844* (Moscow: Foreign Languages Publishing House, 1961); Max Stirner, *The Ego and Its Own* (1844; Cambridge: Cambridge University Press, 1995). See R. W. K. Paterson, *The Nihilistic Egoist Max Stirner* (London: Oxford University Press, 1971) for a commentary on the original translation *The Ego and Its Own*. For the sparse information available about Stirner's life, see John Henry Mackay, *Max Stirner: His Life and Work* (1910; Concord, CA: Preemptory Publications, 2005). For an interesting fictionalized account of a Stirnerite perspective in political discussions with socialist and communist-oriented anarchists, see Mackay's *The Anarchists: A Picture of Civilization at the Close of the Nineteenth Century* (1910; Brooklyn, NY: Autonomedia, 1999).

2. Ludwig Feuerbach, *The Essence of Christianity* (1841; New York: Harper, 1957).

3. Karl Marx and Friedrich Engels, *The German Ideology* (1933; New York: International Publishers, 1972). The discussion of Stirner by Marx and Engels is interesting for what it reveals about the development of Marx's thought. It is not a particularly insightful study of Stirner. It contains significant factual errors, including the preposterous argument that Stirner had a rapprochement with the proto-anarchist socialist, Pierre-Joseph Proudhon that led to Mikhail Bakunin's communist form of anarchist opposition to Marxism. See Lawrence Stepelevich, "Karl Marx and Max Stirner," *Political Theory* 3, no. 2 (May 1975): 159–79.

4. Lawrence Stepelevich, "Max Stirner as Hegelian," *Journal of the History of Ideas* 46, no. 4 (October–December 1985): 597–614. Also see Stepelevich's essays "The Revival of Max Stirner," *Journal of the History of Ideas* 35, no. 2 (April–June 1974): 323–28 and "Max Stirner and Ludwig Feuerbach," *Journal of the History of Ideas* 39, no. 4 (July–September 1978): 451–63.

5. See Stepelevich, "Max Stirner as Hegelian," 614. Also see G. W. F. Hegel, *The Phenomenology of Sprit* (1807; London: Oxford University Press, 1977), which ends with a chapter entitled, "Absolute Knowing," and *The Science of Logic* (1812; Amherst, NY: Humanities Press, 1969), which ends with the chapter on "The Absolute Idea." *The Ego and Its Own* concludes with Stirner's discussion of "The Unique One."

6. Max Stirner, *The False Principle of Our Education, Or Humanism and Realism* (1842; Colorado Springs: Ralph Myles, 1967).

7. Stirner, *False Principle*, 12–13, 21. Jerome Tucille reports in his book, *It Usually Begins with Ayn Rand* (San Francisco: Fox and Wilkes, 1972), that Stirner has been called "Ayn Rand in a bad mood" because of his uncompromising individualism and aggressive form of writing. However, Stirner's writings are laced with references to self-enjoyment just as Rand is concerned with individuals living fulfilling lives. Stirner also displays considerable humor, some of which is acerbic. Humor of any type, acerbic or otherwise, appears seldom in Rand's writings.

8. Stirner, *False Principle*, 12.

9. Stirner, *False Principle*, 15.

10. Stirner, *False Principle*, 15–16.

11. Stirner, *False Principle*, 24.

12. Stirner, *False Principle*, 25.

13. Stirner, *False Principle*, 28.

14. David Leopold, "Introduction," in Max Stirner, *The Ego and Its Own* (Cambridge: Cambridge University Press, 1995), xi–xxxv.

15. G. W. F. Hegel, *The Philosophy of History* (New York: Dover Publications, 1956); G. W. F. Hegel, *Lectures on the History of Philosophy*, vol. 3 (Berkeley: University of California Press, 1990). Also see Leopold, "Introduction," xiii–xvi.

16. Stirner, *The Ego and Its Own*, 63.

17. Stirner, *The Ego and Its Own*, 65.

18. Stirner, *The Ego and Its Own*, 64.

19. Stirner, *The Ego and Its Own*, 66.

20. Stirner, *The Ego and Its Own*, 142. Also see John P. Clark, *Max Stirner's Egoism* (London: Freedom Press, 1976), 64–69.

21. Stirner, *The Ego and Its Own*, 143.

22. Stirner, *The Ego and Its Own*, 150.

23. Stirner, *The Ego and Its Own*, 152.

24. Stirner, *The Ego and Its Own*, 163.

25. Paterson, *The Nihilistic Egoist*. Paterson's work was the first English book-length discussion of Stirner's thought. Paterson accuses Stirner of many philosophic crimes, including nihilism, total atheism, total egoism, and solipsism. For more balanced scholarly treatments of Stirner, see Clark, *Max Stirner's Egoism* and Stepelevich, "Max Stirner as Hegelian."

26. Stirner, *The Ego and Its Own*, 165.

27. Stirner, *The Ego and Its Own*, 271.

28. Stirner, *The Ego and Its Own*, 271.

29. In addition to the tiresome commentary by Marx and Engels in *The German Ideology*, other writers who are extremely critical of Stirner on this point include Albert Camus, *The Rebel: An Essay on Man in Revolt* (New York: Vintage Books, 1956); Karl Löwith, *From Hegel to Nietzsche: The Revolution in Nineteenth Century Thought* (New York: Columbia University Press, 1964); and George Woodcock, *Anarchism: A History of Libertarian Ideas and Movements* (Cleveland: Meridian Books, 1962). Paterson's, *The Nihilistic Egoist*, also pursues this type of critique of Stirner.

30. Stirner, *The Ego and Its Own*, 161.

31. Stirner, *The Ego and Its Own*, 161.

32. Stirner, *The Ego and Its Own*, 99.

33. Saul Newman, "Specters of the Uncanny: The Return of the Repressed," *Telos* 124 (Summer 2002): 115–30.

34. Stirner, *The Ego and Its Own*, 280.

35. Stirner, *The Ego and Its Own*, 282.

36. Isaiah Berlin, *Karl Marx: His Life and Environment* (Oxford: Oxford University Press, 1939), 106.

37. For a positive discussion of the impact of Stirner on Tucker and individualist anarchism in the United States, see James J. Martin, *Men Against the State: The Expositors of Individualist Anarchism in America, 1827–1908* (Colorado Springs: Ralph Myles Publisher, Inc., 1970). Paterson's book, *The Nihilistic Egoist Max Stirner*, includes a lengthy discussion of the presumed influence of Stirner on Nietzsche, but concludes that Nietzsche's philosophy of the Superman cannot be reconciled with Stirner's philosophy of the unique ego.

Chapter Seven

After Multiculturalism

The Logic of Diversity and the Dialectics of Liberty

THE LOGIC OF DIVERSITY IN HISTORY AND SOCIETY

Multiculturalism is a form of pluralism that emerged from the "enlightened antiracism" in the antidiscimination and affirmative action policies of the federal government. The Voting Rights Act of 1964 was particularly responsible for the creation of a rigid system of classifying persons into racial and ethnic blocs. The enforcement of civil rights legislation, specifically that which attempted to ameliorate the disenfranchisement of black voters and discrimination against minority job applicants, required an accountability system to determine the extent of infractions against federal law. A classificatory scheme that purported to place all Americans into ethno-racial blocs was created as an essential component of an accountability strategy in the antiracist agenda. Multiculturalism became the ideological expression of the racial and ethnic schema initially created by the federal government in the United States to measure the incidence of efforts to prevent people from voting or being fairly considered for employment because of their race. Multiculturalism is a vague but broad social movement that has failed to overcome the gaps and divides among the racial-ethnic blocs in the United States.

In *Postethnic America: Beyond Multiculturalism* David Hollinger presents an historical argument for transcending racial and ethnic gaps in the allocation of social desiderata. Most fundamentally, Hollinger, and other theorists who developed similar perspectives, argued that multiculturalism, whatever its contributions to the intellectual and political development of the country, has outlined its usefulness and should be replaced by a perspective called "postethnicity."[1] The postethnic critique of racism and multiculturalism focuses on the antagonism between America's history of racial and ethnic domination and its cultural values that promoted universalism, tolerance, and cosmopolitanism. The postethnic critique provides an important contemporary extension of the content discussed in chapter 2 through 6 of *After Multiculturalism* because it assails the state's role in constructing racial antagonisms and offers a vision of a society beyond the tribalism form of organization found in both racism and multiculturalism.

Postethnicity seeks to redirect some of the thinking about race and ethnicity in a direction that will promote less of an emphasis on "communities of shared descent" and more of an emphasis on "communities of choice," or willed affiliations by people. Toward this end, the concept of "postethnicity" conveys, not regression back to a racist or assimilationist past, but movement toward a future in which ethno-racial identities are loosened and the boundaries are made more permeable. Above all, the postethnicity theorists seek an America that is more cosmopolitan and universalist than either racism or multiculturalism.

> A truly postethnic America would be one in which the ethno-racial component in identity would loom less large than it does now in politics as well as culture, and in which affiliation by shared descent would be more voluntary than prescribed in every context.[2]

The postethnic vision is a "long way from the reality in America" because of the legacy of racism and the potency of the multiculturalist emphasis on communities of descent.

Postethnicity is seen as a potential social movement that could definitively affect public policy in the more voluntarist direction of race and ethnicity articulated by Hollinger and the other postethnic theorists.

Postethnicity is a perspective that favors "voluntary to prescribed affiliations, appreciates multiple identities, pushes for communities of wide scope, recognizes the constructed character of ethno-racial groups, and accepts the formation of new groups as part of the normal life of a democratic society."[3] While it does not seek the elimination of these "communities of descent," postethnicity seeks the deconstruction of racial and ethnic groups to the extent that they are sufficiently flexible to allow persons to affiliate or disaffiliate as they feel inclined. Presumably, individuals in a Postethnic America could legitimately choose to identify self as "other" or "none of the above" as they fill out census surveys or marketing questionnaires. Persons could also legitimately choose to affiliate with any constellation of "nondescent communities" that they choose. At the level of social institutions, efforts to categorize persons into ethno-racial blocs would be eliminated. Choice and permeability, of course, have their limits because postethnicity does not appear to envision circumstances in which individuals in one community of descent might choose to affiliate with another community of descent. Nor does postethnicity seem to envision circumstances in which communities of descent, particularly those that are based on race, might disappear altogether.

In postethnic theory, the problem posed by multiculturalism is the rigidity with which these groups are socially defined. Individuals in American society live their lives as members of many types of groups or social networks simultaneously. The relevance and priority of these groups for individuals change depending upon the specific situations individuals encounter or create for themselves. Therefore, the meaning of the term "we" varies and shifts depending upon time, space, and the highly variable circumstances of individual lives. In the postethnic formulation, for example, the black woman who is a disabled autoworker may find, or choose, that the meaning of "we" varies with changes in the relevance of one or more the four social categories— black, woman, disabled, and autoworker—in her life. Because the problems, challenges, and achievements the person experiences may be shaped by a multiplicity of social categories and dynamics, it makes little sense to reduce persons to one category, or to subordinate them to one overarching master identity. Individuals in postethnic America are continually subject to countervailing and contradictory pressures and experiences. Their loyalties, identities, and sense of belonging cut across many group boundaries. There is no guarantee that the experience of being black, female, disabled, and a factory worker are fully compatible or integrated 100 percent of the time, but the individual is a totality and does not experience the different dimensions of existence as separate political or analytical categories.

While the perspective of postethnicity recognizes the meaning and importance of boundaries delimiting group membership, it resists the rigid ascription of distinctions among persons based on group affiliation, including racial and ethnic groups. Thus, postethnicity opposes ethno-racial particularity and supports the vision of individuality, society, and polity propounded by universalist and cosmopolitan theorists. *Externally*, multiculturalism celebrates separation and division based on racial and ethnic characteristics. Internally, multiculturalism promotes conformity. Postethnicity, on the other hand, acknowledges and supports the cultivation of difference within communities of descent. Postethnicity values diversity above all and "projects a more diverse basis for diversity than a multiplicity of ethnocentrisms can provide."[4] Hollinger characterizes his vision as the promotion of "diversification within diversity."

The critical trajectory of the postethnic perspective is considerably tempered in his treatment of racial groups. Hollinger's concept of postethnicity does not intend to diminish the communities of descent, but instead intends to contribute to their "renewal and critical revision." Postethnicity does not aim toward the dissolution of communities of descent, although Hollinger admits this has largely happened in America for individuals of European descent, but it instead aims toward the strengthening of those racial and ethnic communities where the members believe they need to be strengthened. Postethnicity does not entail a break with either history or biology, but maintains that neither history or biology provide clear guidance for choices individuals make about their affiliations. This point of view challenges the common belief that membership and identification with groups based blood and history are more substantive and authentic than those based on the choice or intentionality of the person. Hollinger emphasizes that the boundaries between groups that are based on choice deserve more, not less, respect than those based on blood, ethnic tradition, or political authority.[5]

The postethnic perspective moves the discourse on race and ethnicity beyond the rigidity and tribalism that is inherent in and reinforced by multiculturalist thought. At the bare minimum, the postethnic perspective envisions a social world that is not divided into camps or blocs separated by race, but is instead characterized by the fluid movement of persons into and out of different group affiliations as they act, think, and feel in their everyday lives. It resists the reduction of personal identity to prescribed social categories in favor of a sense of self that is rooted in voluntary affiliations. In this respect, the postethnic view of individuality is very similar to that of Rand and Stirner, both of whom, despite their many important differences, understood the self to be rooted in the convictions of the individual, not in accidents of biology or history. Postethnicity does not quite completely endorse the constructionist view of race and seems to believe that racial categories have a biological substratum that is independent of human definition. As a consequence, postethnicity retains an element of collectivism in that persons are members of prescribed groups, at least at a biological or precognitive level, despite their thoughts or feelings about it. Thus, postethnicity does not push the logic of diversity in history or society to its absolute limits.

Politically, what concerns postethnicity theorists most of all is that the ethno-racial divides, originally created by racism but now reinforced by multiculturalism, threaten greater social conflict and disorganization. The political project of postethnicity is to mitigate social conflict and disorganization so that the social and political systems can deal effectively with the fundamental problem of American society, which Hollinger believes to be the sharp divisions among the social classes. The political goal of Hollinger's postethnicity is to define away the ethno-racial divides so that the attention of public policy will be refocused on the social class system so that social inequality will be attacked. Conversely, restructuring the social class system is essential to the movement toward postethnicity. As Hollinger says, "by failing to provide sufficient opportunities for poor people of all ethno-racial affiliations, (the United States) is in the process of squandering whatever opportunity it may now have to move in a more postethnic direction."[6] Individualists and libertarians are not likely to support the political element of postethnicity if it elevates social class as the new collective master status defining individuals. They will also likely oppose it if the governmental acquires more power to appropriate and allocate social desiderata. However, movement toward a postethnic America through the progressive deconstruction of ethno-racial blocs has considerable appeal, especially since it entails the delegitimation of the power of the state to define and enforce racial and ethnic categories.

THE LOGIC OF DIVERSITY IN PERSONAL IDENTITY

In his brief but powerful book, *Against Identity*, Leon Wieseltier outlines a philosophic critique of the multiculturalist view of individual identity and the obsession with identity in contemporary America.[7] *Against Identity* focuses on the problems of the construction of self, culture, and community in a society that is oriented toward alleviating anxiety about racial and ethnic identity. The critique of identity helps extend the individualist and libertarian critique of racism and multiculturalism by demonstrating their collectivizing and authoritarian tendencies at the personal level.

Wieseltier is fundamentally concerned with the problems that the fixation on race and ethnicity generate for individuality, civility, and liberty. In Wieseltier's view, the cultural preoccupation with identity is historically relative; it is not a cultural or historical universal. Moreover, identity should not be confused with individuality; individuality is the ancient mediation between qualities attributed by others and those intended by the person, identity is modern version in which the two are collapsed into the socially attributed qualities. Identity emerged as a fixed idea in America with the increased interest during the 1950s and 1960s in social science and in popular culture on how the self was affected by the increased anonymity in urban life, the anomie resulting from social mobility, and the powerlessness of persons who confronted bureaucratic organizations in everyday life. Wieseltier implies that the work of Erik Erikson was a particularly important hallmark in the emergence of identity as a major American preoccupation. Erikson's importance is not due to the particular strength of his scholarship but because of the receptiveness of American culture to his sentimentality. "Erikson's influence on the American obsession with identity was less a theory than a mood. He made identity into a romance."[8]

The preoccupation with identity arose in the same sociohistorical context that served as the source of the multiculturalist view of race relations in America, the decade between the mid-1950s to the mid-1960s. Initially, at least, the emergence and elevation of identity within racial and ethnic minorities was a form of resistance to social and political forces that sought to exterminate or oppress individuals on the basis of a collective identity. In the current milieu, identity has become something quite different. It is less heroic and more narcissistic. Identity is no longer a liberating concept as far as the individual is concerned; it is not particularly helpful in the articulation of a philosophy of individual freedom. Moreover, multicultural notions of identity are particularly pernicious because they militate against the diversity and complexity of individuals.

Wieseltier argues that identity is a euphemism for conformity. In both social science and popular culture, the identity theorists, such as Erikson, offered something in the mid-1950s to the mid-1960s that neither the radical humanists, such as Jean-Paul Sartre and C. W. Mills, nor the structural functionalists, such as Talcott Parsons and Robert Merton, could offer: the promise of a home, a community, and a respite from the chaos and disorganization of advanced industrial society. Coterminous with the inception and expansion of the civil rights movement, identity evolved as a central social psychological category in science and society during the 1950s and 1960s. At the time, alienation and anomie were the chief competitors in the marketplace of explanations of modern forms of anxiety and disgruntlement. Alienation and anomie offered only isolation, conflict, and continued anxiety and disgruntlement, at least until a nebulous, improved social organization could be engineered by politicians and intellectuals at some point in the far distant future. Particularly for racial and ethnic struggles, identity offered a reconciliation of the individual with the external world in the here and now. Identity is the "solution to the problem of individuality" in an advanced industrial society that struggles to manage increasing dissensus and depersonalization.

But the reconciliation of the individual with the external social world comes at a very high price. The promotion of identity in science and society helps to reconcile the person with the ready-made structures of the external world, but the reconciliation amounts to little more than the subordination of the person's internal aspirations to commonplace external facts. Identity "announces a desire to be subsumed, an eagerness to be known primarily by a common characteristic."[9] Thus, identity is a doctrine of commonality, likeness, similarity, and conformism. In racial and ethnic terms, identity is an internal mechanism that establishes the boundaries, membership, and loyalties of the ethno-racial tribes comprising America.[10] It determines who belongs and who does not belong based on a common characteristic that is external to the choices, aspirations, convictions, and activities of individuals.

The formation of group membership based on the attribution and elevation of racial and ethnic commonalities above the convictions and intended qualities of persons is a form of domination and ideological social control. The promulgation of racial and ethnic identity is an ideology and process that maximizes the power and legitimacy of the external world and minimizes the freedom and autonomy of the individual. To the extent that multiculturalism celebrates group formation based on racial and ethnic commonalities, it enforces conformity and adumbrates the diminution of the individual's participation in the process of reality construction. It is a doctrine that undermines the dialectic of social life.

Wieseltier notes that persons who are the same with respect to one dimension or criterion of identity may be very different with respect to another. Human beings are infinitely complex in terms of both the characteristics attributed to them by others and the qualities they choose or intend for themselves. The attribution of identity based on race and ethnicity is a choice, or a consequence of choices, among an infinite array of possible qualities. Human beings are common and different in many ways, but not all these have the same value or significance.[11]

The inherent complexity and diversity of individuals means that the goals of multiculturalism are inconsistent, or it means that diversity stops at the cultural differentiation of ethno-racial groups. For the multiculturalists, the logic of diversity stops at the boundary of the racial or ethnic group. External to the ethno-racial collectivity, multiculturalism, in its most tolerant and celebratory expressions, welcomes diversity, difference, and otherness. However, internal to the ethno-racial bloc, diversity enforces sameness, conformity, and loyalty. Internally, diversity proves itself to be the enemy of multiculturalism because it negates the purity that racial and cultural identities require for their definitive differentiation from each other. For Weiseltier, "Diversity means complexity. Identity means simplicity. Anybody who takes diversity seriously will see that identity is an illusion."[12] The logic of diversity ultimately contradicts multiculturalism because it challenges the elevation of racial and ethnic identity as the sole or predominant quality that defines people. The logic of diversity rescues the possibility of difference and challenge within racial and ethnic groups.

Multicultural thought and identity-based politics propound the contradiction between a diversified, multicultural society and mythical, simplified individuals who populate it. In the multiculturalist formulation, America is a multicultural society comprised of monocultural people. But, Wieseltier argues that the singular "accomplishment of America is not the multicultural society, it is the multicultural individual."[13] Individuals have not just one source of identity but many. Americans, historically, had multiple sources of self, many criteria that served as the foundation of who they were and what they became. Singleness or simplicity contradicts the reality experienced by individuals in American society. Multiculturalism is a reaction to the anxiety posed by the multicultural individual, or the genuine diversity within history and society. Multiculturalism is the fear of heterogeneity at the level of individuals. Extrapolating from Weiseltier's critique of identity, the emancipatory task of antiracist theory is not to validate or perpetuate the elevated significance of race and ethnicity in the process of identity formation and reality construction, but to understand the individual, social, and theoretical expressions of opposition to it. The challenge is to resist the cultural and political imposition of tribalism and reduction of persons to the monocultural individual. The goal of a dialectical libertarianism is to promote the logic of diversity against the forces of homogeneity, rigidity, and conformism. The dialectical libertarian analysis of race employs the logic of diversity to attack racism at the structural, cultural, and personal levels of human existence.

RACISM AND THE DIALECTICS OF LIBERTY: A THEORETICAL FRAMEWORK

Drawing from his studies of Ayn Rand's radicalism, Sciabarra's dialectical libertarian framework envisions a tri-level model that can be used to analyze and critique power relations, including racism, in contemporary American society. This model is presented in figure 1.1 and discussed in chapter 1. Level 1 (L1), at the base of the model, is the personal level of analysis, in which power relations are examined in terms of the cognitive, decision making, and ethical dimensions of individual behavior. Level 2 (L2) is the cultural level of analysis in which power relations are understood through the intersubjective blueprints of everyday life, including language, education, aesthetics, and ideology. Level 3 (L3) is the level of macro-societal political and economic structures, which includes law, the polity, and large-scale social institutions and organizations. The dialectical libertarian model of power enables the three levels to be isolated and abstracted for the purposes of analysis, but they are inseparable and mutually dependent as individuals experience them in everyday life. This model of power relations requires an understanding and critique of each of the three levels and their interaction. Just as individuals must navigate through a cultural and social structural environment on an everyday basis, culture and society are ultimately affected by the decisions and behaviors of individuals. The self, culture, and society shape, and are shaped by, each other in an ongoing process of reality construction. A dialectical libertarian framework enables us to understand that, in a racist society, race and racism exist at each of the three levels of reality, but both race and racism are potentially modified or transformed, depending on the dynamics of culture and society.

The model also contributes to a dialectical libertarian vision of personal, cultural, and societal transformation. Following Sciabarra's analysis of Rand, in opposing the lordship-bondage relationship manifest in all forms of ethno-racial domination, the dialectical libertarian analysis centers on the dialectical concept of the free human subject as the self-conscious, self-determining individual, and it promotes the advent of a "nonexploitative society of independent equals who trade value for value."[14] But the critique must be focused at each of the three levels Sciabarra outlined in the dialectical libertarian model. Sciabarra demonstrates that Rand ridiculed the Anarcho-Capitalists for focusing their critique at the level of social structure and for largely ignoring Levels 1 and 2. Whether Rand's critique of anarcho-capitalism is valid or not, it is futile, from a dialectical libertarian viewpoint to attempt a transformation in race relations by attacking only the structural features of racism, leaving the cultural and personal dimensions intact. It is essential, theoretically and politically, to challenge racism at each of the three levels of reality and to have an alternative vision at each of the three levels, to actualize the experience of political freedom.

Sciabarra's intent is to develop a model of dialectical libertarianism, which he accomplishes through an explication of the radical dimensions of Rand's thought, contrasted favorably with Rothbard's approach. Rand emerges in his analysis as the central theorist in the founding of dialectical libertarianism. The goal of *After Multiculturalism*, however, is to apply the dialectical libertarian model to the analysis of race and racism articulated by the spectrum of individualist and libertarian theorists, which includes Rand but is not limited to her and Objectivist philosophy. Instead, race and racism, as important forms of power relations in contemporary society, can be fruitfully understood from not only Objectivist, but also Anarcho-Capitalist, Libertarian, Individualist Anarchist, and Dialectical Egoist perspectives. In addition, other individualist and libertarian theories may have significant contributions to make to the elimination of racism through the transformation of self, culture, and society.

Figure 7.1 presents a summary of the ideas of each of the five perspectives on race and racism organized according to the three levels of Sciabarra's dialectical libertarian model. The five perspectives can be analyzed comparatively through a focus on what the theorists have said about race and racism, or what their theory implies about race and racism, at each of the three levels in the model. A comparative approach is helpful in identifying the similarities and differences among the five theoretical perspectives, as well as assessing their comparative strengths and weaknesses.

Level of Analysis	Objectivism	Anarcho-Capitalism	Libertarianism	Individualist Anarchism	Dialectical Egoism
Level 3 (L3) Structural: Politics and Economics	Statism and racist legislation are ultimately irrational and immoral. Laissez-faire economics and a limited government are the structural expressions of natural law, reason, and ethics. The predatory state and the mixed economy fragment social bonds.	The interventionist state has created a form of internal colonialism that exploits ethnic and racial minorities. It is the nature of the state to expand its systems of coercion and exploitation.	The minimalist state prohibits both race-oriented legislation and programs that promote preferences. Libertarians advocate for a constitutional amendment to prohibit any form of discrimination.	Anarchists advocate abolition of the state, wage slavery, and the monopolistic tendencies of capitalism. The state legitimates wage slavery and promotes the monopolistic control of the economy, thus generating poverty.	Stirner's egoism rejects all systems because they are systems. He favors the reconstruction of self and society based on the willed relationships by unique individuals within the Union of Egoists.
Level 2 (L2) Cultural: Linguistic and Ideological	Objectivist epistemology suggests that racism is a collectivist and altruist mystification. Because of racist statist cultural ideas, race is a mystique that obfuscates individuality and interpersonal bonds.	Rothbard's methodological individualism suggests that race and racism are abstractions promoted by intellectuals in service to the state.	The old racism has been replaced by a new form that evolved from the government's efforts to respond to the social disorganization in the underclass. The new form of racism legitimates racial gaps and governmental intrusion.	The Anarchists critiqued the constitutionality of slavery and the social contract theory of political legitimacy since both are based on coercion and not the consent of individuals forced to endure them.	All notions of race and racial superiority are critiqued as spooks, or wheels in the head, that fix thought into rigid categories and prohibit freedom of thought and behavior.

Level 3 (L3) Personal: (Cognitive/Ethical)	Rational egoism rejects the collectivizing tendencies of both racism and multiculturalism. Objectivism rejects any form of collective attributions or collective guilt or blame as irrational and unethical.	Anarcho-capitalism maximizes personal autonomy and self-reliance. Ethnic nationalism is viewed as a form of self-reliance and, therefore, it is a form of resistance to internal colonialism.	Libertarians recommend retrenchment of most public policy programs. Murray advocates for a grant program that will promote self-reliance and fulfillment of interpersonal obligations.	Individuals have a right to be free of coercion by the state and a moral responsibility to rebel against the state, including participation in guerilla warfare to end slavery (Spooner) and passive resistance to racism and colonial domination (Tucker).	Notions regarding race and racism are deconstructed and dissolved into the unique individual. The Unique One rebels against all externally imposed fixed ideas.

Figure 7.1. Summary of Individualist and Libertarian Perspectives on Race and Racism

L1 IN THE FOREGROUND: COGNITION AND ETHICS AT THE PERSONAL LEVEL

Beginning with the personal level of analysis in figure 7.1, it is clear that each of the five perspectives places a premium on personal freedom, individual autonomy, and to a greater or lesser extent, self-ownership. Objectivism grounds a critique of race and racism at the personal level in the ethical concept of rational egoism which stipulates that individuals are morally bound to neither sacrifice their life, labor, or decision making to others, nor to expect others to sacrifice for them. Rational egoism rejects the altruism and collectivizing tendencies of racism, as well as the formulations of the collective blame for racism inherent in multiculturalism, affirmative action, and preferential programs. Both racism and governmental action that promotes advantages for select ethno-racial groups inherently rest on an altruist and collectivist view of individuals in a social environment.

Sciabarra may be correct in his assessment that Rand is a superior theorist to Rothbard and other Libertarian thinkers, in part, because Objectivism carefully articulates philosophic positions on all three levels of analysis, while others may focus on the structural level. However, it is also true that the Anarcho-Capitalists and the Libertarians include the analysis of individual behavior in their critique of racism and multiculturalist responses to it. Rothbard's Anarcho-Capitalist critique of racism at the personal level does not focus on universal ethical or psychological principles characteristic of Objectivism, but maximizes an emphasis on individual autonomy and self-reliance as part of the revolutionary heritage of the United States. Rothbard, consequently, was very supportive of ethnic nationalist movements in the United States because he saw them supporting the values of self-reliance and autonomy against the coercive and exploitive internal colonialist practices of the federal government and state-subsidized corporations. In his view, black nationalism was particularly strong in its emphasis on the autonomy of black Americans. Rothbard interpreted ethnic nationalism as a form of revolutionary resistance to a racist state because the nationalist sentiments entail a commitment to resist, work, and live outside of the political and cultural framework of racism. The separatist implications of black nationalism, which are anathema to the universalism of Objectivism, do not appear to bother Rothbard because its adherents were revolutionary antistatists. Perhaps Rothbard does not articulate a psycho-epistemology at the same level of detail that Objectivism provides, but it is not accurate to say that he ignored this important dimension.

The theorists associated with the Libertarian movement in the United States since the 1970s focus more on a social and economic critique of the omnipotent welfare state, but they also articulate an analysis of the implications of this political formation for the behavior of individuals, including those pertaining to racism. For instance, Charles Murray's proposal to eliminate welfare and entitlement systems by providing a grant to each adult, despite its departures from a pure libertarian perspective on public policy, is intended to promote greater self-reliance and cultivate a greater sense of fulfilling obligations to others. At the personal level, Murray's proposal can be understood as a public policy tool that attempts to create the type of circumstances necessary to implement an entitlement theory of justice similar to that propounded by Robert Nozich, even though the proposal is not particularly based on a clearly outlined theory of either human cognition or ethics. However, Murray's proposal clearly has the intent of affecting the ethics that persons practice in everyday life.

The Individualist Anarchists—Tucker, Spooner, and Nock—are also very concerned about the interaction among the three levels in the dialectical libertarian framework and frequently brought the personal level to the forefront of their discussions about race and racism. Tucker and Spooner advocate the abolition of the state and the monopolizing tendencies of capitalism, which they thought are made possible by the exercise of state power. Unlike the communist-oriented anarchists, such as Mikhail Bakunin, Peter Kropotkin, and Emma Goldman, the Individualist Anarchists resist all collectivizing tendencies and advocate for free trade and voluntary exchange. They also reject the profit-seeking foundation of capitalist economics in favor of principles that precluded exploitation and the unbridled accumulation of wealth. Their critique of slavery and collective violence against minorities is founded not only in a political, legal, and economic analysis, but in a utopian vision of interpersonal reciprocity guided by moral precepts. Individuals have not only a right to be autonomous, but they have a moral responsibility to rebel against political domination, including participation in revolutionary and guerilla warfare against slavery and racial violence.

Max Stirner's Dialectical Egoism also carries a forceful analysis and critique of race and racism at the personal level. In Stirner's formulation, "nothing is more to me than myself." Dialectical Egoism attacks every cultural construct and social fact that has an external existence and coercive impact on the person. Stirner is the ultimate individualist or egoist whose intransigence rivals even the rational egoism of Ayn Rand. Stirner's Dialectical Egoism interprets all political, cultural, and ethical codes as antithetical to the self-ownership of the individual. Individuals in this theory do not act morally or immorally, rationally or irrationally, legitimately or illegitimately. Morality, rationality, and legitimacy are all external concepts that function as forms of ideological social control. Persons simply act. What matters to the Dialectical Egoist is not whether the individual is ethical or rational, but whether the individual is sovereign or not, or whether the individual "owns" the act or not. The free subject in Stirner's view is the Unique One, the sovereign individual who is not constrained by natural law, political authority, cultural norms, religion, or fictitious moral codes. At the personal level, Dialectical Egoism deconstructs concepts such as race and culture, or political precepts such as racial superiority, into specters or spooks created by others. All such fictions dissolve into the Unique One who reconstructs everyday life through willed or intentional relationships with other Unique Ones. The Unique One is the implacable enemy of all ideas that seek to impose external meanings and behavioral patterns.

L2 IN THE FOREGROUND: THE CRITIQUE OF CULTURE AND IDEOLOGY

Moving to the cultural level of analysis (L2), other common themes, and differences, emerge in the analysis of race and racism by the five perspectives. Rand's Objectivist analysis clearly argues that racism is a cultural legacy that contradicts the foundational values of American society that emphasized rationality, individuality, self-reliance, and meritocracy. Racism is an ideology that is based on collectivist and altruist values, and elevates force and fraud as legitimate social dynamics. As such, racism mystifies and obfuscates perception and cognition, deteriorates rationality and individuality, and subverts interpersonal bonds. For Objectivists, multiculturalism is the mirror image of racism in that it promotes the same values that force individuals into collectivities and demands the sacrifice of their lives, property, and activity.

Rothbard's Anarcho-Capitalism includes a critique of culture, especially the role that intellectuals play in articulating and legitimating the role of governmental coercion in society. Rothbard views intellectuals in academia, science, the media, and in leadership roles of every social institution as functionaries whose primary job is creating ideological justifications for the "political means" in society. In racist society, this primarily entails the articulation of the necessity and rationality of internal colonialism in all of its facets. His methodological individualism suggests that race and all of the symbols and concepts associated with it are abstractions constructed by the cadre of intellectuals who serve the state. The social role of intellectuals, then, is the creation of culture and ideology that reproduces or reinforces the social relationships required by the structure and function of the state. Multiculturalism is a contemporary variant of this process, particularly since it places a premium on the role of the state in managing the social and economic disorganization created by racism.

In the Libertarian analysis of racism and multiculturalism advanced by David Boaz, James Bovard, and Charles Murray, a new form of racism has emerged in American society that replaced the old form characteristic of slavery and segregationism. The new form of racism evolved from the federal government's efforts to respond to the social and personal disorganization generated by slavery and segregation, especially poverty and discrimination in housing and employment. The major outcome of the efforts of the welfare state was the creation of a permanent underclass. The new racism is a victim-oriented ideology that maintains the underclass through governmental programs that provide housing, food, training, and counseling, all of which function to keep individuals in a state of perpetual helplessness. The Libertarian analysis of culture and ideology focuses on the legitimations for the welfare state and the programs that function to manage the underclass. The Libertarian critique of culture and ideology focuses on the ideas and values that favor governmental intervention into social disorganization. Their cultural critique advocates for the progressive dismantling of the welfare state and the programs that serve the underclass, including multicultural arguments in favor of affirmative action and preferential treatment of select ethno-racial groups.

The Individualist Anarchist analysis of culture and ideology is primarily concerned with the deconstruction of the political legitimacy of slavery and the social contract theory of government. Particularly in *The Unconstitutionality of Slavery*, Spooner deconstructs the legal, political, and cultural arguments that slavery is permissible or legitimate under the *Constitution* of the United States. Using carefully crafted legal reasoning, Spooner demonstrates that there is no provision in the *Constitution* that can be construed as permitting slavery. Spooner takes the critique of the legal foundations of racist society a step further in *No Treason, No. 6*, arguing that the *Constitution* itself has no authority because no one living has consented to be bound by its provisions. In his formulation, contracts have legitimacy only if the parties bound by them have actively and freely consented to them. Succeeding generations of Americans cannot be legitimately bound by a contract created by the nation's founders because they have not freely and actively agreed to it. The *Constitution* has no authority over anyone who did not consent to it. The *Constitution*, the legal apparatus surrounding it, and cultural conceptions about it are a form of ideological control in that they rationalize obedience in the absent of active, voluntary consent. The cultural critique of Spooner, Tucker, and Nock delegitimates the authority of the state and of any political formation that is not founded on the active, voluntary consent of the individual. Slavery and all other forms of racial domination should be challenged because they are based on coercion and the illegitimate appropriate of the lives and activities of human individuals. The role of the critic is to articulate the contradiction between the cultural claims made about political authority and the reality of its foundation in power and coercion.

Stirner's critique of culture and ideology in *The Ego and Its Own* is grounded in his notion of the idée fixe, or the fixed idea. Dialectical egoists are primarily concerned with the power that abstractions acquire in the social process, particularly when they became tools of the state or institutional authorities. Stirner vehemently objects to the philosophic promulgation of abstract terms such as "humanity," "nation," "class," and "race" as though they were real actors in sociohistorical dramas. For Stirner, these concepts are reifications, or alienated thoughts, once used by the Prussian state, its functionaries in academia and the church, and the leadership of the emerging socialist and communist movements to browbeat individuals into submission to external goals and values. These abstractions are little more than anthropomorphisms that structure thought and behavior, thereby, inhibiting the freedom of individuals to think and act for themselves. They are spooks or "wheels in the head" that must be challenged at the psychological and cultural levels if individuals are to live free and fulfilling lives. Stirner's Dialectical Egoism is a rejection of racism and any other ideology or movement that is based on abstractions such as "race," "culture," or "diversity."

L3 IN THE FOREGROUND: POLITICS, ECONOMICS, AND SOCIAL STRUCTURE

At the apex of the dialectical libertarian framework, race and racism are analyzed through the lens of political economics at the macro-level of social organization, revealing several differences among the five perspectives. It also reveals at least one common theme that evinces profound suspicion of the ability and legitimacy of the state to define and manage racial and ethnic dynamics. Rand's political philosophy includes a strong argument that the legitimacy of the state is rooted in natural law, ethics, and human reason. The appropriate role of the state in society is to protect individuals and their property from both internal and external threats. The state does not have a legitimate role in the management or control of the economy, which is appropriately managed by the voluntary, cooperative pursuits of individuals. Racist statutes and any exercise of political power that promotes, subsidizes, or oppresses any ethno-racial group is irrational and unethical. Moreover, in Rand's view, the mixed economy, which allows governmental intervention into the economic life of society, artificially fragments social relationships and creates conflicts among groups and individuals because some benefit by the state's largess while others are victimized by it.

Unlike Rand, Rothbard does not believe that the state has any legitimate role in society. All of the necessary societal functions that the state performs can be performed more effectively and efficiently by private firms. Society should be restructured so that all public functions or services are privatized. Taxation should be eliminated so that individuals seeking these services would pay for them on a fee-for-service basis. The Anarcho-Capitalist analysis of the state argues that a form of internal colonialism exploits and impoverishes ethnic and racial minorities. Internal colonialism is based on coercion, not consensus, and its nature is to expand systems of control and exploitation. The path to improve the life circumstances for all groups is to eliminate the state and allow each person to pursue his or her own interests, affiliating with others as they see fit. The tendencies within the internal colonialist totality that exhibit elements of the new society, such as ethnic nationalist movements that propound individualist values, should be supported by Anarcho-Capitalist revolutionaries.

Libertarianism is more akin to Objectivism and unlike Anarcho-Capitalism in that it articulates a political theory that includes the existence of a limited government. Libertarian political philosophy is based on a the notion of a minimalist, noninterventionist state which, ideally, is exclusively devoted to protecting the rights of individuals and governing from a strict constructionist point of view. The minimalist state is not permitted to create or enforce racist legislation or to promote racial preferences or programs intended to benefit one group over another. At least one prominent Libertarian theorist, Charles Murray, advocates a constitutional amendment that would prohibit the government from participating in any form of discrimination or preferential treatment. While they are not in favor of it personally, the Libertarians would not prohibit discrimination or preferential treatment that occurs in civil society because individuals have the right to affiliate with whomever they choose. However, this general portrayal of Libertarian political philosophy is sometimes compromised in order to achieve other important objectives, such as Murray's proposal to mitigate social disorganization through a federally sponsored grant program.

Individualist Anarchism advocates for the abolition of the state and the promotion of private property and free trade, but unlike Rothbard and Rand, it is not uncritical of capitalism. Tucker and Nock were especially critical of the role that the state played in creating economic monopolies and inhibiting the free economic activity of persons. Tucker believed that capitalism had inherent tendencies toward the concentration and accumulation of capital, which were exacerbated by state intervention in the economy. In Tucker's and Nock's view, the state must be abolished in order to ensure that monopolies do not control civil society and so that individuals can pursue their own interests. For

Tucker, Spooner, and Nock, racism, especially slavery and racial violence, is an important example of how the state promotes the monopolistic control of the economy and how it generates and reproduces poverty and social stratification. Taking their cue from the Abolitionists such as William Lloyd Garrison, the Individualist Anarchists believed that the best response to the social realities of slavery and racism is the abolition of the state and the destruction of the monopolies it created. Tucker and Spooner envisioned a revolutionary transformation of society that, while not capitalistic, would protect individual rights, free trade, and private property, allowing all individuals regardless of ethnicity or race to affiliate freely and to exchange value for value.

Stirner's brand of uncompromising egoism is a type of anarchism that rejects all political systems because they necessarily entail the imposition of political authority in some form. He opposes systems because they are systems. All political systems require some limitation on the self-ownership of the individual. Self-ownership means that the person can freely pursue activities and relationships unimpeded by the state or any other political formation. Stirner favors the reconstruction of self through the Unique One and the reconstruction of society based on the freely chosen or willed relationships found only within the Union of Egoists. Thus, the Dialectical Egoist opposition to racism and multiculturalism is a reflection of the individual's resistance to political authority in any form and a rejection of political and economic processes that place individuals into categories against their will. The political reduction of persons to racial or cultural identities is a form of domination and control and has no legitimacy for the Dialectical Egoist.

RACISM AND THE DIALECTICS OF LIBERTY: TOWARD AN ASSESSMENT

The five theoretical perspectives discussed in this book have many differences, but they are all united in their belief in the ability of individuals to voluntarily work with each other to meet their needs and to solve most, if not all, of their problems, outside the framework of government. They are also united in their opposition to racism and the multiculturalist reaction to it. Each provides an analysis of racism and concludes that it is a social formation based on collectivism and coercion. Each articulates a point of view that warned against replacing the tribalism of racism with new forms of society that are also based on collectivism and coercion. Finally, although there are exceptions, most of the five theoretical perspectives argues in favor of a postethnic future and against the cultural reduction of the individual to an ethno-racial identity.

The discussion of dialectical libertarianism in chapter 1 suggests that theoretical perspectives on racism can be analyzed in terms of the form of critique they offer. Dialectical logic can include an immanent and a transcendental critique of domination. Immanent critique contrasts what a society or social formation says about itself with what it is or what it is becoming. Transcendental critique contrasts societal practice with principles or standards of human behavior, articulated by a theorist, that transcend any one society or historical period. One approach to the assessment of the five perspectives on race and racism discussed in this book is to compare and contrast what each offers by way of an immanent and a transcendent critique of race and racism.

Figure 7.2 provides a summary of the immanent and transcendental critiques of each of the five perspectives. Beginning with the immanent critique of race and racism in American society, the analysis of Objectivism suggests that Rand and her followers offer a clear and focused critique of racism and state intervention on behalf of particular ethno-racial blocs. Rand's critique of racism forcefully contrasts the sociological dynamics of racism in American society with its historical and cultural commitments to individualism and meritocracy. Objectivists also argue against the affirmative action and preferential treatment programs for the same reason. Rothbard, on the other hand, articulates only a weak immanent critique of racism. His treatment of slavery in his historical analysis of the United States, which appears in *Conceived in Liberty*, and his articulation of the theory of internal colonialism are both remarkably atheoretical. Both are grossly detached from the methodology of the Austrian School and the anarchist opposition to authority. Rothbard fails in both of these analyses to include a contrast of prevailing American values with the treatment of minority groups by the major social institutions in the United States. In addition, his support of black nationalism appears to be a political compromise totally unrelated to the Anarcho-Capitalist interpretation of American history, society, and culture. Rothbard neglects to ask how black nationalism provides a real break from racist society, or how it might function to recast racism and political authority in a new form. Mises's critique of anti-Semitism is a superior analysis and is much more of a model of the analysis of racism from the perspective of Austrian economics. In contrast to Rand, Rothbard's analysis of race does not follow from a broader perspective of how cultural values are contradicted by social facts.

The Libertarian theorists, Boaz, Bovard, and Murray, offer lengthy critiques of the contradictions between racism and the statist management of race relations, and historical values in the United States. Each carefully outlines how American cultural values do not include racism or state intervention on behalf of particular ethno-racial groups. Similarly, among the Individualist Anarchists, Spooner's analysis of the unconstitutionality of slavery

Level of Analysis	Objectivism	Anarcho-Capitalism	Libertarianism	Individualist Anarchism	Dialectical Egoism
Immanent Critique	Rand articulated an immanent critique through her argument that both racism and statist efforts to legislate equality of life circumstances contradict the basic values in the founding of American society.	Rothbard articulates only a weak immanent critique of racism. His history of the American Revolution is remarkably atheoretical, as is his analysis of internal colonialism; both fail to contrast prevailing American values with historical events and political processes.	The Libertarians, especially Bovard and Murray, provide lengthy discussions about the contradictions in the management of race relations in public policy. Bovard, Boaz and Murray also describe how core American cultural values contradict racism. All three contrast the realities of racism with American ideology.	Spooner's analysis of slavery is a model of immanent critique. He uses legal methods to deconstruct the legitimacy of slavery and demystifies racism as social practice. The historical meaning of the founding documents contradict slavery. Nock's analysis of lynching is another example.	Stirner is ruthless in his demonstration of the contradiction between racism and prevailing philosophic constructions of history, God, and humanity. Stirner provides a critique of ideology that consistently lays bare the social and human roots of master concepts, such as race.

Transcendental Critique	In her articulation of the core ideas of Objectivist thought, Rand clearly demonstrated that racism is inconsistent with Objectivist principles because it is fundamentally collectivist and irrational.	Rothbard's transcendental critique of statism and governmental intervention is very strong. He provides considerable detail about the functioning of the ideal society. Racism contradicts the principles of Austrian economics and anarchist thought.	Nozich outlined the basic philosophic principles of a libertarian utopia, which indirectly relate to the analysis of racism. Murray's effort to improve society through public policy initiatives has libertarian goals, but these initiatives require the coercive power of the state for their implementation.	Tucker identified some the elements of a transcendent critique in his concept of equal liberty. He uses the notion of "equal liberty" as the standard to critique the state, capitalism, and ideological forms of control, such as religion.	Stirner's deconstruction of ideology contradicts the whole notion of a transcendent critique; he does not and cannot outline the elements of an ideal society or eternal principles for human behavior. His notion of the unique individual and the union of egoists are as close as he can get to a transcendental critique.

Figure 7.2.   Immanent and Transcendental Critique: Summary of the Five Perspectives on Race and Racism

is a model of this type of critique. Spooner uses legal methods to deconstruct the presumed legitimacy of slavery. He succeeds in demystifying racism as a form of social practice. Nock's analysis of lynching and racial violence is another masterful expression of immanent critique since it reveals a social practice that conflicts with the libertarian principles of the American founding and how it functions as a device to divert the lower social classes from challenging the upper echelons of the social stratification system. Stirner was ruthless and unrelenting in his critique of racism and the constructions of humanity, God, and history prevailing in his time. His critique of ideology consistently reveals the human and social base of master concepts, such as race.

Both Rand and Rothbard offer strong transcendental critiques of racism. It is clear that racism and state intervention are inconsistent with the core ideas and principles of both Objectivism and Anarcho-Capitalism. Both Rand and Rothbard outline the basic elements of the appropriate functioning of social institutions; racism and state intervention on behalf of ethno-racial collectivities have no role in either. Rothbard outlines in considerable detail how an Anarcho-Capitalist society might function. Racism clearly contradicts the principles of Austrian economics and his market-based version of anarchist thought.

The transcendental critiques of racism that Rand and Rothbard offered are the result of a careful discussion of basic philosophic premises about humanity, society, and economy. This is not the case with the Libertarians, the Individualist Anarchists, and Stirner. Among the Libertarians discussed in this book, only Nozich outlines even the broad philosophical principles of a libertarian utopia. Unfortunately, these principles are never directly related to an analysis of racism or race relations. Murray's efforts to improve society through public policy initiatives may have some libertarian elements, but they are based on the coercive and redistributive power of the state for their implementation. Among the Individualist Anarchists, only Tucker identifies some of the elements of an ideal society; at the minimum, he differentiates the anarchist vision from socialism, capitalism, and communist anarchism. Nock occasionally addresses transcendent political values and uses them to critique racial violence.

Stirner's philosophy is also weak from a transcendental point of view. The deconstruction of ideology by Stirner and Dialectical Egoism contradicts the whole notion of a transcendental critique. Dialectical Egoism does not, and perhaps cannot, outline the elements of an ideal society or any transhistorical principles for human behavior. Stirner's notion of the unique individual and the union of egoists are as close as Dialectical Egoism can get to a transcendental critique. In fact, Stirner's critics argue that he was inconsistent in his treatment of the Unique One and the union of egoists as behavioral ideals since his whole philosophy is built on an opposition to behavioral ideals of any sort. The fluidity and indeterminacy of the unique individual and the Union of Egoists preclude a meaningful transcendental critique.

A balanced assessment of the five perspectives cannot elevate any one of them as the absolute model of a dialectical libertarian theory of society and individuality. Each perspective includes elements of a dialectical libertarian analysis of racism and a vision of a society that ameliorates the most violent and inequitable facets of racism. Social change may be partially dependent upon changes in how people think, but, fortunately, the creation of a society that does a better job of articulating the role of ethnicity and race in the everyday lives of its citizens is not dependent upon a perfect theory that is true throughout all time and space. For those who are committed to social changes that improve the everyday lives and quality of interactions among diverse people, the five theoretical perspectives discussed in this book, despite their many shortcomings, offer new vistas and the promise of a radically different path to pursue individual freedom and social justice than what we have historically experienced in the United States. For that reason alone, the notion of a dialectical libertarian analysis of race and racism is worthy of serious study and debate as we consider the multiculturalist opposition to racism.

NOTES

1. David Hollinger, *Postethnic America: Beyond Multiculturalism* (New York: Basic Books, 1995); "Group Preferences, Cultural Diversity, and Social Democracy: Notes Toward a Theory of Affirmative Action," *Representations* 55 (Summer 1996): 31–40; and *Cosmopolitanism and Solidarity: Studies in Ethno-racial, Religious, and Professional Affiliation in the United States* (Madison: University of Wisconsin Press, 2006); Jeffery Alexander, "Bringing Democracy Back In: Universalistic Solidarity and the Civil Sphere," in *Intellectuals and Politics*, ed. Charles Lemert. (Newbury Park, CA: Sage, 1991); Neil J. Smelser and Jeffery Alexander, *Diversity and Its Discontents: Cultural Conflict and Common Ground in Contemporary American Society* (Princeton, NJ: Princeton University Press, 1999); and Paul Gilroy, *Against Race: Imaging Political Culture Beyond the Color Line* (Cambridge, MA: Harvard University Press, 2000).

2. Hollinger, *Postethnic America*, 129.

3. Hollinger, *Postethnic America*, 116.

4. Hollinger, *Postethnic America*, 107

5. Hollinger, *Postethnic America*, 119. Also see Mary Waters, *Ethnic Options: Choosing Identities in America* (Berkeley: University of California Press, 1990), Richard Alba, *Ethnic Identity: The Transformation of White America* (New Haven, CT: Yale University Press, 1990), and Maria Root *Racially Mixed People in America* (Newbury Park, CA: Sage, 1992).

6. Hollinger, *Postethnic America*, 16. Also see F. James Davis, *Who is Black?* (University Park: Pennsylvania State University Press, 1991) and Paul Spikard, *Mixed Blood: Intermarriage and Ethnic Identity in Twentieth-Century America* (Madison: University of Wisconsin Press, 1989).

7. Leon Wieseltier, *Against Identity* (New York: William Drenttel, 1996).

8. Eric Erikson, *Childhood and Society* (New York: Norton, 1950); *Identity and the Life-Cycle* (New York: International Universities Press, 1959); *Youth: Challenge and Change* (New York: Basic Books, 1963).

9. Wieseltier, *Against Identity*, 4.

10. Wieseltier, *Against Identity*, 6.

11. Wieseltier, *Against Identity*, 4.

12. Wieseltier, *Against Identity*, 38.

13. Wieseltier, *Against Identity*, 38.

14. Chris Matthew Sciabarra, *Total Freedom: Toward a Dialectical Libertarianism* (University Park: Pennsylvania State University Press, 2000), 383.

Selected Bibliography

Alba, Richard. *Ethnic Identity: The Transformation of White America*. New Haven, CT: Yale University Press, 1990.

Alexander, Jeffery. "Bringing Democracy Back In: Universalistic Solidarity and the Civil Sphere." In *Intellectuals and Politics*, edited by Charles Lemert. Newbury Park, CA: Sage, 1991.

Allport, Gordon. *The Nature of Prejudice*. 1954. New York: Perseus Books, 1979.

Antonio, Robert J. "Immanent Critique as the Core of Critical Theory: Its Origins and Development in Hegel, Marx and Contemporary Thought." *British Journal of Sociology* 32 (Fall 1981): 330–45.

Berger, Peter, and Thomas Luckmann. *The Social Construction of Reality: A Treatise in the Sociology of Knowledge*. New York: Doubleday, 1966.

Bergland, David. *Libertarianism in One Lesson: Why Libertarianism Is the Best Hope for America's Future*, 9th ed. Cartersville, GA: Advocates for Self-Government, 2005.

Berlin, Isaiah. *Karl Marx: His Life and Environment*. Oxford: Oxford University Press, 1939.

Bernstein, Richard. *Dictatorship of Virtue: Multiculturalism, Diversity and the Battle for America's Future*. New York: A. A. Knopf, 1994.

Best, Steven, and Douglas Kellner. *Postmodern Theory: Critical Interrogations*. New York: The Guilford Press, 1991.

Bloom, Allan. *The Closing of the American Mind: How Higher Education Has Failed Democracy and Impoverished the Souls of Today's Students*. New York: Simon and Schuster, 1987.

Boaz, David. *Libertarianism: A Primer*. New York: Simon and Schuster, 1997.

———, ed. *The Libertarian Reader: Classic and Contemporary Writings from Lao-Tzu to Milton Friedman*. New York: The Free Press, 1997.

———. *Toward Liberty: The Idea that is Changing the World*. Washington, DC: The Cato Institute, 2002.

Bonilla-Silva, Eduardo. *Racism without Racists: Color Blind-Racism and the Persistence of Racial Inequality*. Boulder, CO: Rowman and Littlefield, 2003.

———. "The (White) Color of Color Blindness." *Race, Ethnicity, and Education: Racism and Anti-Racism in Education*, edited by E. Wayne Ross. Westport, CT: Praeger, 2006.

———. *White Supremacy and Racism in the Post–Civil Rights Era*. Boulder, CO: Lynne Rienner, 2001.

Bovard, James. *Attention Deficit Democracy*. New York: Palgrave McMillan, 2006.

———. *The Bush Betrayal*. New York: Palgrave McMillan, 2004.

———. *Feeling Your Pain: The Explosion and Abuse of Government Power in the Clinton-Gore Years*. New York: St. Martin's Press, 2000.

———. *Freedom in Chains: The Rise of the State and the Demise of the Citizen*. New York: St. Martin's Press, 1999.

———. *Lost Rights: The Destruction of American Liberty*. New York: St. Martin's Press, 1995.

———. *Terrorism and Tyranny: Trampling Freedom, Justice, and Peace to Rid the World of Evil*. New York: Palgrave McMillan, 2003.

Camus, Albert. *The Rebel: An Essay on Man in Revolt*. New York: Vintage Books, 1956.

Clark, John P. *Max Stirner's Egoism*. London: Freedom Press, 1976.

Collier, Peter, and David Horowitz. *Second Thoughts about the Sixties*. New York: Summit Books, 1990.

Feuerbach, Ludwig. *The Essence of Christianity*. 1841. New York: Harper, 1957.

Darder, Antonia, and Rodolfo Torres. *After Race: Racism after Multiculturalism*. New York: New York University Press, 2004.

Davis, F. James. *Who is Black?* University Park: Pennsylvania State University Press, 1991.

Den Uyl, Douglas. *The Fountainhead: An American Novel*. New York: Twayne Publishers, 1999.

Doherty, Brian. *Radicals for Capitalism: A Freewheeling History of the Modern American Libertarian Movement*. New York: Public Affairs, 2007.

D'Sousa, Dinesh. *The End of Racism*. New York: The Free Press, 1995.

Dyson, Michael Eric. *Debating Race*. New York: Perseus Books, 2007.

Ellis, Richard J. *The Dark Side of the Left: Illiberal Egalitarianism in America*. Lawrence: University of Kansas Press, 1998.

Foster, Lawrence, and Patricia Herzog. *Defending Diversity: Contemporary Philosophical Perspectives on Pluralism and Multiculturalism*. Amherst: University of Massachusetts Press, 1994.

Fredrickson, George. *Racism: A Short History*. Princeton, NJ: Princeton University Press, 2003.

Friedman, David. *The Machinery of Freedom: Guide to Radical Capitalism*. 1973. Chicago: Open Court Publishing, 1995.

Gilroy, Paul. *Against Race: Imaging Political Culture Beyond the Color Line*. Cambridge, MA: Harvard University Press, 2000.

Giroux, Henry A. *Living Dangerously: Multiculturalism and the Politics of Difference*. New York: Lang, 1993.

Glazer, Nathan. *We Are All Multiculturalists Now*. Cambridge, MA: Harvard University Press, 1998.

Gregory, Steven, and Roger Sajek. *Race*. New Brunswick, NJ: Rutgers, The State University, 1994.

Hegel, G. W. F. *Lectures on the History of Philosophy*. 1830. Berkeley: University of California Press, 1990.

———. *Phenomenology of Spirit*. 1807. London: Oxford University Press, 1977.

———. *The Philosophy of History*. 1837. New York: Dover Publications, 1956.

———. *The Science of Logic*. 1812. New York: Routledge, 2004.

Herrnstein, Richard, and Charles Murray, *The Bell Curve: Intelligence and Class Structure in American Life*. New York: The Free Press, 1994.

Hollinger, David. *Cosmopolitanism and Solidarity: Studies in Ethnoracial, Religious, and Professional Affiliation in the United States*. Madison: University of Wisconsin Press, 2006.

———. *Postethnic America: Beyond Multiculturalism*. New York: Basic Books, 1995.

Hospers, John. *Libertarianism: A Political Philosophy Whose Time Has Come*. Los Angeles: Reason Press, 1971.

Kant, Immanuel. *Critique of Practical Reason*. 1788. Cambridge: Cambridge University Press, 1988.

———. *Critique of Pure Reason*. 1781. Cambridge: Cambridge University Press, 1988.

Kelley, David. *The Contested Legacy of Ayn Rand: Truth and Toleration in Objectivism*. New Brunswick, NJ: Transaction Books, 2000.

———. *The Evidence of the Senses*. Baton Rouge: Louisiana State University Press, 1986.

Kierkegaard, Søren. *The Concept of Dread*. 1844. Princeton, NJ: Princeton University Press, 1957.

Kimball, Roger. *Tenured Radicals: How Politics Has Corrupted Our Higher Education*. New York: Harper and Row, 1990.

Kivisto, Peter, ed. *Multiculturalism in the United States: Current Issues, Contemporary Voices*. Thousand Oaks, CA: Pine Forge Press, 2000.

Lacey, A. R. *Robert Nozick*. Princeton, NJ: Princeton University Press, 2001.

Leopold, David. "Introduction." In *The Ego and Its Own* by Max Stiner. 1844. Cambridge: Cambridge University Press, 1995, xi–xxxv.

Long, Roderick. "The Benefits and Hazards of Dialectical Libertarianism." *The Journal of Ayn Rand Studies* 2, no. 2 (Spring 2001): 395–448.

———. *Reason and Value: Aristotle versus Rand*. Poughkeepsie, NY: The Objectivist Center, 2000.

Löwith, Karl. *From Hegel to Nietzsche: The Revolution in Nineteenth Century Thought*. New York: Columbia University Press, 1964.

Machan, Tibor. *Ayn Rand*. New York: Peter Lang, 1999.

———. *Libertarianism Defended*. Aldershot, UK: Ashgate Publishing, 2006.

Mackay, John Henry. *The Anarchists: A Picture of Civilization at the Close of the Nineteenth Century*. Brooklyn, NY: Autonomedia, 1999.

———. *Max Stirner: His Life and Work*. Concord, CA: Preemptory Publications, 2005.

McElroy, Wendy. *The Debates of Liberty: An Overview of Individualist Anarchism, 1881–1908*. Lanham, MD: Lexington Books, 2003.

McLaren, Peter. *Revolutionary Multiculturalism: Pedagogies of Dissent for the New Millennium*. Boulder, CO: Westview Press, 1997.

Martin, James J. *Men Against the State: The Expositors of Individualist Anarchism in America, 1827–1908*. Colorado Springs: Ralph Myles Publisher, Inc., 1970.

Martindale, Don. *The Nature and Types of Sociological Theory*. Boston: Houghton-Mifflin, 1960.

Marx, Karl. *Economic and Philosophic Manuscripts of 1844*. Moscow: Foreign Languages Publishing House, 1961.

Marx, Karl, and Friedrich Engels. *The German Ideology*. New York: International Publishers, 1972.

Melzer, Arthur, Jerry Weinberger, and M. Richard Zinman, eds. *Multiculturalism and American Democracy*. Lawrence: University of Kansas Press, 1998.

Menger, Carl. *Principles of Economics*. 1871. Glencoe, IL: Free Press, 1950.

Michaels, Walter Benn. *The Trouble with Diversity: How We Learned to Love Identity and Ignore Inequality*. New York: Metropolitan Books, 2006.

Michels, Robert. *Political Parties*. 1911. New York: The Free Press, 1966.

Mises, Ludwig von. *Human Action: A Treatise on Economics*. 1949. San Francisco: Fox and Wilkes, 1996.

——. *Omnipotent Government: The Rise of the Total State and Total War* 1944. Grove City, PA: Libertarian Press, Inc., 1985.

Mosca, Gaetano. *The Ruling Class*. 1896. New York: McGraw-Hill, 1939.

Murray, Charles. *In Our Hands: A Plan to Replace the Welfare State*. Washington, DC: American Enterprise Institute, 2003.

——. *Losing Ground: American Social Policy, 1950–1980*. 1984. New York: Basic Books, 1994.

——. *What It Means to Be Libertarian: A Personal Interpretation*. New York: Broadway Books, 1997.

Myrdal, Gunner. *An American Dilemma: The Negro Problem and Modern Democracy*. Somerset, NJ: Transaction Publishers, 1995.

Newman, Saul. "Specters of the Uncanny: The Return of the Repressed." *Telos* 124 (Summer 2002): 115–30.

Nock, Albert Jay. "Anarchist's Progress." In *State of the Union: Essays in Social Criticism*, edited by Charles Hamilton. 1927. Indianapolis: Liberty Fund, 1991, 34–51.

——. "The Criminality of the State." In *State of the Union: Essays in Social Criticism*, edited by Charles Hamilton. 1939. Indianapolis: Liberty Fund, 1991, 269–75.

——. *Free Speech and Plain Language*. 1931. Freeport, NY: Books for Libraries Press, 1965.

——. *Memoirs of a Superfluous Man*. New York: Harper and Brothers, 1943.

——. *Our Enemy, the State*. 1935. Caldwell, ID: Caxton Publishers, 1959.

——. "What We All Stand For." In *State of the Union: Essays in Social Criticism*, edited by Charles Hamilton. 1913. Indianapolis: Liberty Fund, 1991, 139–48.

Norris, Christopher. *Against Relativism: Philosophy of Science, Deconstruction, and Critical Theory*. Malden, MA: Blackwell, 1997.

——. *Reclaiming Truth: Contribution to a Critique of Cultural Relativism*. Durham, NC: Duke University Press, 1996.

Nozick, Robert. *Anarchy, State, and Utopia*. New York: Basic Books, 1974.

Omni, Michael, and Howard Winant. *Racial Formation in the United States from the 1960s to the 1990s*. New York: Routledge, 1994.

O'Neill, William. *With Charity Toward None: An Analysis of Ayn Rand's Philosophy*. Totowa, NJ: Littlefield, Adams, & Co, 1972.

Oppenheimer, Franz. *The State: Its History and Development Viewed Sociologically*. 1908. Somerset, NJ: Transaction Publishers, 1999.

Paterson, R. W. K. *The Nihilistic Egoist Max Stirner*. London: Oxford University Press, 1971.

Peikoff, Leonard. *Objectivism: The Philosophy of Ayn Rand*. New York: Penguin, 1991.

Raimondo, Justin. *An Enemy of the State: The Life of Murray N. Rothbard*. Amherst, NY: Prometheus Books, 2000.

Rand, Ayn. *Atlas Shrugged*. 1957. New York: Penguin, 1992.

———. *Capitalism: The Unknown Ideal*. New York: Penguin, 1967.

———. *The Fountainhead*. 1943. New York: Bobbs-Merrill, 1993.

———. *Introduction to Objectivist Epistemology*. New York: Penguin, 1979.

———. *Philosophy: Who Needs It?* New York: Penguin, 1982.

———. *Return of the Primitive: The Anti-Industrial Revolution*. 1975. New York: Penguin, 1999.

———. *The Virtue of Selfishness: A New Concept of Egoism*. New York: Penguin, 1964.

Rawls, John. *A Theory of Justice*. Cambridge, MA: Harvard University Press, 1971.

Root, Maria. *Racially Mixed People in America*. Newbury Park, CA: Sage, 1992.

Rosenau, Pauline Marie. *Postmodernism and the Social Sciences: Insights, Inroads and Intrusions*. Princeton, NJ: Princeton University Press, 1992.

Rothbard, Murray N. "The Black Revolution." *Left and Right* 3, no. 3 (Spring–Autumn, 1967): 7–17.

———. "Black, White, and 'Polish': The Cry for Power." *Left and Right* 2, no. 3 (Autumn 1966): 11–14.

———. *Education: Free and Compulsory*. 1971. Auburn, AL: The Ludwig von Mises Institute, 1999.

———. *Egalitarianism as a Revolt Against Nature*. 1974. Auburn, AL: The Ludwig von Mises Institute, 2000.

———. *The Ethics of Liberty*. Atlantic Highlands, NJ: Humanities Press, 1982.

———. *For a New Liberty: The Libertarian Manifesto*. New York: The Macmillan Company, 1973.

———. *Individualism and the Philosophy of the Social Sciences*. San Francisco: The Cato Institute, 1979.

———. "The Irish Revolution." *Left and Right* 2, no. 2 (Spring 1966): 3–7.

———. *The Irrepressible Rothbard: The Rothbard-Rockwell Report Essays of Murray N. Rothbard*. Edited by Llewellyn H. Rockwell. Burlingame, CA: Center for Libertarian Studies, 2000.

———. *Ludwig von Mises: Scholar, Creator, Hero*. Auburn, AL: The Ludwig von Mises Institute, 1988.

——. *Man, Economy, and State: A Treatise on Economic Principles*. 1962. Auburn, AL: The Ludwig von Mises Institute, 2001.

——. "Robert Nozick and the Immaculate Conception of the State." *Journal of Libertarian Studies* 1 (Winter 1977): 45–57.

——. *The Sociology of the Ayn Rand Cult*. Port Townsend, WA: Liberty Publishing, 1987.

Rushton, J. Phillippe. *Race, Evolution, and Behavior: A Life History Perspective*. Port Huron, MI: Charles Darwin Research Institute, 2000.

Sacks, David, Peter Thiel, and Elizabeth Fox-Genovese. *The Diversity Myth: Multiculturalism and Political Intolerance at Stanford*. Oakland, CA: The Independent Institute, 1996.

Savich, Vincent, and Frank Miele. *Race: The Reality of Human Differences*. Boulder, CO: Westview Press, 2004.

Schmidtz, David, ed. *Robert Nozick*. Cambridge: Cambridge University Press, 2002.

Sciabarra, Chris Matthew. *Ayn Rand: Her Life and Thought*. Poughkeepsie, NY: The Objectivist Center, 1996.

——. *Ayn Rand: The Russian Radical*. University Park: Pennsylvania State University Press, 1995.

——. *Marx, Hayek and Utopia*. Albany: State University of New York, 1995.

——. "The Rand Transcript." *The Journal of Ayn Rand Studies* 1, no. 1 (Fall 1999): 1–25.

——. *Total Freedom: Toward a Dialectical Libertarianism*. University Park: Pennsylvania State University Press, 2000.

Shiell, Timothy C. *Campus Hate Speech on Trial*. Lawrence: University of Kansas Press, 1998.

Sidel, Ruth. *Battling Bias: The Struggle for Identity and Community on College Campuses*. New York: Penguin Books, 1994.

Smelser, Neil J., and Jeffery Alexander. *Diversity and Its Discontents: Cultural Conflict and Common Ground in Contemporary American Society*. Princeton, NJ: Princeton University Press, 1999.

Sollors, Werner, ed. *The Invention of Ethnicity*. New York: Oxford University Press, 1989.

Spooner, Lysander. *No Treason, No. 6: The Constitution of No Authority*. 1870. Larkspur, CO: Pine Tree Press, 1965.

——. *A Plan for the Abolition of Slavery*. Boston: Author, 1858.

——. *Poverty: Its Illegal Causes and Legal Cure*. Boston: Bela Marsh, 1846.

——. *Revolution: The Only Remedy for the Oppressed Classes of Ireland, England, and Other Parts of the British Empire*. Boston: Author, 1880.

——. *To the Non-Slaveholders of the South*. Boston: Author, 1858.

——. *The Unconstitutionality of Slavery*. New York: Burt Franklin, 1860.

Stepelevich, Lawrence. "Karl Marx and Max Stirner." *Political Theory* 3, no. 2 (May 1975): 159–79.

——. "Max Stirner and Ludwig Feuerbach." *Journal of the History of Ideas* 39, no. 4 (July–September 1978): 451–63.

——. "Max Stirner as Hegelian." *Journal of the History of Ideas* 46, no. 4 (October–December 1985): 597–614.

——. "The Revival of Max Stirner." *Journal of the History of Ideas* 35, no. 2 (April–June 1974): 323–28.

Stirner, Max. *The Ego and Its Own.* Cambridge: Cambridge University Press, 1995.

——. *The False Principle of Our Education, or Humanism and Realism.* 1842. Colorado Springs: Ralph Myles, 1967.

Stotsky, Sandra. *Losing our Language: How Multicultural Classroom Instruction Is Undermining Our Children's Ability to Read, Write and Reason.* New York: The Free Press, 1999.

Taylor, Charles, ed. *Multiculturalism: Examining the Politics of Recognition.* Princeton, NJ: Princeton University Press, 1994.

Taylor, Jared, and George McDaniel. *A Race against Time: Racial Heresies for the 21st Century.* Oakton, VA: New City Foundation, 2003.

Tierney, William. *Building Communities of Difference: Higher Education in the Twenty-First Century.* Westport, CT: Bergin and Garvey, 1993.

Thernstrom, Stephan, and Abigail Thernstrom. *America in Black and White: One Nation, Indivisible.* New York: Simon and Schuster, 1997.

——. *No Excuses: Closing the Racial Gap in Learning.* New York: Simon and Schuster, 2003.

Tucille, Jerome. *It Still Begins with Ayn Rand: Part Two of a Libertarian Odyssey.* Mill Valley, CA: Pulpless.Com, 1999.

——. *It Usually Begins with Ayn Rand.* San Francisco: Fox and Wilkes, 1972.

Tucker, Benjamin R. *Instead of a Book by a Man Too Busy to Write One: A Fragmentary Exposition of Philosophical Anarchism.* 1897. New York: Haskell House Publishers, 1969.

Waters, Mary. *Ethnic Options: Choosing Identities in America.* Berkeley: University of California Press, 1990.

Welsh, John F. "Reification and the Dialectic of Social Life: Against the Berger Group." *Quarterly Journal of Ideology* 10 (Spring 1986): 12–23.

——. "The Unchained Dialectic." In *Neoliberalism and Education Reform,* edited by E. Wayne Ross and Rich Gibson. Cresskill, NJ: Hampton Press, 2007.

West, Cornell. *Democracy Matters.* New York: Penquin, 2004.

——. *Race Matters.* Boston: Beacon Press, 1993.

Wieseltier, Leon. *Against Identity.* New York: William Drenttel, 1996.

Wilkinson, J. Harvie. *One Nation Indivisible: How Ethnic Separatism Threatens America.* New York: Addison Wesley Longman, 1997.

Willett, Cynthia. *Theorizing Multiculturalism: A Guide to the Current Debate.* Malden, MA: Blackwell Publishers, 1998.

Wolff, Jonathan. *Robert Nozick: Property, Justice and the Minimal State.* Stanford, CA: Stanford University Press, 1991.

Wood, Peter. *Diversity: The Invention of a Concept.* San Francisco: Encounter Books, 2003.

Woodcock, George. *Anarchism: A History of Libertarian Ideas and Movements.* Cleveland: Meridian Books, 1962.

Wreszin, Michael. *The Superfluous Anarchist Albert Jay Nock.* Providence, RI: Brown University Press, 1972.

Yarros, Victor. "Philosophical Anarchism: Its Rise, Decline, and Eclipse." *American Journal of Sociology* 41, no. 4 (January 1936): 470–83.

Zeitlin, Irving. *Ideology and the Development of Sociological Theory.* Englewood Cliffs, NJ: Prentice-Hall, 1968.

Index

About the Author

John F. Welsh is an independent scholar living in Louisville, Kentucky. He recently retired as professor of higher education from the University of Louisville where he taught courses in the administration and finance of higher education and mentored doctoral students through their dissertation projects.

He publishes widely in social science and higher education research journals, including the *Journal of Higher Education*, *Race, Ethnicity and Education*, *Journal of Higher Education Policy and Management*, *Journal of College Student Retention*, *Community College Review*, *Community College Journal of Research and Practice*, *Assessment and Evaluation in Higher Education*, *Campus-Wide Information Systems*, *Community College Enterprise*, *Trusteeship*, *Cultural Logic*, *Quality Assurance in Education*, *Connection: The New England Journal of Higher Education*, *Midwest Quarterly*, *Humanity and Society*, *Free Inquiry*, and *Quarterly Journal of Ideology*.

He has also published chapters in recent books on topics including dialectical logic, the future of public education, innovation in information technology in higher education, how the war on terror is affecting higher education, and the dialectics of race and liberty.

He received several teaching, research, and service awards during his career.

In 2003, he won the "Red Apple Award" for outstanding teaching and mentoring at the University of Louisville. He also won the award for Excellence in Online Teaching from the Kentucky Virtual University in 2003 and 2006.